'I was ten years old when introduced to the principles of working smart by psychologist, Greg Nicholson, at an after-school tutoring centre, Edworks. Even then, I had a grand passion: I wanted to become a doctor. Today, thanks to Edworks, I am about to realise my dream.

Edworks taught me how to fly!'

Pallavi Prathivadi
Fifth year medical student, Monash University

REACH FOR THE SKY

Discovering the power of Working Smart!

'From the very beginning, you encouraged me to strive for excellence. In so doing, you instilled in me not only academic and "book smart" skills, but key elements that make me "life smart" too.' **Tracy, Year 10**

REACH FOR THE SKY

Discovering the power of Working Smart!

Greg Nicholson

Forewords by Dr. Tui McKeown
and
Professor Frank Vajda

Illustrated by Prue Sobers

OLD TREES ✧ Melbourne

First edition published in Australia by Pineapplehead Publishing 2004

Second edition 2012 (updated 2014) published by Old Trees Press
(Melbourne, Australia)
PO Box 1008
Camberwell, Victoria, 3124, Australia
enquiry@OldTreesPress.com

Cover design by Said
www.said.net.au

National Library of Australia Cataloguing-in-Publication entry:

Nicholson, Greg (Gregory Steven)

Reach for the sky : discovering the power of working smart! / by Greg Nicholson ; foreword by Dr Tui McKeown and Professor Frank Vajda ; illustrated by Prue Sobers

2nd UK/Australian English ed.

ISBN 9780987210494 (pbk.)

Study skills.
Time management.
Life skills.

Sobers, Prue
McKeown, Tui
Vajda, F.J.E. (Frank J.E.)

371.30281

For my favourite teacher, Patricia Nicholson

And for Gabriel, Tristan, Aidan, Dylan, Harrison,
Tianna, Lola, Sienna and Jalisa

The Edworks principles that follow, and the guidelines for 'working smart', are also dedicated to you, the student owner of this book.

The Achieve® Program, 'Learning for a brighter future', delivered to the Caribbean by author, psychologist and educator, Greg Nicholson, wholly reflects the Edworks principles which he developed. Caribbean readers please note that some terminology, such as school grade levels, may differ.

In Barbados,
Classes 3 and 4 are the equivalent of Grades 5 and 6 (Upper Primary) in this book, while Forms 1–6 in Barbados are the equivalent of Years 7–12 levels (Secondary and Seniors) stated herein.

Happy learning, and always remember to look up and reach for the sky!

ACHIEVE
BARBADOS

When are we going to get it right?

Schoolwork is boring, repetitive, irrelevant and of no value—except for the social life. These were widespread views found by researchers at Australia's Flinders University in a landmark study of declining male student achievement and retention rates in 60 state and private schools.[1]

That school is an unpleasant waste of time where adults fail to listen, were among the telling blows dealt to the school system from a cross-section of 1800 secondary male students, reflecting a global education culture long in denial and out-of-step with a changing world.

The study eloquently described classroom tedium; that work was always the same, lesson after lesson, day after day, year after year: pupils read a novel, for example, and then did a review about it, then read another and did 'a review about it', or saw a movie and did 'a review about it'. Sometimes 'they just get you to do assignments' one after the other or to sit in the classroom and 'copy out of books or from other people'. That's 'all we ever do', the study reported.

Author of 'Listening to the Boys', Dr. Malcolm Slade, said that adults were not genuinely listening to each other, to the world or to the young; that the prevailing global education crisis could not be solved merely by demanding more resources and assuming quality education depended upon traditional structures and accreditation processes.[2] He asserted it was naïve to consider strategies for reform or responses to existing problems that did not address a threefold need: to clean up the mistakes of the past, to do more with less and to embrace liberalising and revolutionising technologies.

That was more than ten years ago.

So what of today? Despite schools promoting diversity and government voices proclaiming educational reform, critics lament authentic change is still nowhere to be seen.[3]

☆

In the UK, strident calls to abolish statutory testing have been raised since the nineties. A University of Leeds study noted 'teaching to the test' undermined student initiative, creative thinking and a need to foster a love of teaching and learning.[4] A decade on, Ofsted (the Office for Standards in Education) observed teaching to the test saw children missing out on a well-rounded education as schools sought to inflate their league table standing.[5]

Chief inspector of schools, Christine Gilbert, said some pupils were drilled to pass written tests at the expense of speaking and listening skills. Ofsted inspectors found that in maths, a narrow focus on meeting examination requirements had pupils passing tests while lacking the ability 'to apply their knowledge independently' and were ill-prepared for further study. Some teachers instruct children in techniques to pass the tests while failing to ensure pupils know what they are doing, their report said.

Today, evidence of failing schools and claims that Britain has produced a lost generation of young people who lack employable skills are supported by a Chartered Institute of Personnel and Development report in which employers argue education skills are too focused on testing and written examinations, believing 'many school-leavers don't possess communication skills.'[6]

☆

In a climate of declining academic achievement, over two decades ago, US researchers warned American education was in crisis,[7] claiming children in the main were learning little, and a teacher's lot spelled long hours for meagre reward. Despite government recognition of the problem as critical, solutions were perfunctory, with the major national initiative of the era, the *No Child Left Behind* program, producing faint effect. Current findings of the Center on Education Policy reveal forty-eight per cent of public schools are failing under the law.[8] Every year, 1.3 million high school students drop out of school.[9] Literacy problems now cost the US economy $300 billion a year.[10]

Professors Henry Levin and Cecilia Rouse write in *The New York Times* that the US lags behind while its economic competitors rapidly increase their graduation rates.[9] They argue that given the pace of technological progress, educated workers are critical as sources of innovation, productivity and economic growth. Wise investment of public dollars to reduce high school dropouts, they declare, must be central to any strategy to raise economic growth, reduce inequality and return fiscal health to the nation. On a human level, the writers observe staying at school helps individuals lead 'healthier and more productive lives.' However, acknowledging those who do stay the course, a John Hopkins University report said that 'too many graduates are still unprepared for the needs of college and high-wage employment.'[11]

☆ In a recent news article, a 13-year-old, Year 8 student complained he could not cope with school. The problem? Things had changed since primary school. His teachers were now seeking his *opinions* on a variety of issues and topics. Trouble was, he didn't have any opinions! More importantly, eight years at school had not prepared him for this stage of his education.

A word to soothe the critical eye
Whilst every effort has been made to minimise small variations in spelling and terms between Australian and British English, please note that 'pupil' and 'student' are interchangeable throughout this text, and 'programme' is used in its shorter form, 'program'. Where the third person, 'we', is used, this may denote the author and students, Edworks or Achieve, or the author and his editor. The first person, 'I', naturally represents the advice or opinions of the author. The text contains some words not normally capitalised that are used for emphasis and easier recognition by pupils—eg 'complete your Plan'. Please note that essay titles follow the formal convention of title inside quotation marks with no full stops unless two sentences occur in the title. Where an essay is cited as written by a named pupil, its entire text, as well as the title, is enclosed in quotation marks.

The author also emphasises that where some guidelines are prescribed, for example, the use of 'The Two-Factor Model' or the 'Funnel Approach' and so on, they are not intended as the only structure or means of achieving a desired outcome. Rather, the author has set out to identify and conform to the requirements of an education system that will determine student success or otherwise.

The concept of 'working smart' in the following chapters should be regarded only as a stepping-stone to developing a pupil's personal style and work methods; there are many different ways to achieve an end. Thus ultimately, in spite of guidelines that may be prescriptive, by offering pupils skills that foster thinking and independence, 'Reach for the Sky' and its working smart principles seek to build a mental set for diversity.

DISCLAIMER:
The information in this book is offered as a guide to students seeking to improve their academic performance. The interpretation by the author of the requirements for the criteria discussed and the associated examples reflect the experience and understanding of the author and have not been endorsed by the Australian Department of Education, the US, UK or Caribbean Departments of Education, or other relevant bodies. However, the author's working smart principles, guidelines and structures have been successfully used or supported by students, universities, teachers and parents for over two decades.

The information is a guide only. Pupils are reminded to ensure that any work they submit for school and for external assessment is their own.

Contents

Contents (continued)

Foreword

Reach for the Sky—Discovering the power of Working Smart! is a book I wholeheartedly endorse.

Today, the thinking parent knows that a person's ongoing employment and well-being is linked, more than ever, to his or her ability to learn and adapt. In our era of competitiveness and change, parents are acutely aware that for their children to succeed at school and beyond in their careers, their goals must transcend the short-term aim of passing exams, to acquiring a vital skill of working life: *the ability to learn.*

But where do we turn? Where do we go to learn 'how to learn'? Such a skill is not, paradoxically, to be readily found in the classroom, where pressures of cost, time constraints and ever-expanding curricula are burdensome features of both private and public schools.

Here, *Reach for the Sky* fills a time-long void. The book provides an opportunity for students to achieve personal advancement through a friendly, readily grasped, systematic approach which I believe they will enjoy. For interested parents who read *Reach for the Sky,* it offers a thorough and practical support tool to assist their children, and rewarding experiences for both. In fact, this time-effective, self-directed learning approach is one where I suspect parents will gain as much as the children they seek to help.

While the book is aimed primarily at upper primary and secondary school students, it has much broader appeal. I am particularly keen that my students read the section in Part 3 on essay writing. The lessons of *Reach for the Sky* are as applicable to the tertiary student and adult who realise they have missed the 'learning to learn' part of their education.

Psychologist, Greg Nicholson, offers a 'how to' of learning based on a simple philosophy: learning is life-long and should be an enjoyable experience. Often the challenge is just getting started. I warmly recommend you continue to read on, now that you have taken the first step.

Tui McKeown, PhD.

Dr. McKeown is a senior lecturer, Department of Management, Faculty of Business and Economics, Monash University, Melbourne.

☆

Through the experience of my son, a former Edworks pupil, I can bear testimony to the excellent benefits of Edworks Tutoring. It is timely that founder, Greg Nicholson, has written a book to bring the concept of 'working smart'—a distillation of Edworks' teachings—to a wider public.

These teachings offer the student the potential not only to achieve the glittering prize of scholastic achievement, but importantly, greater coping skills in the preparation and performance of everyday tasks and assignments. Learning how to think and read constructively, discovering the pleasure of motivation, optimising study time and importantly, learning the art of written communication through essay writing—these and more, are in the kitbag of skills presented in *Reach for the Sky*.

This book will not only be of immense value to students who want to become achievers. *Reach for the Sky* is for the procrastinators and worriers of the student world, for pupils who question the reason they should attend school at all, and for those who aspire to be more successful, but are confused as to how to go about it. It is also a handy reference book for parents who want to help and guide their children but to date, through lack of user-friendly resources and sensible, practical advice, have been unable to do so.

The opening excerpts suggesting the failure of conventional education to clarify and offer greater understanding of tasks set in class, provide an immediate insight into the book's purpose: to show students how to move beyond being merely passive receptors and storers of vast quantities of information, to becoming thinkers, where learning is an active process and where making mistakes plays a positive role as a stepping stone to success.

This is, in no way, a criticism of the work of dedicated teachers who perform an essential social service to our community. Rather, I believe that teachers whose pupils adopt the working smart guidelines will find they offer complementary support to their teaching methods. The book gives striking examples of students who, in following the working smart precepts, have been able to correct their approaches to intellectual tasks by analysing information, focussing on key words, extracting information and structuring their written responses to achieve a desired result.

All educational subjects involve essays.

In my observation and experience as a lecturer and medical fraternity consultant, the creation of the English essay during school years becomes the paradigm for teaching communication skills across most other subjects.

Although the sciences and, to a lesser degree, the humanities, require factual knowledge, the means of expressing it becomes just as important as the knowledge itself if it is to be communicated effectively. Here, *Reach for the Sky* will be of great value to students during their school years and beyond, whatever their chosen fields.

The presentation of *Reach for the Sky* is simple, basic and common sense. It is highly motivational and uses the language of the psychologist in the guise of a teacher. As such, the guidelines often delve deeper than one might otherwise expect from such a book, providing a sense of personal support, encouragement and know-how to student readers who may question their own ability to perform, or who need to change their attitudes towards others.

The book is a feast of brilliant tacit knowledge not usually found in works of its kind. I submit that the skills reflected in its pages will be of benefit not only to upper primary and secondary students, but also for students at tertiary level who may possess sound knowledge of their chosen disciplines, but perform less well in the area of written communication. On reflection, *Reach for the Sky* contains valuable guidelines that some of my former pupils at the University of London may well have found highly useful. Indeed, I would have found them of great value myself during my own studies as a medical student.

'The world belongs to people who are organised,' paraphrases the words of an icon of Australian medicine, P.F. Bladin. Such organisational skills are expertly presented in this book in language appropriate for students who, after all, represent future participants seeking their places in a competitive world. As the book reveals, a pupil at examination time sitting alone in front of the paper was comforted by a single thought: 'What would Edworks tell me to do?' I recall doing my medical exams as a young student, relying on my revered and learned mentor in a similar way. For Edworks' founder and author of *Reach for the Sky*, Greg Nicholson, it is the ultimate compliment.

Frank Vajda
Royal Swedish Order of the Polar Star Officer First Class, 2002;
Member of the Order of Australia (AM), 2012
MD (Melb) FRCP (Ed) FRACP

Professor Frank Vajda, Consultant Neurologist and Neuropharmacologist, is founder and former Director of the Australian Raoul Wallenberg Centre for Clinical Neuropharmacology, St. Vincent's Hospital, Melbourne, and current Professorial Fellow, Dept of Medicine, University of Melbourne.

A word to parents and guardians

Thank you for giving a few minutes of your valuable time.

The quality of student learning has rarely demanded greater scrutiny. In the swiftly-evolving, high-tech world of our twenty-first century, the symbols of fresh beginnings and exciting times nonetheless coexist with disturbing signals of the unknown challenges and uncertainties of the future.

No one quite knows what the decades will bring: what new technologies and industries will emerge, what production and workplace demands will be, what economic, environmental and social concerns will put us, and our children, to the test. It appears certain however, there will be greater complexities and more issues to face, more problems to solve, and more decisions and choices to make, than ever before.

Who will flourish, who will flounder?

It should not be difficult to predict who will flourish and who will flounder in what promises to be a highly competitive business and social environment. Understandably, most parents believe that there are educational systems in place to prepare the youngsters of today and tomorrow for the rigorous times ahead. But are there?

As little as a decade ago, rote learning was still at the height of popularity. This acquiring of knowledge through passive memorising and regurgitation embodied traditional learning for centuries. For most of the 1900s, student success continued to be measured in quantitative terms: *the more you know, the smarter you are. Don't worry if you don't understand. Just get it right!* Teachers' ticks and crosses and the words, 'well done', and 'more focus, please', generally characterised the response to a pupil's work. In concert with examination results, these became the yardstick of a student's level of achievement.

From Prep year on, it was the pupils with the fastest answers who received the pats on the head. The others were simply told, 'try harder!' Success within the classroom was purely answer-driven, whether it meant calling out the answer, filling in the gaps or writing it in full. It was within this teaching environment that young impressionable minds quickly learned if they wanted to be seen as bright, they had to put their hands up first.

Content delivery

Essentially, this method relied on a pupil's natural ability to memorise, store and retrieve vast quantities of 'knowledge' throughout school life. The focus was on content delivery: an exercise in transmitting volumes of information. That it provided little room for critical thinking and analysis, the assessment of issues and problem solving—and consequential personal development—none within the educational halls of power, it seemed, felt it necessary to question.

Having studied early childhood learning and as an experienced young teacher and psychology graduate, I reached a pivotal point in my career when it struck me that, in the face of a rapidly changing global environment, this time-worn and mechanical teaching paradigm was still being practised—worse, that there was a widely-held belief it was equipping our youngest citizens for the dynamic challenges of the new world. Perhaps even more disquieting was that the youth of the day were all too soon becoming tomorrow's teachers, instilling the same deeply entrenched methods and habits into the minds of a new generation. The secondary students of the nineties are already well into adulthood!

Edworks Tutoring for Success

I set up Edworks in 1990, a tutoring organisation, offering students a practical point-of-difference in education that focussed on awareness, stimulation and a genuine extension of student skills.

Through a personally tailored program for each pupil, Edworks' young people are encouraged to take that step beyond innate ability to a new level of awareness where they discover how to 'work smart'. They are challenged, guided and empowered to become thinkers. They learn how to dissect, analyse and evaluate issues, to produce discerning opinions, solve problems, make informed decisions and become effective communicators. These are the essential elements that shape the independent learner.

Nothing succeeds like success! Not unexpectedly, as pupils develop their skills, confidence blooms—and with it comes increased critical, creative and independent thinking. Importantly, beyond our centres, these skills allow students to effectively judge and refine their own performances, offering a pathway to greater autonomy and future personal growth.

Why are such skills not available to every child?

Indeed, in an uncertain world, where the vagaries of an economic climate see good times plummet to gloom and doom, as a parent you might ask, who will be the resilient, recession-proof employers and employees at such times? It will be those who can assess and prioritise problems, who can communicate, innovate and solve issues—who can resolve conflict and effectively manage time. It will be those who can take the initiative and think on their feet!

The average pupil of rote learning, however, has few skills on which to call, being essentially reactive, rather than proactive. Typifying this experience, tertiary students in employment have observed of their tutors: 'They try to stuff us with information. Employers have complained that we are like robots, lacking in independent thinking and disinterested in the things happening around us.'[12] In the educational arena, it's also been noted that with universities producing more would-be teachers than there are positions to accommodate them—the case for many years—some graduates emerge with not only 'a head full of educational theory', but 'questionable classroom skills'.[13] How will this impact future outcomes?

How do you read, Gabe?

Recently, I asked 12-year-old Gabe, a new pupil whom I knew to be having tennis lessons, how he executed a serve. The boy spent a lively two minutes explaining to me in front of his mother, how to hold the tennis racquet, where and how to stand, how high to toss the ball and so on. Then I asked: 'When you read, Gabe, how do you go about that?'

Gabe was perplexed and gave it some thought. He finally shrugged and said: 'I don't know, I just . . . read.' His mother was curious. I then suggested that after attending tennis school for a period of seven-plus years, if her son had still been taking wild hit-and-miss swings at the ball, she would no doubt be rightly concerned.

Gabe was in Year 7. Yet he was unaware that for reading exercises, it was not enough to passively understand the text. He had no idea that as a secondary school student his reading should have been an active process: identifying key words, extracting information, predicting outcomes and verifying the content—a process he should have begun to learn in simpler form at primary school.

Disturbingly, little has changed

Our tutors are reminded daily at Edworks that disturbingly, most school students still operate on a 'hit-and-miss' basis. In more than two decades little in education seems to have changed.

The signs of rote learning and content-based teaching are plainly evident when new pupils are reluctant to undertake or show their working out, for fear of appearing 'dumb'. Of course, this process reveals the steps students take to arrive at their answers, and to emphasise its importance during problem solving, our pupils are encouraged to use good quality paper for their computations. For new enrolees, it's a novelty and welcome relief to no longer be expected to produce the fast answer, but to arrive at solutions through analysing the question, deductive reasoning and concrete thinking.

Driving a desire for greater learning

For many students, our programs provide a genuine awakening. What excites youngsters is their sudden sense of control over the learning process. For some, it's like turning on a light! They begin to grasp that learning is meaningful, that it has a purpose—that it is not just an endless series of questions and answers. The program strategies and skill building lead to a new appreciation of learning which drives the desire for achieving and learning more. Students' parents, themselves conditioned by the question-answer routine of rote learning, are often surprised by their children's new-found enthusiasm—and as observers are intrigued.

There is another rote learning legacy obstructing the learning process.

I see it regularly: many pupils fail to understand the *nature* of questions. Here, I would ask, 'How can they therefore perform the tasks expected of them? How can they predict outcomes, for example, if they know nothing of how to look for cues?' *If students do not understand the question*, they cannot possibly become involved in *the process of constructive thinking.*

How you can help

This book is not only designed for students seeking to change their lives through a competitive edge. It offers you as a parent a chance to participate in your child's quest.

The book's format is simple and clear. Aside from in depth essay discussions for senior students, it can be read in a relatively short time, and will provide a sound appreciation of your child's academic challenges. Hand in hand with the book's working smart guidelines, your awareness will enable you to discuss and perhaps assist older students in their study, or to guide younger pupils in the step-by-step processes that will allow them to flourish and reach their potential.

Stumbling blocks of parenthood

A worried parent of a Grade 5 pupil commented to me recently that not for the first time had his daughter, Aimee, asked him for help on a class project.

'What can I do,' he shrugged, 'but sit with her in the evening at the Internet trying to find information? Even then, I am not quite sure what the teacher's expectations are.'

I asked the father whether Aimee had been shown a mock project in class as a guide. Apparently not. Had the class been shown how to read the question to establish the key components of the task? Were they guided in the process of scanning texts to identify the relevance of research information? Had they been taught how to take notes, to plan the essay project before committing it to paper? When asked, Aimee shook her head in bewilderment.

Perhaps Aimee was wrong. Perhaps she hadn't paid attention when these issues were explored in class. Perhaps. But if you've ever been caught in a similar situation, you will know that Aimee and her father are typical of students and their parents who struggle with these issues all the time.

In view of our successes, the book's 2004 first edition had been long overdue. Regrettably, it was not possible to present all of my teachings in the one volume. However, I selected important aspects to assist any student from Grade 5 onward, and particularly senior secondary students and tertiary students, to dramatically and effectively lift their game—in particular, to improve their written communication skills which, in my opinion, are the greatest predictors of success. I hope this newest edition proves equally valuable.

Replacing old habits with new

This book's primary goal is to give families key skills to future-proof their children. Such skills demand not the passive memorising of content but active *critical and creative thinking*. Above all, they offer a springboard to success. They are not difficult to learn, but like tennis lessons, require regular short-term practice to become second nature; removing old faulty habits and building a strong skills repertoire is our goal. Once learned, the skills can be applied time and time again in new situations both in and outside the classroom and so are vital for achievement in tertiary education and beyond.

As a concerned parent, there is an opportunity here for you to impact your child's future. You might perhaps consider a role as support coach to offer guidance, motivation and comfort where needed. But approach it with care. It's important you allow the impetus for working smart to come initially from your child. It should be seen as her or his personal quest for improvement as s/he is the one who will be learning the skills and achieving the results.

Notwithstanding, secondary students should be made aware of the strong competition they will face as they progress to tertiary level. This may provide you with an ideal starting point for a family discussion. In spite of being well qualified to commence their undergraduate degrees, Australian school leavers have as low as a fifty per cent chance of completing their courses and graduating,[14] and in the United Kingdom, student numbers abandoning higher education once begun, are soaring, one university estimating that less than fifty per cent of its pupils would finish their degrees.[15] A spokesperson tellingly commented that dropping out does not benefit 'the student, the university or society.'

In the United States, the picture is bleaker. When the Organization for Economic Cooperation and Development (OECD) tracked the results for the number of students completing their college courses, of eighteen countries including Slovakia and Poland, the US finished last with up to 46 per cent.[16]

Whilst cost is a factor in some cases, the high student drop-out rates in first year tertiary bear testimony to a challenge that is more than many bargain for.

So where do the reasons lie?

It is reported that some within the teaching profession view a teacher's primary goal as merely presenting information to students, where students are viewed as passive recipients of bodies of content, and where, at best, they become a vessel into which knowledge is poured. This mindset is a reflection of thirty years ago when teaching was described as 'scattering seeds to the wind rather than transferring them to specific containers' where 'all that is required of a teacher is that he deliver himself of his nuggets of wisdom.'[17] Critics of this content-based practice rejoin: 'It is all very well to scatter the gems of wisdom to the winds, but what if they are not caught or fall on barren ground?'[18]

Barren ground, indeed! More than a decade has passed since this book's first edition and like other observers I continue to hold that Western education is still in crisis.

In spite of governments and school bodies paying lip service to change, or implementing assessment systems or greater school resources as token progressive moves, encountering students as I do every day, fresh from the classroom and across a broad socio-economic and age range, I see the evidence of change is still alarmingly absent.

That the educational landscape is devoid of genuine revolutionary reform should be as greatly concerning as global regions that flail in a haemorrhaging economy. Surely our cues could not be more glaring.

At all costs, education must become engaging, inspirational and innovative for it to be universally relevant in the coming years. True revolution means changing the way *teachers teach* so that pupils will *want to learn*—so that they will become passionate and competitive about learning—and thus be equipped to not only successfully navigate the contours of their future lives, but to contribute meaningfully towards building safe, prosperous and harmonious communities in which to live.

To offer our youth less, is irresponsible. We know what we should be doing and we know how to do it.

What is left but to act!

Greg Nicholson
Melbourne, Australia, 2014

A note to students and teachers

This book challenges the notion that school, even at senior level, means hard work. For students who explore what it has to offer, it will bring greater awareness, meaning and pleasure to learning and greatly facilitate and complement the work of their teachers.

Psychologist and educator, Greg Nicholson, in an engaging, easy-to-read style, offers *Reach for the Sky—Discovering the power of Working Smart!* as a powerful guiding light to students from upper primary to senior secondary years. The text is packed full of skills tailored to meet and beat the demanding challenges of an often stressful academic pathway. They are skills little practised in the classroom.

This is not to reprove teachers or their teaching. It is more that the skills in question do not fit the paradigm of traditional teaching. That is, classroom practice exists within an educational culture where teaching methods place weighty reliance on the passive 'practice effect' and a student's innate ability to store and mechanically retrieve volumes of knowledge.

Former university lecturer and secondary school teacher, Roderick Bruce, observes that curricula are biased towards 'knowing'; that students demonstrate their knowledge by rote learning where there is no understanding of such knowledge's significance. Bruce remarks that school leavers lack the ability to think and learn independently, which elicits criticism from tertiary teachers and employers.[19] In a cross cultural study, US researchers, Professors James Stigler and James Hiebert, report that before giving a problem solving task to students, American teachers almost always demonstrate the problem solving procedure *first,* so that it can be practiced.[20] The impact of the challenge and the opportunity to learn through grappling with and thinking through the problem is therefore greatly reduced.

This book is about learning *how to think to solve problems* and not the parroting of answers through the practice effect. In fact, the right answers are more consistently achieved through appreciating what underpins the learning process. The good news is, once learned, the skills are life long and can be used in and out of the classroom in a variety of situations, over and over again.

You may well ask the reason 'content delivery' is still deeply ingrained within the classroom. As with so many long-held practices, the answer lies in our traditions and culture—and it affects us all. Teaching methods and processes have evolved over the years through a blending of formal teacher training with teachers' cultural experiences during the thirteen years of their own schooling. That is, the ideas, beliefs and rituals of youth have passed through time to fuse with the disciplines of teacher tertiary training.

As pointed out by Stigler and Hiebert, teaching in their view can be likened to cultural events such as participating in family dinners—that it is unconsciously learned over long periods through the informal sharing of events with others; that teachers learn more readily what to expect and how to play their roles by having participated within an educational culture, than through formal study. Thus, within the context of our modern world, these old methods are clearly out-of-pace and less than effective.

The challenges for change, not only for teachers, but governments, education boards, parent councils and administrators alike, are immense and complex. *Reach for the Sky* is therefore offered in a spirit of contribution towards this change, and as a tribute to pupils and to the critical role which teachers play.

Using his vast knowledge and professional experience in teaching and psychology, Greg Nicholson shares some of the strategies and programs he has developed as CEO of Edworks, offering a trove of skills and resources to augment a student's curricula learning. His refreshing teaching philosophy, focussed on empowering students to think, analyse, evaluate and problem solve, is well supported by national and international research.[19-23]

Inspired by his pupils' continuing successes, Greg has selected what he believes are the most significant aspects of his teachings. He stresses that of these, the skill of *written communication,* is paramount. In fact, in his broad experience involving thousands of students, Greg hails writing skills as the greatest predictor of success in school life and beyond.

'Without such a skill,' he asks, 'how is one's knowledge or understanding of an issue to be effectively expressed whatever the subject, be it English, geography, history, maths or the sciences?'

Within the book's pages, students will discover powerful and proven strategies for working smart: the spending of *less time and effort for better results.* In developing their skills, they will learn how to avoid procrastination, how to eliminate the fear of failure and how to reduce stress. Using The Two-Factor Model, they will be shown how to prioritise their workloads; and they will be offered efficient note-taking short cuts to save valuable study time.

These skills add up to students acquiring greater self-reliance and the capacity to become independent learners—thinking for themselves and taking the initiative. These are vital qualities for students who seek long-term success.

Without them, they will be ill equipped to face the important challenges of tertiary education after the comparative 'spoon-feeding' of school life. That is, students will need the skills to manage demanding assignments, to navigate information resources, to meet tutor expectations and to excel in the face of course-based student rivalry.

The early stages of this book are punctuated with numerous short and easy exercises designed to foster pupil confidence and motivation. There are four chapters devoted to upper primary students, offering them a head start to their secondary years, whilst a greater part of the second half of the book is dedicated more (but by no means exclusively) to senior secondary students wishing to refine their essay writing skills for the immediate challenges of their final years—or for younger secondary students, the challenging years in store.

A glance at the Contents and a flip through the last chapter and the Appendix, will give pupils, teachers and interested parents, an idea of the innovation and detailed assistance offered through helpful practice programs which includes a step-by-step ten-week daily program of 15 minute exercises. Together with the advice for working smart, these programs have the potential to create success not only during a student's academic life, but throughout the complex and competitive adult years ahead.

PART 1

Ready . . .

Congratulations! You've done it!

You've just opened the book that can change your life. The fact that you are reading this suggests a couple of very encouraging things. Number one: you want to take a look at improving your academic performance *right now.* Two: you're keen to learn the skills that can spell success for you also in the years ahead. Incidentally, that should read, the *complex* years ahead—in case you've had your head in the sand.

But more about that shortly.

Remember! The years ahead belong to you. It is *your* future. It may be hard to imagine at the moment, but believe it or not, what you choose to do now, today, can greatly influence your future choices. This might involve a whole string of significant future issues including your family, your lifestyle, your level of achievement and your level of wealth.

The odds are fairly predictable.

Today's decisions and the path you take will impact on how you shape up to tomorrow's challenges; how quickly and deftly you can solve the problems—big or small—that crop up for you in the future. In turn, this will be a measure of how happy you are likely to be with who you are, and who or what you become. More to the point: today's action can affect the number of doors that swing open to you in your career, in your social and family circles and so on, as your life unfolds.

Being proactive!

'Why is this so important?' you may ask. 'Why should I become proactive at this early stage of my life?'

Let's take a closer look.

Have you ever really seriously considered what it's going to be like? The mountain of choices, the issues and decisions you will face in your life? Perhaps you *have* tried to think about them. Or perhaps you're that old ostrich who prefers not to dwell on intangibles—those things you can't immediately see or feel. Fair enough! But just for a minute, prise your mind open a wedge and contemplate the nature of our developing world.

Okay. The growth of the Internet and globalisation are shining examples. One-time small companies and individuals can now capture international markets and operate big time. Trouble is, in many fields, competition is slick and steep. It's a busy corridor and the elbows are jutting like limbs in a jungle; not everyone can get through.

The players? The players are high-tech! They're lean and hungry. And they're profit-driven. Potentially, they span every corner of the globe. This has forced businesses to shape up, shave off their baggage and emerge as lean and mean as their global competitors.

It's happening now and it will continue to happen in the future: labour forces demanding longer hours and seeking only the highly skilled workers: the ones who can handle the stress of the job, who know all about effective time management, state-of-the-art technology and staying properly trained.

Fields like marketing, IT, business, science, research and development are becoming more dynamic and competitive every day. Employers want people with multi-faceted training and experience. An ad for a career job might warn: *'Only people with a double degree in Business and Engineering need apply.'*

Consider for a moment: if you really want to land the top jobs in your chosen field, you will have to be a sharp operator: proactive; someone with vision who can think ahead. Someone who can see a problem and take action before it gets out of hand.

Reactive individuals who sit around dozing won't get a look in.

So apart from being proactive, you will have to be a cool problem solver. You'll need to be a clear thinker who knows how to identify problems. You'll have to be an effective communicator. You will need to know how to prioritise action and manage time—all with a minimum of stress and fuss.

Pretty formidable, isn't it?

Discovering the secrets

What can we do about it? How do we tackle the pursuit of our potential to cope with it all? How do we begin to define our goals for this complex future? In other words, how can we improve our academic performances to realise our dreams?

You might guess that I'll say: 'Batten down the hatches and get ready for some solid hard work *and plenty of it!'*

Right?

Wrong! If you've read this far, give yourself a pat on the back! You are on the brink of discovering the secrets to improved grades without putting in the mammoth long-term effort you'd expect.

Working smart

When you hear students complain about having to study hard or the grind of school life, you can bet they've never heard of 'working smart'. That is, the skill of spending *less time and effort* on tasks while achieving *better results.*

Again, that's—*less* time and effort. *Better* results!

Fantasyland? Gobbledygook? Impossible? Not at all! Consider this: what do operators like Bill Gates, Richard Branson and Mark Zuckerberg have in common? They are specialists at *maximising results,* while *minimising effort and cost.* In the world of business, people call it *leverage.* We call it *working smart.*

At our tutoring centres, we have living proof that working smart really works. We have a multitude of success stories from our pupils—and many of them joined us for the very same reason you have opened this book. As you flip through its pages, you will notice there is no fine print, no complicated theories and procedures.

Success is rarely attributed to mind-boggling processes, anyway. Rather, it comes through being able to break complex procedures into small, easy-to-follow tasks. So success does *not* mean you have to double your workload to achieve it. The key simply lies in grasping the strategies and putting them to work for you.

Sound good?

Success stories to whet the appetite

Clarissa found the key

Now, Clarissa is a great example! She was a C-minus grade, 18-year-old student doing her final year. She came to us a few months before exam time. Despite attending a top private school, Clarissa was very worried. She knew her C-minus average grades would not gain her the university course of her choice.

That all changed within a few short weeks. At one of our centres, Clarissa was taught how to work smart. She soon began to proudly report she was performing faster and more efficiently than ever before, saving up to 45 minutes on every essay. That's three to four hours each week on homework alone!

Not only was Clarissa saving time and reducing her workload. A few days after the state-wide final exam results were announced, Clarissa's parents got in touch. They sounded absolutely delighted!

And, Clarissa?

Clarissa was over the moon!

She had achieved a score of 97.1 out of a possible 99.7. With her top subject English, she had attained a total score allowing her to review her nomination of university courses. In fact, Clarissa performed so well, she was eligible to select courses that just three months earlier had been beyond her.

Jack hit the target

When Jack first stepped through our doors, clearly, he wanted to do well. However, he was unsure of himself and had very low self-esteem. Above all, he was dreading the thought of yet more schoolwork after school.

The first thing we did was to show Jack he had nothing to fear; that he wasn't in for more of the same. In his classroom, he was struggling with bare passes. He knew he could do better, but didn't know how to go about it. As time had gone by he had lost more confidence, and things became worse. The problem was, Jack was relying on a hit-and-miss approach to try and get him through. In English, he wrote essay after essay. Each time his mark was a C or a D and each time his English teacher told him, 'Try harder next time, Jack. Concentrate on the topic!'

Was Jack given important strategies for improving his writing skills? Was he taught how to plan his essays, or how to give them structure? Was he shown how to analyse issues, how to assess reader expectations of his writing or how to project personality? Unhappily, no!

Consequently, as Jack attempted each new essay topic, he was second-guessing as to where he had failed the time before. He was concentrating like mad. He was trying so hard that it hurt! Why had he only achieved a C-minus for his last essay? Poor Jack! He had no idea.

Jack spent his final school year with us, attending once a week after school. As he began to take on the working smart strategies, he gained self-confidence. Experiencing a degree of success, he soon became self-motivated and more focussed. Following his first round of compulsory assessment tasks, Jack's mother wrote to us excitedly that Jack had obtained all A+ results in his first round of assignments and that his younger sister who also came to Edworks, had achieved three scholarships.

Today, Jack is in his third year at university enjoying Media Studies. During his vacation periods, he works for a large corporation where he continues to apply the strategies he learned for working smart to the job at hand: particularly, how to think on his feet, and how to critically analyse and evaluate the consequences of issues and policies.

The corporation is clearly impressed! In fact, it well may be that Jack has already created his own springboard to success in the future.

Anju became a risk taker

Anju was a quiet girl, not seen by her teachers as having scholarship potential. She was very average in class and had very poor composition skills. In fact, when Anju came to us in Grade 5, she seemed to have forgotten that sentences started with a capital letter, and in general her writing was, well, pretty shabby.

We immediately saw the reason for Anju's below-average results: in the classroom she was afraid to take risks and get things wrong, so she sat quietly in the shadows feeling like a failure, and continuing to do poorly.

During our sessions, we showed Anju that taking risks was a part of learning. We also used her strengths as opportunities to praise her, to help her self-esteem. By the end of just her first session, Anju had begun to look brighter and much happier—and before long, she was picking up her pen with real enthusiasm. We showed Anju that education wasn't about getting answers wrong or right. It was about learning how to think, how to solve problems and how to communicate effectively. We moved her focus from being purely answer-driven, to using *strategies* to achieve her results.

The transformation was remarkable: Anju began to write imaginative, well-structured compositions, and improved her maths marks by 50 per cent. She acquired the tools to refine and evaluate her performance. She became a risk taker and realised that even when she got an answer to a problem wrong, her success was growing; she was achieving simply by moving towards more effective, consistent ways of thinking.

It was a pleasure to see the looks on the faces of Anju's parents when they reported her scholarship results: the offer of two half-scholarships plus acceptance into an accelerated program at a leading secondary school. Not bad for a shy young under-achiever!

Only a myth

Clarissa, Jack and Anju are only three of thousands of our pupils who have learned the easy-to-grasp strategies that put them in the fast lane to study success; to the achievement of scholarships, and selective school entrance and university placements. Like our other students, they also discovered that the widely held belief, *success means hard work,* is no more than a myth.

Incidentally, another important aspect of working smart can also be achieved. If you stick with this book, you will come to understand and appreciate it. Your school years need no longer be a drag, to be tolerated and endured as best they can. Working smart can transform your outlook. Whether you have years or only months to go, your school time can become a satisfying and enjoyable experience. It can be a period in your life you will look back upon in years to come with nostalgia and pride.

'Oh, come on now, that's really stretching a point,' I hear all the doubting Thomases cry. Right. Time to find out whether I'm bluffing.

Are you ready?

PART 2

On your mark . . .

CHAPTERS 1 - 20

ALL STUDENTS

Understanding yourself and getting organised

CHAPTERS 21 - 24

UPPER PRIMARY

Learning to think, reason and write

Dear Student,

In Part 2, whether you're a procrastinator, a perfectionist or both, whether you're stress prone, simply disorganised, or even have good intentions—if you are a student seeking a better understanding of topics and how to improve your skills for higher levels of success, Chapters 1 to 20 are for you.

Older students:

Older students should also note the following: Towards the end of Part 2, Chapters 21 to 24 have been written to mainly assist upper primary students. However, these chapters may offer benefits for you also that you have not previously considered. In fact, it's a perfect (undercover) way to swot up on gaps in your knowledge without losing face. Explore its possibilities.

Younger students:

At the same time, in other chapters, younger students may find references to subjects or issues they have not yet reached in their schooling. Don't worry! You'll find plenty written just for you to read in depth, right through to Chapter 24 and beyond. So scan the few areas you don't need at this stage and move on to find your special areas of interest and enlightenment. Keep the book safe. You will need it again before long.

Let's take a look.

1

Problems, problems . . .

Problems?

'Why start with *problems?'* you ask. 'Isn't that being a bit negative?'

Not so! Let's look at sport, for example. A very significant ingredient for success in sport is self-diagnosis. Many coaches play a vital role in this process by helping sports stars identify and overcome their weaknesses and problem areas.

In the academic arena, the process and benefits are very similar. So let's invest a few minutes seeing where your strengths and weaknesses may lie.

You'll need a pen or pencil. Over the next 60 seconds, simply jot down in the following box what you see as the main problems or difficulties you commonly face when studying. Put them in order from the hardest. For example: getting started, managing your time, completing the task, and so on. (Don't be concerned about writing in this book; that's what it's for.)

The situation should apply to you, personally, and not necessarily reflect the examples given. (One young man told me he couldn't find time to study because he loved computer games too much! His mum and dad soon fixed that problem.) Give it some thought. A minute of honest self-analysis is a vital lead up to working smart. So go on. What's number one?

1.
2.
3.
4.
5.

Now, using the item numbers for identification, categorise those problems under the headings in the next table. For example, 'getting started' needs motivation, whereas 'time management' would be a matter of skill.

MOTIVATION	SKILL

If you have any trouble with this one, read Chapter 3, 'Motivation', first, and then come back to it. Otherwise, you have now identified whether your problems are a matter of *motivation* or *skill*. Well done! This will assist you to better understand where your strengths and weaknesses lie; what aspects you already have in place and, to coin an old phrase, what could do with a little spit and polish.

Stay with me.

So far, so good.

2

Good intentions are not enough!

Good intentions to succeed are admirable.

Unfortunately, they aren't enough to get us where we want to be. We all know that. The reality is, like a New Year's resolution, even the best of intentions can wane and slip by the wayside—and that's often followed by a deepening sense of self-doubt and failure. 'What a wimp! Can't keep a promise, even to myself,' sort of thing.

What we need is something to keep us going when our good intentions wear thin. And because 'wearing thin' can happen all too swiftly, the next chapter or two will put things into perspective—fast!

. . . Well, what are you waiting for?

3

Motivation

You've been promised something you really want!

That 'something' occupies your every thought. But—there's a price to pay. You must complete a chore in exchange. The chore is irksome. In fact, it's gross! It's dirty, time consuming and requires hard work, sweat, and a systematic approach to getting it done.

Do you do a deal? Of course, you do! That coveted prize at the end of the task, beyond your reach until now, shines before you like a beacon every second of the chore. Each step you take, the job becomes lighter and lighter, your reward closer and closer. This is classic *motivation* at work! When it comes to doing things we dislike, motivation gives us the kick-start we need to get us going. Call it, aiming at a greater purpose beyond the job itself.

Studying for exams or an assignment can be irksome for some, requiring a systematic approach to getting it done. It might even be considered gross. But it's not a dirty job, it doesn't require hard work if you're smart, and in doing so, you won't need to sweat a single bead. Nevertheless, you'd be a lone star if you didn't need a little motivation. Let's examine the motivating factors behind your need to study. They're simplified perhaps, but make the point:

When I study:

1. I will be well prepared for my exams.
2. Thorough preparation means the potential for good results.
3. Good results mean personal satisfaction, and a likely positive relationship with my parents (which can be helpful), teachers (productive), and my peers (the ones who count, anyway).
4. Continuing good results mean sound qualifications.

5. Sound qualifications can lead to a good job and a favourable career that will allow me to also contribute meaningfully to society.

6. A good job offers prospects for higher levels of achievement, more credibility and a solid income—possibly considerable wealth.

7. The above factors in point 6 can open doors to rewarding relationships on many levels both personal and professional, a successful family life, an attractive lifestyle, flexibility to make choices, having *wider* choices, and so on.

Points 1 to 4 are assumed to be short-term goals. By points 6 and 7, we are considering future long-term goals, perhaps ten or 15 years or so from now. Whether short or long-term, you can see how motivation can be defined as a force that propels you towards the *greater purpose* beyond the task.

For now, the task at hand is study.

The greater purpose is the achievement of your goals.

4

Goals

Some students thrive on setting goals. They get a high from the power of motivation. Others think goals suck. If you've begun reading this with a yawn and both eyes half closed, you'll no doubt be grumbling, 'Who needs goals! Why worry about them?'

If you're not used to setting goals, that's a very good question. Perhaps it can be explained like this: when you take a car trip, you usually have a pretty good idea where you're headed, right? If not, you'll likely go nowhere of note and waste a whole heap of time in the process. So, it makes sense. You plan. You have a goal or a destination in mind.

The same goes for the journey you're on right now as a scholar: 13-plus years of schooling designed to prepare you for adulthood and your life ahead. The difference is, it's probably the most important journey you're ever likely to undertake!

However, consider this further analogy for a moment: what if the car ride *were* taken aimlessly, without forethought or a sense of direction? Where would you be? Peering at a solid brick wall in some dark and distant back street might be close to the mark!

So too, the school journey, taken without aims or goals, without planning, without preparation, could land a person at some future time in a place they'd rather not be: Dead End Alley.

Are goals important?

You bet they are!

5

Your crystal ball

Let's take a leap ahead into your future. The aim: to work on some of your goals.

If you've never given it much thought, take time out for a few minutes. Sit back and dream a little. Gaze into your mental crystal ball and imagine several future scenarios under different headings: Your future career. Future relationships including friends and loved ones. Children. Leisure pastimes and interests like sport, helping others, hobbies. Personal possessions, like owning a house or a yacht. Exotic locations, if that's what you yearn for.

When you've finished visualising your future, look at the following circle (or, crystal ball). At each of the four points on the circle, write down a particular goal that you hope to have achieved in, say, ten or 15 years' time.

It's interesting that many pupils, and even adults, find this activity difficult. But there's a consolation prize: the harder you find it, the more beneficial it will be.

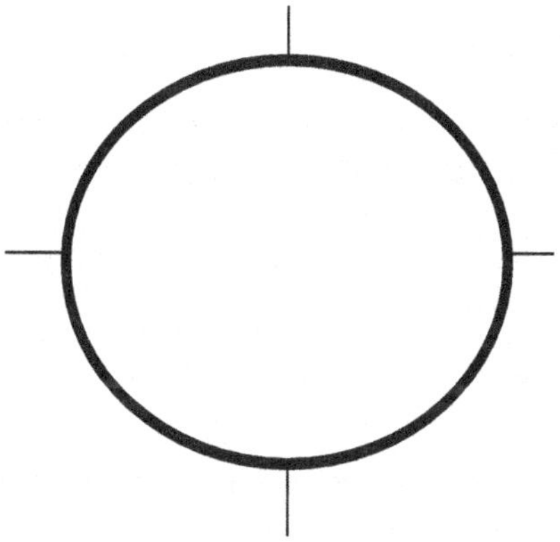

Well done! You have just taken a first step in taking control of your life. Let's look at the others.

6

Steps to achievement

Fear not. Your future has not just been set in concrete. You can change your goals any time. The great thing is: you're headed in the right direction!

You will recall on pages 8-9, the step-by-step list of motivating factors (short- and long-term goals) that were linked to the task of study. This plotting of sequential events is called *mind mapping.* That is, each motivational step in the chain ultimately brings you to the achievement of your long-term goal, or goals. The reverse is called *perting.* This means you start at the end result (that is, your long-term goal) and work backwards through each step to the present time. This is the best way to appreciate what you will need to do to achieve your goals.

Let's try it. Select and record one of your goals from the activity on the previous page. Then fill in the key prerequisites step-by-step. Starting at Step 4, one down from your long-term goal, at each step simply ask yourself, 'What do I need to do, to achieve the result in the box above?'

For example:

MY LONG-TERM GOAL IS ⇨	**To become a successful movie director.**
STEP 4:	Use my credentials and reputation as Assistant Director to work for the best in the field.
STEP 3:	Use my degree and creative flair to achieve work as an Assistant Director.
STEP 2:	Undertake and achieve a much coveted, university degree in filmmaking.
STEP 1:	Achieve good academic results in the final, school year.

Here's another example:

MY LONG-TERM GOAL IS ⇨	**To own and manage a winery.**
STEP 4:	Become a wine expert in order to develop a successful business.
STEP 3:	Travel abroad to study techniques and gain more experience.
STEP 2:	For experience and to save money for travel abroad, get a good job in the field.
STEP 1:	Achieve good academic results to undertake a university degree in wine making.

Now it's your turn. Record more than one goal if you like:

MY LONG-TERM GOAL IS ⇨	
STEP 4:	
STEP 3:	
STEP 2:	
STEP 1:	

MY LONG-TERM GOAL IS ⇨	
STEP 4:	
STEP 3:	
STEP 2:	
STEP 1:	

It's no surprise that you've noted a common thread. The foundation for a number of your goals is *good educational results.* Whether it is getting into the course of your choice or competing against 100 other applicants for a job, the reality is that it is a competitive world. So, if you want to succeed and achieve your goals, you need to take stock right now.

At Edworks we have borrowed an old adage: 'Winners *make* it happen. Losers *let* it happen'. Perhaps this is a good time to ask:

'Which one are you?'

7

The three Rs: Responsibility. Recognition. Rewards.

Let's face it: long-term goals are essential in the scheme of things. But on a day-to-day basis, you would have to be super-human to stay focussed on long-term goals for any length of time. We need short-term goals to keep us going and, of course, the rewards that go with them!

This is a good part: the three Rs. But it's not what you may think. The three Rs are: responsibility, recognition and rewards.

Responsibility:

What is it? What does it mean? In my practice as a psychologist, I find that people's gloomy attitudes and discontentment with life can often be related to two things: a lack of control and denying responsibility.

Such people are often very, very miserable. Typically, they have chosen to abandon all control over their own lives. This means they not only blame others for every negative situation; they also give others responsibility for the positive things that happen to them. The first clue to this lies in their responses when I ask them: 'What does responsibility mean to you?'

How would you respond to this question? Test it and see:

Responsibility means:

Most people write something to the effect that it means 'taking the blame' or 'being accountable for one's actions' when things go wrong.

However, did you realise that the negative, 'blame' aspect of responsibility is only half the equation? This is where recognition comes in.

Recognition:

Recognition allows us to see the other side of responsibility. The positive side. The rosy view. When we do well, being able to recognise and acknowledge that *we* are the ones who have been responsible for our success, is a very significant step towards building self-esteem and continuing to do well.

The problem is, to do this we often have to overcome deeply entrenched ways of thinking. Many parents and teachers have traditionally focussed on and taught only the negative parts of responsibility: the *blame syndrome.* But there's more to it than that. Pivotal to our personal growth is also recognising and taking responsibility for our *achievements.*

It's not as hard as it seems.

We simply reframe our thinking. For example, the next time you complete a challenging task or have some success in your life, don't wait for others to pat you on the back.

Do yourself a favour. Congratulate yourself!

RECOGNISING RESPONSIBILITY

⇩ POSITIVE THINKING ⇩

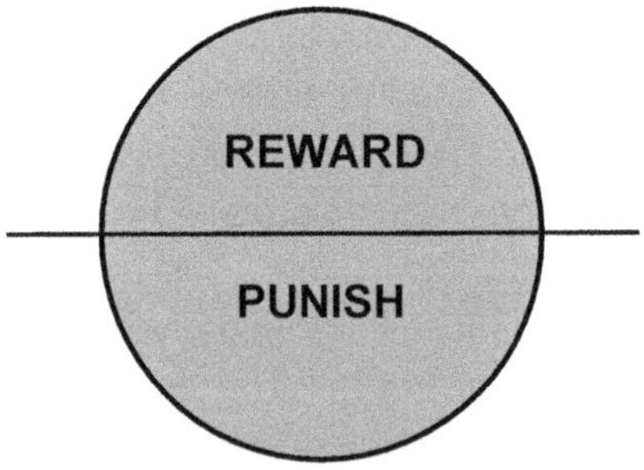

⇧ NEGATIVE THINKING ⇧

Rewards:

Perhaps you link rewards only to chores completed at home or the (sometimes, undeserved) spoils of being a grandchild. If so, and if you view your education and school life as largely depressing and fraught with stress, get ready for a surprise. It need not be that way. Being a student can have its rewards.

Shock! Disbelief! What did you say?

Well, it's in your hands. But learning to reward yourself during your school years is good practice if you want the most out of life and to enjoy it to the max.

If I've piqued your curiosity, have a look.

First thing: find a small pocket book—buy one if possible; this will show you're serious and put you right behind the wheel. Next, when faced with assignments, study or exams set some short-term goals. It's understood, of course, you'll give your best to all tasks—that means within the time frames and according to the task directives.

Jot down brief notes in your pocket book: the assignment, time frames, goals, self-rewards and so on. Then, when you have achieved your goals, (more of that later) go ahead; reward yourself. You'll have earned it!

In a nutshell, what we have learned in this chapter is: 'Responsibility' goes beyond simply owning up when we've done wrong. It also includes 'recognition' for something we've done right! To reinforce the most *rewarding* step in this formula, in large letters, fill in the missing word.

Being a totally responsible person means I should give myself _____________ when I do things well and achieve my goals.

Use a pencil for the next one. Your choice of rewards might change.

A choice of three rewards I could give myself for completing—to the best of my ability—my next study task or assignment:
1.
2.
3.

Come on then! What did you choose? Your mum's chocolate cake? All weekend with your favourite apps—or a good book? Time out with friends? *Fried brains on toast?*

To each his own!

Let's get down to tackling some of the stumbling blocks to success.

8

Overcoming procrastination

We all know the wisdom of the old saying: 'Procrastination is the thief of time'. Seldom are these words truer than when applied to study.

Everyone has been guilty of procrastination at some time—putting off that undesirable job, for instance, that threatens to be time-consuming, smelly, uninspiring, exhausting or just plain boring. Procrastination is part of human nature—an acceptable flaw in our human make-up. That is, as long as it's held in check; as long as it doesn't become a ruling force in our lives.

Students who typically put off studying for assignments or exams may shift in their seats at the memory: the last minute panics, the rushes of adrenaline, the anxiety—and yes, all too often, less than optimum results. Adrenaline highs and burning the midnight oil are meagre substitutes for thorough preparation and planning.

What makes a chronic procrastinator?

Are they born that way? Influenced by parents or siblings? Is it other aspects of their environment; something they've eaten, perhaps? You may well smile.

But if you can face the following, steel yourself.

Let's look at the theory I developed demonstrating one of the likely origins of the syndrome: 'The Brussels Sprouts Theory of Procrastination'.

This is based on the notion that when faced with irksome tasks we have three basic strategies. Indelible imagery aids my case: a dinner plate of food including a nice serving of little green highly odorous Brussels sprouts. What child has ever licked his lips at such a sight? I suspect none! Who has *never* tried to avoid eating the little blighters? Again, I suspect the answer is no one.

To improve our understanding, let's consider some avoidance strategies we might have used in our early childhood when faced with the delectable Brussels sprout.

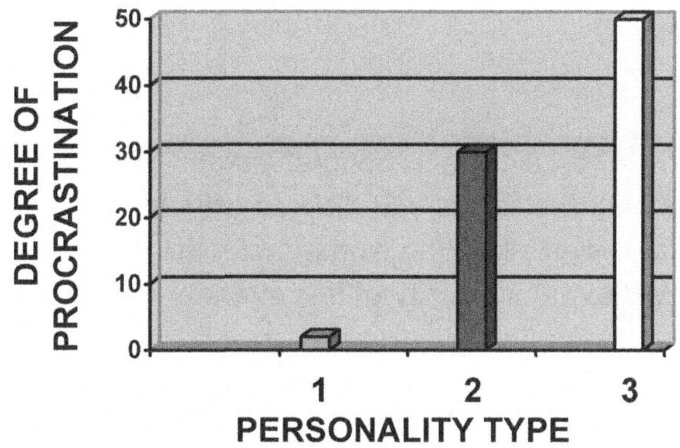

Which personality type are you?
When confronted with Brussels sprouts, how did you react?

Type 1:
You shrugged your shoulders and accepted the inevitability of it all. You ate the Brussels sprouts, keeping your favourite foods till last.

Type 2:
You shrugged your shoulders, but were not quite ready to put them in your mouth. So you spent time (delay tactics) attempting to disguise the sprouts' unique flavour by chopping them, mashing them, mixing them, *pulverising them into putty* with the other foods on your plate—before finally eating them.

Type 3:
You looked the Brussels sprouts in the eye. You then began to eat what you liked most. Determined to avoid the little green balls at all costs, you devised ingenious strategies: hiding the sprouts in your pocket; slipping them under the table to Fido, the dog, who fainted at first whiff, or stealing off to the bathroom for half-an-hour in the hope that all the dinner plates would be gone by the time you returned.

The Brussels Sprouts Theory of Procrastination Interpretation:

Type 1:

If you identified yourself as a Type 1, congratulations! Even at an early age, you faced and dealt with the things you disliked without delay. Only then did you proceed to reward yourself. At the dinner table, the rewards took the form of foods you liked. While the simplicity of this strategy is obvious, it was very effective.

Type 2:

Those who saw themselves as Type 2 personalities tended to labour the point when dealing with the Brussels sprouts. In general, such people appear to have no set strategy and are hindered by procrastination to some degree. It suggests Type 2s are not aware of the benefits of taking full responsibility, of biting the bullet (small green ones in this case) and then rewarding themselves. Recognising your Type 2 personality now, will help you to overcome Brussels sprout-type issues even into adulthood.

Type 3:

Alarm bells should be ringing if you've found yourself in the final category. As a child, your strategy for dealing with unpleasant issues was to ignore them, hoping they would go away.

Still sounds familiar? Many of us continue to employ the same pointless strategies today. It's futile. But we do it! We know deep down such tactics only prolong the situation. We know they make us more resentful. This resentment relates partly to Type 3's experiencing feelings of being out of control.

You will recall I see people in my practice whose suffering revolves often around blaming others for their woes. Is this you, too? When confronted with difficult circumstances your typical responses might be: 'It's not fair; they just don't understand me!' or 'She makes me feel *so* mad!'

If this strikes a chord, think for a moment: life is not and has never been *fair!* We may conduct ourselves with integrity. We may always have the best of intentions. We may strive to do the right thing by people. But, there is no rule that says others must treat us in the same manner. The truth is, we do not have full control over our day-to-day environment. (No one asks, for example, to be harassed by the school bully.)

Fortunately, however, we do have full control over how *we choose* to deal with situations. By this I mean, we need to ensure our thoughts and not our feelings direct our lives. This is where the empowerment lies.

When we don't have control over situations, *we can still be in control*—by having power over our thinking. In turn, this helps us to manage stress.

This is an important message. Why not write this thought down in your pocket book to serve as an everyday reminder:

'I should allow my *thoughts*, not my feelings, to direct my actions.'

When confronted with things we dislike, rather than letting our feelings get in the way, we need to be more positive. An example: when studying, imagine that for whatever reason, you are feeling a little anxious. You may want to blame someone for this: a teacher for setting the task, or a young sibling for causing distractions—distractions, by the way, that you have perhaps unconsciously encouraged).

If you allow your feelings to rule, anxiety can mushroom into physical discomfort like muddled thinking, a cracker of a headache, feeling sick in the stomach, and so on. A worse case scenario is unadulterated panic and falling in a heap; nothing accomplished except a barrel load of stress. What folly!

Here's the solution: If you find yourself in this situation, take a few deep breaths to calm yourself. Then gather your thoughts into order:

Thought 1:
The task seems complex and difficult, but I have a bag of skills to tackle it. (Don't worry! You will learn these skills as we go.)

Thought 2:
I will break the task into smaller parts and complete them one at a time.

Thought 3:
I have access to references including the Internet to assist me.

Thought 4:
I have allowed myself enough time. I will not procrastinate further. I will begin this assignment now.

You see. It's not an insurmountable task after all. In other words, when you permit logical thoughts and not your emotions to determine outcomes, you immediately *take control* of the task or the issue at hand. In achieving this in practice, you will not only accomplish your assignment, you will have learned a valuable strategy that can be applied across many areas of your future life. And the bonus?

Your self-esteem will soar like a bird!

9

Fear of failure

That's not all there is to procrastination, of course.

An aversion to the task at hand is not the only reason people put things off. Perfectionists may also avoid doing things until the last minute. These delay tactics are a direct response to the *fear of failure.*

It is not uncommon. Such fears are felt and seen not only in the classroom, but by people of all ages through all walks of life. Renowned psychologist, Doctor Albert Ellis, recognised this and did some important work on it. He helps us to see things more clearly.

In summary, Doctor Ellis highlights humankind's foibles by suggesting that some people live their lives according to beliefs that defy rational thought. In other words, they live by unrealistic codes that don't make good sense. His proposed 'Ten Irrational Beliefs' include such ideas as:

- it is easier to avoid life's hardships than face them
- we should depend on people stronger than ourselves
- the world should provide our wants and needs, and so on.

Remember, these are Doctor Ellis's *proposed irrational* beliefs. The second of his 'Ten Irrational Beliefs' reads: 'I must be unfailingly competent in all that I do, if I am to consider myself worthwhile.'

In short: 'I must be good at everything, or I'm worthless.' Subconsciously, some procrastinators think they must do *everything* well to be seen as worthy. Irrational thoughts like this can be a gigantic stumbling block when it comes to study. Some pupils want to be seen by their teachers, parents or peers as eternally brilliant in all that they do.

But they can't get started on the task!

They begin to fear failure of assignments or exams and, worse, the perceived disgrace this would bring.

Such perfectionists overlook a very important fact. William Shakespeare highlighted it when he wrote, 'to err is human'. In other words, we are all human and therefore we make mistakes. In turn, making mistakes is one of the best ways we learn.

What happens when we take our first step as an infant, or attempt to ride a bicycle for the first time? Of course, we fall over. But the experience gives us the sense of balance we need to stay upright a little longer the next time we try. Having the will and the courage to try, accepting that we may not get it quite right the first time, is fundamental to the learning process. The irrational belief can therefore be replaced by a realistic thought:

'It would be good to do everything well, but being human means making mistakes.'

When this is learned at a conscious level, would-be perfectionists, including students at study, can discard the barriers of procrastination and advance without fear towards achieving their goals.

Do you think you may be just a bit of a perfectionist? If so, it may help to jot down the rational statements mentioned, in your trusty pocket book. Or keep a card with affirmations (statements) in your wallet for easy reference. Check it regularly.

Here's another suggestion: small coloured stick-on paper dots put around your room or elsewhere, are great reminders of rational statements. Different colours can represent different statements. Such pointers become practical reminders to make your new affirmations at a conscious level. In other words, stop, repeat them to yourself and believe in them. Here are others that may be relevant to you.

☺ **Look on the sunny side; the worst rarely happens.**
☺ **Making mistakes allows me to learn.**
☺ **I hate frustration but I can bear it.**
☺ **To enjoy life more, I'm prepared to take *calculated* risks.**

A perfectionist's equation: **Fail = to be a failure**
A rational person's equation: **Fail = being human**

10

The ultimate reward: time on your hands

Along with your sense of accomplishment, the ultimate reward of overcoming procrastination is—free time!

Yes!

Time to devote to yourself—to indulge yourself; do what *you* want. Take in a movie. Play tennis. Catch up on the latest sci-fi novel. Visit your beloved grandparents. Go cycling. Dust off your skate board and hit the vert ramp.

Just think: time away from studies to relax and revitalise your life through family, friends, interests and hobbies.

I guess some mouths have dropped open. Remarkably, many pupils see studying as an endless production line: one assignment after another. As soon as one is completed, another waits to be done. Such students believe there's no choice; that completing tasks ahead of schedule only means the next one will be staring them in the face.

Wrong!

That is definitely *not* what overcoming procrastination is all about. Remember the old saying: 'All work and no play make Jack a dull boy'? If that were not written to alert compulsive students of study, then it may well have been. Removing the shackles of procrastination means freeing up time so that your well-deserving self can pursue the interests that will enhance your quality of life. Not only that, it will bring balance into your everyday living to make you a better person.

Showing how time can be used to advantage, the simple diagram below, spells it out loud and clear. When you move from Student A to Student B, you will spend less time studying and earn more time to use as you please.

ALLOCATION OF TIME

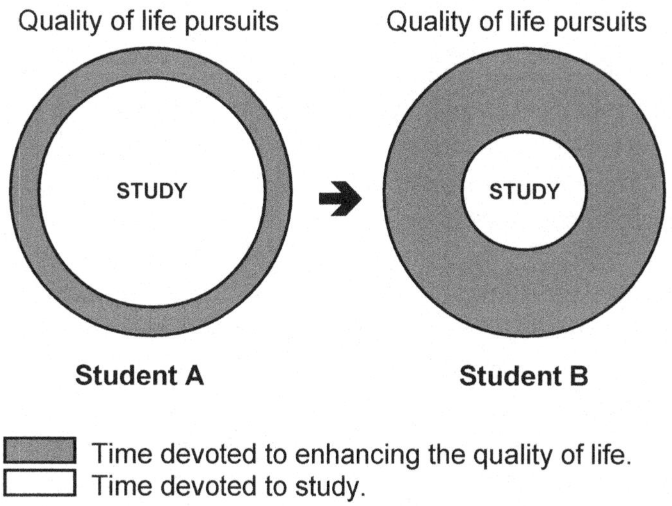

Studying doesn't have to leave you drained and stressed out. However, if you equate study to years spent in hard labour, then beware, that's what it probably will be! Life is what you make it. But remember:

You have the power to choose.

11

The power of working smart

What is your idea of success?

Making the cover of Time magazine? Becoming the world's top model or wealthiest business tycoon? Achieving a 'Sportsperson of the Year' award? Winning a Pulitzer Prize?

Few mortals, of course, achieve such lofty goals. The point is, definitions of success vary. But for those already at the top, there is usually a common success formula comprising key factors where leverage, or working smart, is high on the list.

You will remember we spoke of working smart in Part 1 *Ready . . .*, on page xxxvii. Working smart through leverage empowers us to be successful using *less time, effort and energy* than we generally thought possible.

Have you ever watched someone change a flat tyre on a car, for example? If so, you will know that loosening the nuts on a wheel requires a fair degree of effort. How then can truck drivers loosen the wheel nuts of huge trucks with only the same effort as that needed for a car? The answer is *leverage!* To cope with the greater demands of a truck, we simply increase the length of the wheel brace. In turn, this gives us greater leverage and the wheel nuts can be loosened with ease. Smart? Without a doubt!

Here's another idea:

What about singers and writers? Do they stroll around cities and towns singing their songs and telling their stories over and over again, like days of old? Of course not! We've come a long way since the Dark Ages. Today, artists use leverage. Working smart, they create CDs, DVDs and books, often using YouTube and e-books on the Internet to significantly expand their customer base. Instead of reaching a minority, they may sell their works to millions of people! Less time! Less effort! *Incomparable* results!

Let's have a look at the components of working smart as they apply to you as a student. What are the essentials for success at school, while using less time, less effort and less energy than we normally do?

Working smart is comprised of:

1. **Awareness**
2. **Motivation** and
3. **Skills**

Motivation has already been introduced. Let's examine the remaining two factors in more detail and the reason we need them:

Awareness

Awareness is our starting block. It simply means having an understanding or knowledge of something. But *knowing* is one thing. Knowing *how* in terms of developing competent skills is quite another matter. If you've ever had golf, ballet or tennis lessons, for example, you will probably agree. It might take just a few minutes for a golf pro. to remind us how to swing a golf club; or for a ballet teacher to demonstrate a delicate pirouette; or a Serena Williams DVD to show us how to hold that racquet.

But then what? We spend years trying to translate our awareness (hampered perhaps by bad habits or poor co-ordination) into everyday skills. So much so for knowing what to do! You can see why learning *how* to do things comes in handy. Perhaps the next story will convince you as we look at skills.

Skills

Imagine this: Dermot had never bothered to learn how to swim. He was quite happy just to float on top of the water or splash around. One balmy summer's day, he was paddling blissfully in the sea when a sudden movement caught his eye. To his horror he could see a large menacing fin cutting through the water and headed his way at an uncomfortable rate of knots.

Panicking, Dermot turned to the shore, his motivation to swim rocketing by several thousand per cent! But his poor skill level meant that all he could muster was a splashing good dog paddle, and . . . unfortunately . . . the lucky shark got his lunch.

Clearly the message is that awareness and motivation alone won't get you across the line (or to shore for that matter), unless you have the skills to follow through. The good news is that unlike sport, the skills needed for study and the results that ensue aren't nearly as difficult to achieve.

At our centres, where the lives of many pupils have been transformed, *awareness, motivation* and *skills* have each played their part. However, they are not always needed in that order. In fact, in some cases, students certainly have the motivation and the ability to do well. They simply lack the awareness and the supporting strategies (the skills) to accomplish successful study and achieve optimum results.

Once they are shown the way, everything falls into place. Remember, Clarissa, Jack and Anju? Many of our pupils progress in leaps and bounds. After achieving a very good mark for his assignment, one Year 8 boy told his father excitedly: 'Dad, I really don't know how I could get any smarter!'

Here's the equation you might want to jot down:

Awareness + Motivation + Skills = Working Smart

Importantly, part of awareness is knowing that *planning and managing study time* are fundamental keys to success. We will look at them in the next chapter or two.

With a little skills practice, you'll be adding a new feather to your cap!

12

Heeding Father Time

Have you ever thought what would happen if we ignored Father Time in our everyday lives? You've got it!

Chaos!

Life would be one big untidy tangle of events—lumping and bumping together, twisting and turning, piling one on top of the other like a gigantic plate of spaghetti! In fact, organised society as we know it could not exist.

Imagine the world of business without clocks! Busy directors would miss board meetings. Reps would miss customer appointments and lose sales. If time were ignored, workers would roll up for work any old hour of the day. Executives would plump for the long lunch (if restaurateurs opened in time to serve them, that is). But restaurant service would be the least of our worries.

What of emergency services? If time were totally disregarded, police or ambulances might take a day before they reached you. Shock, horror! You could be hit over the head or stung by a jelly fish! Hospitals could be on skeleton staff—the surgeon at golf, mindless of the hour (and on the putting green alone, incidentally, if his colleagues failed to show).

Public transport systems would be a wipe-out! Buses, trains and planes would never arrive or leave on time. Shops would open and close on a whim. Schools? (I'll let you ponder that one!) Cinemas and television? Now, there's a thought! They'd run features at random, string them together like beads, show them at weird times. You couldn't rely on a program; and think of the length of the ads! Advertisers would make them as long as the features.

Is heeding time important? Of course it is! In fact, it's like a system of government. Without it, confusion and disorder would reign supreme and we would all have headaches bigger than the state of Texas.

You will realise by now I'm hinting at the impact of time when it comes to study. For example, how long would it take you to write a good creative essay, say, a page-and-a-half? Two hours? Three hours? If so, consider the following.

Our pupils, trained to work smart, can deliver in 30 minutes! That's brainstormed, planned and final copy (as if conducted in an examination setting). Thirty minutes, max.

How do they do it? For starters, they are skilled at time management. They know how to break assignments into segments: into smaller manageable tasks. They have learned how much time they should devote to each segment. They instinctively check their watches. They practise. They bring other skills they have learned into play. (We'll examine those in the coming chapters.) The results are well-constructed, thoughtful, individualistic pieces, worthy of high marks and of which any student would be proud.

Want to know how it's done? Keep reading! You are on the verge of developing a primary skill for working smart.

Now we can match words with action.

13

The Two-Factor Model

'Be prepared!'

This nifty little motto has been used worldwide by the scouting movement for more than a century. Its message is that if we are ready for the events that cross our path, outcomes will likely be brighter. Being prepared for study is no exception; and planning with timetables will give you an edge.

Timetabling your assignments is an important part of working smart. But firstly, we need to prioritise our weekly workload.

Despair not if you've always avoided this task or are unsure how it works; a model is already set up for you.

With minimal practice, once you have reviewed the advice, it should take you no more than five or six minutes to prioritise your work and complete a timetable for two weeks of assignments. When you have achieved this, you can amend it each week as you finish tasks and add more. This ensures work is completed in an orderly way, on time, *and* with time up your sleeve.

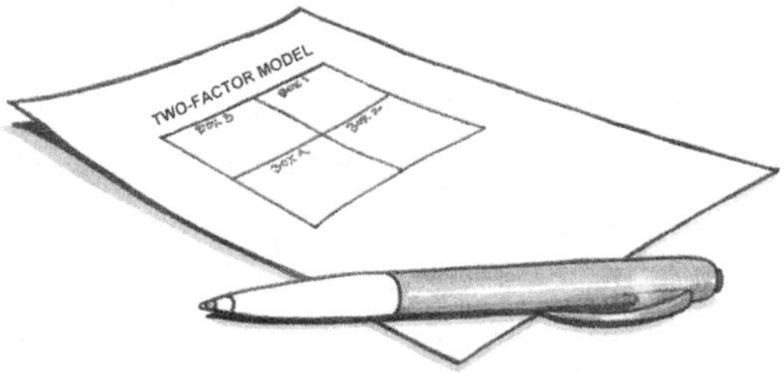

For younger students, even if you are not yet in secondary school, prioritising and timetabling your projects now, will greatly assist you later. Ask your teacher or family to assist you.

Let's have a closer look.

Prioritising your work using:

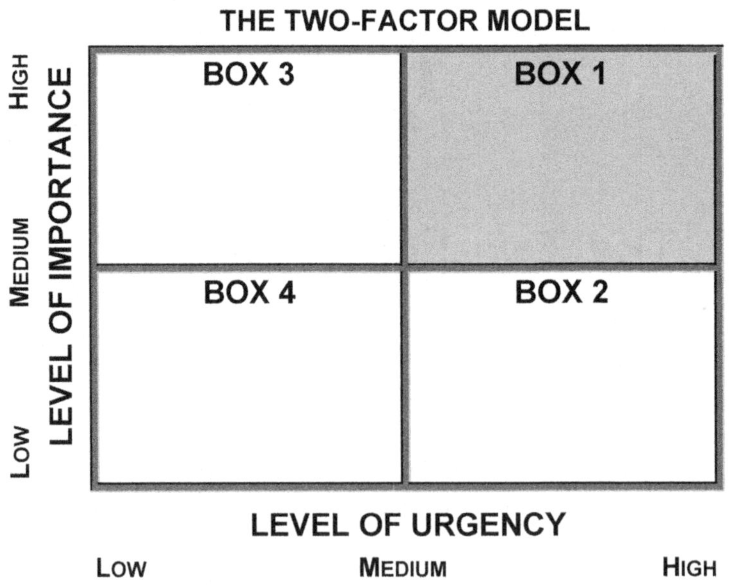

As you can see, The Two-Factor Model comprises a grid of four boxes, numbered 1 to 4. The two factors that show how to prioritise your work are:

1. Level of **Importance**
2. Level of **Urgency**

Importance reflects the value of an assignment. (That is, the percentage points it contributes to your end-of-term, or end-of-semester grades, eg ten per cent, 25 per cent, and so on.)

Urgency denotes the time you have to complete the task, depending on the due date—four days, a week, etc.

When handed a class assignment, you are also given its value and due date. Therefore, you can immediately assess its two-factor status.

Younger students are given a due date for a project which is marked on completion. However, such work usually doesn't have a percentage value attached. If you explain to your teacher that you would like to put in some practice for the years ahead, s/he may be happy to give you an idea of the overall value of a project in relation to its subject.

From Low to High, the left-hand vertical of The Two-Factor Model shows Level of **Importance**. (For example, an assignment worth ten per cent would be considered of Low Importance; 25 to 35 per cent, of High Importance.)

The bottom horizontal shows Level of **Urgency** from Low to High. (That is, an assignment due in three days would be considered Urgent, whereas one due in two weeks, Non-urgent.)

One box, for example, would hold tasks that are both Important (having high percentage values) and Urgent (almost due for handing in). Another box would contain work of Low Importance but that was nonetheless, Urgent. Which boxes are these? That's right. **Boxes, 1** and **2,** respectively.

Let's look at them together:

Box 1: Important-Urgent assignments (shaded).

Box 2: Low Importance but **Urgent**.

Box 3: Important but **Low Urgency** assignments.

Box 4: Low Importance-Low Urgency.

Of course, the value of an assignment remains constant. The Level of Urgency changes, however, as the due date draws closer. Therefore, as assignments in **Boxes 1** and **2** are completed and leave your timetable, work in **Boxes 3** and **4** can be transferred across to **Boxes 1** and **2** as they move from Low Urgency to Urgent. Any new assignments are also assessed and slotted into their appropriate boxes.

An example: if you have an English essay, we'll call Task A, due in three days' time and worth 25 per cent of your final marks, then it would be high in both factors and therefore placed in **Box 1**.

A history essay, Task B, also worth 25 per cent, but not due for three weeks, would be slotted into **Box 3**. In two weeks' time, Task A would be well finished and Task B moved across into **Box 1**.

Yet another assignment, Task C, worth, say, only ten or 15 per cent and due in 5 days, would go into **Box 2**, while a Task, D, worth 15 per cent and due in four weeks would be relegated to **Box 4**. Task C drops off the table on completion and Task D moves into **Box 2** as it become an urgent factor.

Got it?

Great! But before we practise, do read the next brief chapter.

Then it's time you had a break!

14

Recharging your batteries

'Samantha yawns a lot,' sighed Mr. Witherspoon.

'She sits long enough in front of her books, but her grades don't reflect it.' An anxious parent was telling me of his Year 9 daughter. 'Half the time she seems to be in a bit of a daze,' he said. 'But she plods on.'

Such parental concerns often cross my desk.

Students will sit for hours taking great pains to 'put in the effort'. But their grades seldom reflect the time spent on assignments. Not knowing how to work smart, students often overlook the importance of recharging their batteries when studying. 'Putting in the hours' is false economy if it's not accompanied by good common sense. To keep the concentration flowing, you need to stoke up your energy stores.

A part-answer lies in a simple strategy: *Move!* Get up! Move about. Go to the kitchen for an apple. S-t-r-e-t-c-h those limbs. Do some sit-ups. Take a minute to breathe deeply. Fill your lungs with some clean fresh air. Hold it in! One-two-three-four-five and release. But don't stop there: Shake a leg. Raise an arm. Roll a punch (at the punching bag). Dance a step. Nip outside. Get the idea? It's called the renewing Five-Minute Break or FMB. It should come about 45 minutes after sitting at your desk. The FMB is not only healthy practice, it's a vital part of working smart.

Keep the TV *off*, and if you visit the kitchen during your break, don't be tempted by fatty high-sugar and salty junk food. Leave the chips and fizzy drinks and grab a piece of fruit. Sip on some juice. Nibble a nut. Revitalising our body cells with oxygen through deep breathing, mild exercise and wholesome snack foods is an energising combo when studying. They clear the cobwebs, refresh the body and restore our wit and humour.

Like a car engine, your brain needs premium grade fuel for a top performance. And like a car engine, it will likely get sluggish if idle too long. So take an FMB—but then grab your bag.

That engine of yours needs putting through its paces to keep up its spark.

15

Skill 1: Smart prioritising

Refreshed? Good. Let's get down to business:

Imagine you are set homework assignments in class on August 2nd.

Starting below is an example of such assignments. Due dates range from 6th to 16th August. A sample Two-Factor Model is on page 38 for you to complete, using the homework information provided.

Box 1 is already done for you as a guide. Your job is to allocate the remaining assignments into their respective boxes within five minutes or less. But, whoa! Hold on!

It's important you scan the homework example *first*. Then, on the next page, read 'Breaking down tasks' carefully, before attempting to tackle the task.

AUGUST

SUN	MON	TUE	WED	THU	FRI	SAT
1	2	3	4	5	6	7
8	9	10	11	12	13	14
15	16	17	18	19	20	21
22	23	24	25	26	27	28
29	30	31				

[shaded box] = Homework due

HOMEWORK

Week commencing Monday, 2nd August

French:

Translate the short story on pages 27 and 28 from your French textbook.

- ❒ Due date: 11th August.
- ❒ Value 10%.
- ❒ Suggested time taken:
  ① Translation—1 hour.

Maths:

Produce a graph comparing the sugar, fat and salt content of five brands of breakfast cereal. Interpret your results stating which cereal is the healthiest and give reasons. Are any of the manufacturers misleading the public? (300 words)

- ❒ Due date: 9th August.
- ❒ Value 35%.
- ❒ Suggested time taken:
  - ① Researching and collecting data—1½ hours.
  - ② Interpret and write report—2 hours.
  - ③ Edit and final copy—½ hour.

Art:

Following our visit to the National Gallery complete the questionnaire.

- ❒ Due date: 6th August.
- ❒ Value: 10%.
- ❒ Suggested time taken:
  - ① Answer questionnaire—2 hours.

Geography:

Salination is a global problem: What farming methods have contributed to salination? Include maps and graphs to show how the situation has worsened over recent decades. What are some practical ways farmers can assist in overcoming this problem? **(400 words)**

- ❒ Due date: 13th August.
- ❒ Value: 15%.
- ❒ Suggested time taken:
  - ① Research—1½ hours.
  - ② Note-taking—1 hour.
  - ③ First draft—1½ hours.
  - ④ Editing and final copy—2 hours.

English Essay

Title: 'The most embarrassing moment in my life was when . . .' **(800 words)**

- ❒ Due date: 16th August.
- ❒ Value 20%.
- ❒ Suggested time taken:
  - ① Brainstorm and plan—½ hour.
  - ② First draft—2 hours.
  - ③ Edit and final copy—½ hour.

Breaking down tasks

You will notice that at the end of each subject under, 'Suggested time taken', the assignment is broken down into small manageable units.

This serves several purposes:

Firstly, the task is not overwhelming! The smaller units allow you to plan realistically *what you think you can achieve within a given time frame.* Secondly, you can then assign time-frames for completing each segment of the task. Finally, you can monitor how well you are sticking to the times. That's working smart! In other words, you progress *one step at a time.*

Sports people use this approach to maintain focus and motivation. Mountain climbers pace themselves in the same manner. They aim for first base to begin and proceed accordingly, base-by-base.

Imagine if they set their sights on achieving their goals in one go. Mountain peaks would never be conquered!

The same step-by-step approach will help you to maintain and follow an established timetable and ensures that you apportion your time and pace yourself in the right manner. If you aren't too certain, ask your teachers or someone at home to assist you to break down the tasks.

Once you have allocated the tasks to their respective boxes, you can then simply prioritise each task segment.

I recommend that you look at tasks from **Boxes 1** and **Box 2,** first.

THE TWO-FACTOR MODEL

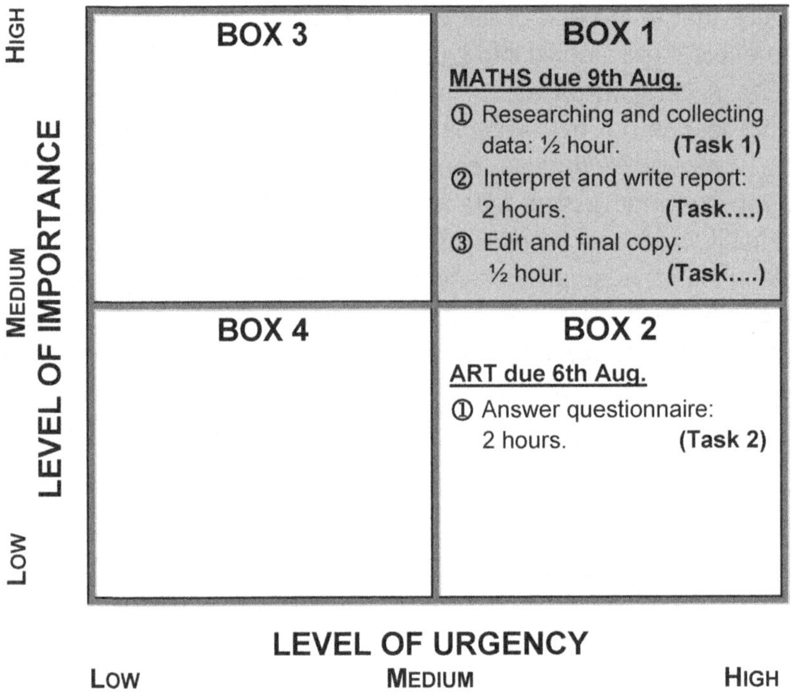

In the **Box 1** example, beginning early in the week at one sitting (with breaks), we aim to complete:

Maths:

① Researching and collecting data—½ hour, and then undertake:

Art:

① Answer questionnaire—2 hours.

You will notice the other segments in **Box 1**, (Maths ② and ③) have not yet been allocated task numbers. Those task numbers will not be known until you have filled out the entire model with the homework given. However, as they are in **Box 1**, (Important-Urgent) they should be completed in the early stages of the week.

You should also aim to tackle segments from **Box 3** and **Box 4,** as soon as time permits. This means you can keep on top of all tasks and have some of them already underway by the time they move across to **Boxes 1** and **2.**

Remember, start early in the week.

Would you like to compare your effort of prioritising the homework assignments with ours? You'll find our suggested guidelines in the Appendix, the first tool of 'Brain-boosters for Working Smart', page 231.

There is also a template of The Two-Factor Model in the Appendix, page 235. You can photocopy and enlarge it to use as often as you wish. Alternatively, print one from Edworks' website at edworksglobal.com; click on the 'Checklists and Templates' tab. Keep your Two-Factor Model for prioritising assignments in a special book or file and up-date or replace it on a regular basis.

Let's finish off the job with Skill 2, by filling in the timetable.

16

Skill 2: Smart timetabling

Timetabling itself is pretty straightforward.

After prioritising, using your own shorthand (eg *M-3, 2h* meaning *Maths, Task 3, 2 hours*) simply transfer your prioritised schedule onto a timetable. A timetable template is provided in the Appendix, page 236, for photocopying and enlarging for your everyday use. Practise here, with the timetable below.

WEEKLY TIMETABLE

🕐	MON	TUE	WED	THU	FRI	SAT	SUN
9 am							
10 am							
11 am							
Noon							
1 pm							
2 pm							
3 pm							
4 pm							

5 pm							
6 pm							
7 pm							
8 pm							
9 pm							

Remember, working smart means you should aim to complete your set tasks in as short a time as possible. However, this should never be at the expense of the quality of your work.

Recapping, the guidelines discussed so far for 'Skill 1: Smart Prioritising', 'Skill 2: Smart timetabling' plus settling down to study are:

1. Break assignments into smaller tasks.
2. Prioritise those tasks.
3. Transfer tasks to your weekly timetable.
4. In your pocket book, record three tasks and the reward/s you aim to give yourself on completion.
5. Begin as soon as possible.
6. Monitor the time.
7. Allow an FMB every 45 minutes or so; get up and move around.
8. Eat only sensible snacks such as fruit.
9. Be balanced! Allow time for recreation and hobbies.

Using real homework assignments, with practice, you will develop skills that will soon be second nature. By now you will understand that prioritising with The Two-Factor Model and timetabling are designed to:

- Focus you on relevant tasks (even those you normally put off till last).
- Keep you on track for *all* assignments.
- Avoid procrastination.
- Save time for other activities.
- Produce better results.
- Reduce stress.

The last point is particularly important.

We should not overlook that a key function of The Two-Factor Model is to *reduce stress.* That is not to say a little stress from time to time cannot be useful—it may even sharpen your wits.

However, should you feel the sweat on your brow and your concentration fizzing like a headache pill in water as your workload builds up, it will pay you to be aware of what is happening to your body and how to manage the symptoms.

It's normal. But you'll need 'fight-back'.

17

What is stress?

Stress is normal, as I said. Perfectly natural; an inherent part of life.

For example, confronting one's secondary years after primary school can be stressful for some: a time when cheerful classroom projects smelling of paste are suddenly traded for the whiff of ink and written assignments that seem to pile endlessly like the Eiffel Tower.

It's a time for knuckling down. For getting serious. A time for exams—and a bunch of symptoms, too, that might come with them. Take your pick: a throbbing headache, feeling sick or dizzy, a pounding heart, breathlessness, sweaty palms, confusion, a blank memory. Ah, the turbulent mind seeking order. Stress, stress, stress!

For some, as deadlines draw near, the prospect of study alone can signal stress symptoms.

In Chapter 8, page 20, we discussed that some stressful situations are beyond our control. However, a lot of stress is avoidable. Indeed, some stress—*good* stress, that is—actually works in our favour. For example, stress is the mover and shaker that gets us up in the morning; it's what motivates us to achieve. We'd certainly be lost without that! Looking forward to a holiday raises the heartbeat. Falling in love sets it aflutter. Winning a major prize can be breathtakingly stressful. Can these things be bad? Of course not! They are all good motivating stuff; they make us feel excited and happy.

Actually, much of this pleasant stress produces similar biochemical reactions (chemical changes inside the body) to those caused by the unpleasant stress in our lives—the fear, the anger, anxiety, resentment, frustration, panic and so on. The human body readily adjusts to good stress responses. We can even handle the unpleasant stresses in life fairly well, provided they're short-lived. (Realising in the dead of night that a noise is only a cat, for example; the heartbeat pretty quickly gets back to normal. No harm done.)

Interestingly, until quite recently, scientists believed laughter to be stressful.

But now they know its physical action actually *reduces* it. So enjoy that comedy; have a good belly laugh at a funny joke. It can be very therapeutic!

The main trouble is that our modern lives are fraught with *ongoing,* unpleasant stress or *distress.* It is almost relentless. Just by watching television or reading the media, we are exposed to the stresses of aggressive advertising or distressing films or news items.

Doctors know too well the health impact of distress on today's society: We humans get sick from it. We are injured by it. Unpleasant stress contributes big time to heart disease, cancer, lung ailments, accidental injuries and suicide. They are all among our leading causes of death. Three of the top-selling drugs today, are a tranquilliser, an ulcer medication, and a blood pressure pill. These are all designed to help people cope with chronic (ongoing) stress.

In Chapter 8, you may recall our discussion and strategies to overcome stress due to procrastination (pages 20-21). Look back on this chapter again as a reminder, if necessary. From this, we learned that stress is actually a very personal condition. Its presence or intensity is measured by how an individual may respond to the *cause* of the stress.

The event or factor causing the stress is called the *stressor.* (So, if you suffer stress being goaded by the school bully, or chased by a neighbourhood dog, the bully and the dog would be the stressors.) Our stress responses have a taxing effect on the body. Being of a personal nature, we may each react differently.

Personality types

You've probably heard people described as Type A or Type B personalities. Stress researchers slot these types into these two classes: Type A people often suffer higher stress levels trying to get too much done in too short a time. Consequently, it's common also for them to become easily irritated.

Type B personalities, on the other hand, are more serene. They display calmness and the ability to *roll with the punches.* (Guess which type copes better with stress?)

Even for those in between, responses can vary depending on personal circumstances. For example: a red traffic light may be accepted calmly by you as a driver, yet with annoyance by me, who is late for an appointment.

A novice skier, putting on skis for the first time, may suffer a severe attack of nerves (stress). Yet, a veteran skier with skills that match an expectation to perform well may feel just enough to get the adrenaline pumping. Similarly, the prospect of sitting for an exam may be accepted calmly by some pupils, anxiously by others.

Like the veteran skier, the calm students have their skill levels and performance expectations nicely balanced. High skill levels and expectations for strong performances. No fear. No jangling nerves. There is little, if any stress at all.

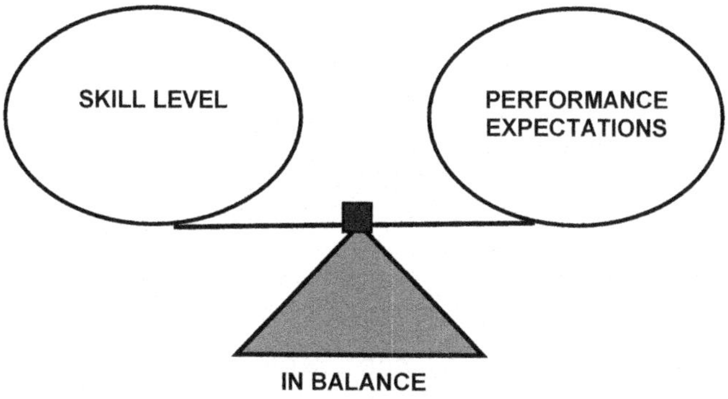

The anxious students have sound reasons to be worried. Yet, their anxiety can be caused for different reasons:

1. Some have lacked motivation during the year, are poorly skilled and are ill-prepared for the exam. Naturally, they expect to fail and are feeling the strain.

2. Others have been achievers, but they've lost the plot. Their motivation and self-confidence have taken a nose-dive. Stress is up.

3. Then there are still others, like Bianca, whom we'll meet in the next chapter. Here, there is strong motivation; but there is no awareness of working smart: no smart skills to pass the exams with the flying colours she had worked so hard to achieve.

4. Yet other students are under pressure for a totally different reason: stress also results when we expect more of ourselves than we can actually deliver. In other words, when we have a higher expectation of our performance than our skills will allow.

Let's look at point 4 for a moment:

Such expectations are irrational. Like those of the perfectionist discussed in our 'fear of failure' chapter, page 22, they don't make good sense. In this case, the scales are unbalanced: low skill levels outweigh expectation levels.

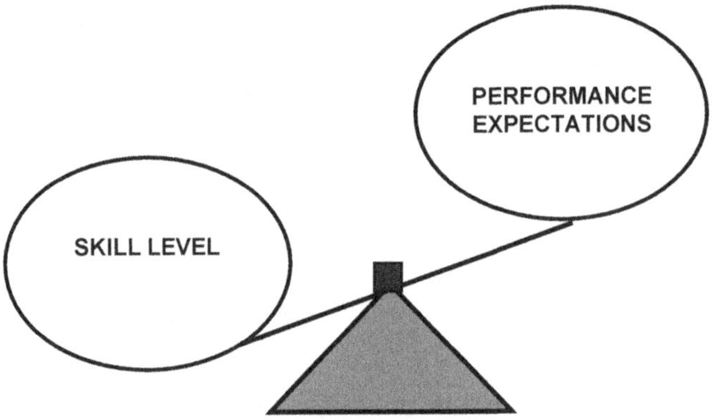

Stress can be considerable for people with distorted beliefs about their own ability to perform.

For example, children of highly successful parents may suffer this syndrome. They think that to be held worthy or have credibility themselves, they must reach the same heights as their accomplished parents.

This can occur even though, being only young, they have had neither the advantage of many years' experience, nor the passage of time to develop the parents' skills. Adults with this syndrome who fail to achieve a parent's attributes, may simply lack the parent's innate talent for success. (A similar syndrome can also affect the sibling of a high-achieving brother or sister.)

As we have seen, overcoming irrational beliefs is something we can learn. If the belief can be nipped in the bud, all the better.

Step one requires some honest self-appraisal. Those concerned need to look reality in the eye.

Step two involves learning to recognise and accept your personal strengths and weaknesses as defining who *you* are. Adopting a more realistic view then allows you to judge what you should expect of yourself.

These steps take courage! But taking them removes the conflict of ideas and the tensions disappear. For pupils facing this issue, making a conscious decision to take control in this way can be exhilarating! Some have described it as akin to being released from a ball and chain. It means being free to accept that:

- ☺ it's good to do everything well, but
- ☺ to err is human, after all.

And provided you are well prepared with the skills for working smart, stress during study and exam times, will be allowed to diminish to manageable levels. In fact, it will melt away like ice on a warm day.

However, being aware of stress and how or why it may affect us does not provide all the answers. The world is a big place. Issues can be complex when dealing with individuals and some go beyond the scope of this book. Nonetheless, in the next chapter you will also discover:

- why shadow behaviour is bad
- how mirror behaviour can be good, and
- how visualisation, particularly at study time, can be practised to combat rising stress.

Add these pearls of wisdom to your armoury for working smart.

18

Skill 3: Managing stress

Control. And good management. That's what it's all about.

The key to coping with stress in pursuit of your goals is: *learn to control it!* Then it becomes manageable. In other words, stress won't interfere with your performance if you can *lower* your responses to it—or remove it altogether!

Recently, a Year 12 pupil, we'll call Bianca, wrote to a news editor after her mid-year exams. Bianca had studied her subject diligently for well over a year. She had swotted solidly for a month before the exam. When faced with the exam paper however she had panicked. She rushed through the paper and didn't read the questions properly. As a result, she was left in the doldrums with a very average mark.

Bianca blamed herself. She said she became frazzled and choked on the exam. But she claimed had she not been under such pressure to perform, she could have done the exam in her sleep. What had happened? What had caused this unfortunate outcome?

Bianca had crumpled in a heap because the exam she blew was worth a good deal: a third of her final mark. In spite of being 'well prepared' for the exam, she'd allowed anxiety about her results and their importance to affect her ability to perform at her best. Panic, stress, panic! Bianca was yet to learn a cold hard fact of life: worrying is futile and can only make things worse!

There are two points to make here:

Firstly, did Bianca know how to work smart? She may have studied long and hard. But had she developed the right skills? How ordered was her memory bank? Was her thinking structured in such a way she could retrieve information reliably and systematically? Had she practised, for example, (like a marathon runner facing a gruelling event) breaking down the task into manageable units and taking them step-by-step?

Secondly, she let her feelings take over. Her dominant thoughts about the exam's importance to her final mark mushroomed into overwhelming anxiety.

This worked against any positive energy she might have harnessed to keep her normal stress response to the exam in check.

How do you view it?
Is it a threat or a challenge?

Had Bianca been able to see her exam in perspective as a challenge rather than a threat to her final mark, the results may have been different. Her peer group had no problems. Bianca's high stress level was self-generated.

However, it *was* controllable.

Incidentally, there was no call to remove it completely. A little adrenaline would have given her a nice edge. That is, being 'in control' allows you to function efficiently, even in the face of a little stress.

Importantly, this is a lesson of life.

Recent scientific studies suggest that in learning how to deal with stress in our lives, we develop mental toughness and strength against future stress. Be it for exams, business or in sport, when competitors' skill differences are only marginal, it is not the person who blacks out under stress who wins the day. It's the one who can maintain focus and keep a balanced perspective. It's the person with the ability to achieve, *one step at a time.*

Note the words 'balanced perspective'. This means being positive and motivated without losing your cool. Many sports coaches learned this lesson the hard way. Before sports psychology became popular, they believed the more rousing their motivation techniques, the better their athletes would perform.

Bitter experience proved them wrong.

Such stimulating up-beat techniques prior to big events raised stress to undesirable levels. Players' performances peaked, and then flagged dramatically, causing them to lose. These days, many sports people are instead seen engaged in various forms of relaxation therapy before major competitions.

The following table on the next page shows just how stress levels can affect performance. Performances are raised to a certain level during well-managed stress. But when stress overload cuts in, performances plummet. In other words, too much stimulation can be unproductive, causing stress overload to work against you.

STRESS PERFORMANCE INDICATOR

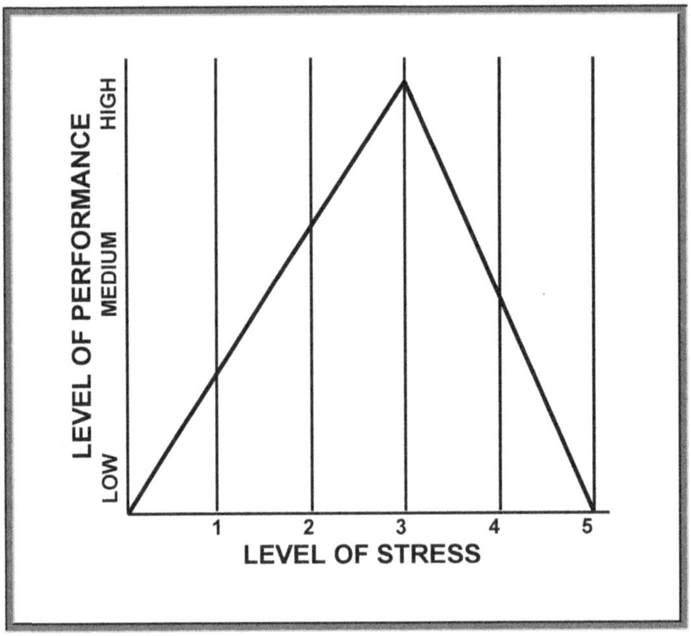

Becoming self-aware

How does this translate for you as a student? It means for peak performance, you need to be self-aware—to listen to and understand your own body so that you can reach and maintain an optimum level of performance where manageable stress can work in your favour.

A number of tried and true therapies can help us to become more self-aware and be useful in reducing stress when important events loom ahead. Skills developed now, will aid you for a lifetime.

Let's investigate some of them:

➢ **Be a naturalist (in your own room)**

Getting back to nature by listening to soothing sounds has helped many people to restore calm and to cope with their busy everyday lives. Find a CD of therapeutic sounds, for example, from nature. Rolling waves crashing against rocks, birds singing in a forest setting, water gurgling in a brook, the sound of rain and so on, can all be very calming. Try it.

Well ahead of exam time or any big pressure event, find some privacy, perhaps in a bedroom or study. Put on your CD, get comfortable and allow yourself to be transported wherever your imagination takes you for about 15 minutes. These natural treatments have been shown to slow the heartbeat and lower blood pressure and are considered an antidote to tension.

➢ Be an optimist

Learning to become an optimist, someone who thinks positively, is pleasant to be around, will have a positive impact. Even should things go awry, if you are normally well-balanced and happy with friends and strong family support, you will be well placed to cope with potentially stressful situations.

Some researchers believe, too, that when we experience negative circumstances such as bad news or suffering some kind of adversity (for example, surviving a bad car accident), being able to respond in a positive manner can actually strengthen our bodies and lead to higher levels of health and perhaps, longer life.

Don't forget!

Strike a healthy balance between work and play. Relaxing the mind and body through other means like exercise, yoga, tai chi, religion, meditation and so on, can offer excellent opportunities to relax and unwind. Check out your local media, library or phone book and join a club!

This is supported by a US study at the Mayo Clinic in Minnesota of 839 people over a period of 30 years. The study showed that the happy optimists in the group had a greater life expectancy than their grumpy, pessimistic cohorts.[24] ('Cohorts' are 'colleagues' or 'people banded together in a group'.)

➢ Mirror behaviour

We can actually learn to control stress through a happy frame of mind—*even if we have to copy, or mirror the behaviour of, someone else!*

Observing others, like friends or relatives who have cheerful pleasant personalities and show confidence and self-control, may help us to change our own dispositions. US psychology professor at Hope College, Dr. David Myers, suggests that simply *acting* 'happy' may help us to *become* happier. But he warns: 'You can't just sit around waiting for inspiration to become happier. You need to get up and start acting the way happy people act and talking as happy people talk.'

There's also a bonus up for grabs: as mentioned, the ability of the body to control and lower stress appears to be a health-building process:

Studies suggest that hormones in our bodies are able to trigger factors that restore rather than destroy life processes. But without stress-management skills, chronic stress (the persistent kind) can stimulate destructive chemicals in the body that can have an impact on our current and future well-being.

Becoming an optimist or mirroring behaviour to be a happier person is all well and good. But what if these positive strategies fail us on the day? How do we lower the stress at crucial times like exam time to allow us to perform at our most productive levels? Is there a skill to be learned?

➤ Visualisation: 'stop' technique

One way a stressful situation can be controlled is to use the 'stop' technique. This means putting up a 'stop' sign in your mind to block out the negative thoughts that may try to enter. Then, you allow pleasant thoughts to take their place.

Remember, our frazzled Bianca at exam time? Using her lamentable experience as an example, following is a re-enactment of her likely thoughts, and the strategies she *could* have used to take control of the situation. If you ever find yourself in a similar situation, all you have to do is follow our lead:

Bianca (on taking up her exam paper):
'This is worth a third of my final mark... Oh dear, my mind is so muddled... If I don't do well I'll really look stupid after getting A plus's all year. What will my friends think? And mum and dad? Look at those questions. If I don't get them right, I'm cooked.'

Control strategy—the 'stop' sign

Sit up. Rest an elbow on the desk, fingertips lightly over the forehead to cut out the light and allow a little privacy. Close your eyes. Breathe quietly, slowly, deeply. Visualise a large 'stop' sign. This is like saying firmly to yourself: *'Stop these negative thoughts. Worrying doesn't solve a thing. Relax.'*

Next, think of a soothing scene. People often use thoughts of floating on a billowing white cloud, waves lapping gently onto a beach, or resting beside a lake in a wooded setting, and so on. Allow your relaxing thought to replace the stop sign. *All this need only take one minute.* Then, have a little faith. Believe in yourself! Remind yourself you are well prepared for your exam; that you have the information you need stored ready to address the questions.

Remember, in order to answer a question correctly, you must first understand it. Read it thoroughly: slowly, carefully, completely. You're doing well. You feel more relaxed. Your mind has restored order. You are in control . . . and you're on your way.

The 'stop' visualisation technique can be used in other stress situations to calm the body and allow you to take control—or simply when you want to relax away from the daily routine. It may not happen properly, the first time. Like any skill, it must be repeated several times before it becomes automatic.

So put in a little practise every day. In time your new habit will be as comfortable as old boots and you'll have another skill to add to your skills bag.

Having said this, some students may find themselves suffering enormous stress and exhaustion towards the end of the academic year as a result of poor study habits, tough exams and over-extending themselves.

If stress persists alarmingly and cannot be eased, it is important to heed the body's warning signals and seek professional help. A psychologist is well qualified to assist in the replacing of bad habits with new effective ones; remember that a little preventative maintenance could change your life.

For those whose stress is more manageable, however, skills such as visualisation should be enough to reduce anxiety and restore the status quo.

Once the skill is acquired, not only will it give you power over control, but resilience, a positive outlook and potential for greater happiness. In fact, once you learn to manage stress and then go on to achieve your goals—it will not only be good for your body's inner health.

You'll feel on top of the world!

19

Skill 4: Smart note-taking Steps 1 and 2

'I hate it! It's boring and frustrating.' Zak suddenly grinned apologetically.

I had mentioned note-taking to a pupil and asked him what he thought.

'I seem to spend hours at it,' Zak confessed. 'I end up copying huge slabs of text into my notes and half the time I don't even know what it is I'm supposed to be looking for.'

I started to tell Zak he could do note-taking in one of two ways but he beat me to the punch line. 'I know!' he nodded. 'The wrong way or the right way! Right?'

'Well, what's it to be?' I asked. 'Do you want to play it smart? Do you want to save time and effort? Do you want to find out what it is you're supposed to be looking for? Or do you want to keep doing time and hard labour?'

Zak's response should come as no surprise. He chose to do it right—and today, in fact, he's a bit of a note-taking whiz, approaching research assignments with confidence and enthusiasm.

Where had Zak gone wrong before learning how to work smart?

Zak had the misconception that he was getting somewhere by keeping busy copying out copious research notes. But he was getting nowhere! All he was doing was wasting precious time.

In fact, Zak had simply become a human photocopying machine. His note-taking was no more than a mindless copy of the research text. No thinking required! His research contained no awareness of the need for analysis: no identifying what was relevant to the discussion topic. No wonder Zak was completely at sea.

As you've seen, all was not lost. Once we pointed him in the right direction, Zak became quite a high achiever. But not all students are as fortunate as him, or perhaps as lucky as you. Not everyone is shown the way.

When I began university, I was amazed at how quickly the student car park went from being full to comparatively empty. Even before my third assignment was due, I could drive in and park with ease. As the year had progressed it became easier still.

Where had all the students gone?

Home, probably. They had simply dropped out—and why? It was all too hard. Sure, they had scholastic ability. But they'd overlooked one crucial thing: they didn't know how to manage time. I remember the lecturers smiling knowingly when we first ambled in, fresh and eager to begin our new academic era. 'Look to your left and look to your right,' one of them had said, gesturing to our group, 'because only one in two of you will be here in the end to collect your degree.' I thought he was joking. But he was right! Half of the students dropped out.

When you get to tertiary level, there won't be just one task or so needing completion at any one time. There may be five or more, big pressing assignments on the table at once. You'll be expected to read huge amounts of text: lecturers may require that an essay's bibliography contain up to 15 or 20 references. That's 15 to 20 separate texts, each of which may be as long as your arm. And of course the information you reference has to be included as part of your discussion. Unless you can manage time effectively, be warned: it *will* run out! Assignments will be due and you'll be forced to submit rushed, poorly presented work. Worse, if you miss a deadline altogether you may well be one of those leaving an empty space in the university car park.

But fear not, help is at hand!

Let's get back to Zak. We soon showed him how to address his problem: if he became skilled at researching, note-taking and essay writing the smart way, he would then be motivated and eager to tackle the tasks.

At his opening session with us, Zak learned that note-taking was not the initial step in addressing the text. The first thing was to become aware of how a text was structured. That is, if he wanted to write a good essay, he first had to understand the writings of others.

This is how it works:

Step 1:
Understanding text structure

Generally, each paragraph has one main idea. This is normally but not always in the first sentence or two. Having introduced the main idea, authors then fill in the supporting or substantiating details in the same paragraph. Usually, paragraphs contain at least three or four sentences. However, that is not to say a paragraph cannot be short. For instance, a one- or two-liner, can sharpen meaning and impact, or make a point stand out, as this book shows.

The following diagram shows our General essay writing plan, or G-Plan. This represents a short text comprised of six paragraphs: an introduction, four main body paragraphs and a conclusion. It shows that by stripping away the words (the flesh, so-to-speak) to reveal the skeleton, we can learn how experienced writers structure their texts.

SKELETON G-PLAN (GENERAL)
PARAGRAPHS FOR AN ESSAY

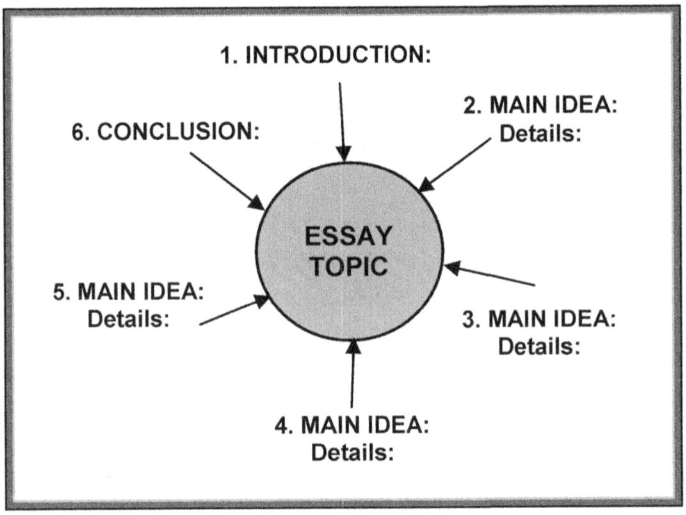

Next time you have to read a text in preparation for writing an essay, you should now know what to look for in each paragraph:

1: A Main Idea
2: The Supporting (or Substantiating) Details

In a moment, we'll put this new information into practice. Read and complete Step 2; then we can tackle Step 3 in the following chapter.

Step 2:
Highlighting your text

Beginning at the bottom of page 58 you will find four paragraphs of text about oxygen and health. Choose two different coloured pens or highlighters—one for Main Ideas, the other, Supporting Details. Next, highlight or underline in one colour, each Main Idea contained in the paragraphs. Ensure you highlight only the Main Idea's *key* words, not whole sentences (saving time is as important as identifying Main Ideas). Then with your second colour, circle or highlight the key words of the Supporting Details.

We're doing fine! Continue reading into the next chapter to include Step 3. Then you can complete the given exercises.

20

Skill 4: Smart note-taking Step 3

Do you make the most of the Internet?

As a research base for any student, the Internet is a remarkable resource. Some have likened it to having 150 million consultants right at your fingertips, virtually free-of-charge. Thing is, with all that knowledge at your disposal, how can you possibly cope with such a load? How do you sift through all that information to extract exactly what you need? You can't, of course! Take any subject and there are usually thousands of references you could bring up. Sometimes millions. Even if you retrieve just a few, there is still a problem: you have access to the information; but you haven't been taught how to use it.

This is where note-taking skills are so invaluable. Pick an internet reference, scan the text and simply by looking for the Main Ideas in the first few paragraphs, you can quickly get a grasp of the text's content. But, wait! Do you know what you're looking for? Are you researching the right subject? Have you read the topic question thoroughly? It makes sense: unless you *understand the question*, it's a waste of time looking for information to provide your answer. I often say to pupils: 'When you begin to read a question, don't assume that whatever concept first pops into your head, must be the right one. Look at a chair, for example. Just because it has four legs, doesn't make it an elephant.'

Thinking *is* a challenge. It requires input and effort. A good thinker will explore all possible criteria. If a question fulfils just one criterion in your thought process, (such as something having four legs), you must *read on*. There may be a number of criteria involved. What are they? If you misunderstand the question and charge up the wrong track, 'putting in an effort' won't count for much when your work is being assessed. At senior level, you will simply fail.

So, remember! You need to understand the question thoroughly!

With this in mind, completing an assignment can therefore be seen as a two-step process:

1. Ensure you understand the question: it may have a number of components.

   If you don't understand the question, consult your teacher *before* you leave class. Outline what you believe the question is asking and inquire if this is correct. Don't make the mistake of asking what it means. It's your job to work that one out. However, teachers are usually happy to acknowledge whether you are right or wrong.

2. Research and write up your answer. (We'll cover these aspects in due course.)

It's time for Step 3. Then we can get on with some practice.

Step 3:
Recording your notes

From the previous chapter, we identified and highlighted the Main ideas and Supporting Details in the sample text below. The next step is to record the information in a structured format. On the opposite page you will find a simple table designed for student notes. Our pupils like this method because it's easy and it's effective. Importantly, when it comes to essay writing, it will give you an edge. By note-taking as outlined your essays will evolve in a similar structured format. Try it: having used your highlighters as suggested, write a brief summary in the relevant areas. Record details in *as few words as possible* to save time and effort.

The key is this:

1. Record enough detail to allow an accurate account in your essay.
2. Keep each detail clear, but as brief as possible.

As you will see in the Table, the first paragraph has been done for you. Check it out to get the idea. Put your notes into your own words. This avoids copying and shows you understand the text.

'Oxygen

Oxygen is the elixir of life! When we breathe it into our lungs from the air, it is transported in the bloodstream to every single cell in our bodies. Here, it becomes an essential factor in the "burning" of fuel (food) to create energy. Without a constant oxygen supply, we would die. When we don't get enough, the quality of our lives is impaired: depending on the degree of oxygen deprivation and the time involved, this can affect us in a variety of ways.

Mentally, we may become tired, forgetful or irritable. In newborn babies, lack of oxygen may result in retardation. As adults, if the brain is starved of oxygen for long enough through poor blood circulation a stroke may result—or even death.

Oxygen can affect our well-being and happiness. Without sufficient in our systems we can become lazy, despondent, overweight, lacking in self-esteem, hard to live with and well, rather boring! To put it plainly, oxygen-deprived people tend to let life slip by—instead of hitching a joy ride.

If you recognise any one of these symptoms in yourself, it's possible a lack of oxygen is the problem. Your poor body needs more of the stuff! And to get more oxygen in your life, you'll have to take more than a deep breath. If you really want to be an improved human being, positive action is needed for the rewards to be reaped—and the number one change must start with *diet.*'

THE WORKING SMART NOTE-TAKING TABLE

PARAGRAPH 1
MAIN IDEA:
Oxygen essential → life.
SUPPORTING DETAILS:
Breathe air → blood carries ox. to cells.
Ox. vital → helps burn food → energy
Lack ox.—can threaten life.
When ox. ↓ qual. life ↓. Effects vary:
Depends how long/degree of ox. shortage.
PARAGRAPH 2
MAIN IDEA:
SUPPORTING DETAILS:
PARAGRAPH 3
MAIN IDEA:
SUPPORTING DETAILS:
PARAGRAPH 4
MAIN IDEA:
SUPPORTING DETAILS:

How did you do? Here are our suggestions:

THE WORKING SMART NOTE-TAKING TABLE

PARAGRAPH 1
MAIN IDEA:
Oxygen essential → life.
SUPPORTING DETAILS:
Breathe air → blood carries ox. to cells.
Ox. vital → helps burn food → energy
Lack ox.—life not supported.
When ox. ↓ qual. life ↓. Effects vary:
Depends how long/degree of ox. shortage.
PARAGRAPH 2
MAIN IDEA:
Ox. deprivation affects health.
SUPPORTING DETAILS:
May get—weary, lethargic, impatient, vague.
Posbl. retardatn. if infants deprived ox./birth
Brain no ox. long enough → posbl. stroke or death.
PARAGRAPH 3
MAIN IDEA:
Ox. affects state of mind, happiness.
SUPPORTING DETAILS:
Not enough → *can* be listless, depressed, fat, low s-esteem, moody.
People short/ox.—→ unhappy/miss life's opports.
PARAGRAPH 4
MAIN IDEA:
If lack/ox a prob. → need more in system.
SUPPORTING DETAILS:
Deep breathing not enough
Want feel better? Chang/vital
Need/proactive → new life pleasures
Chang diet—# 1.

Note-taking should be lean. The aim is, use key words to prompt concepts to spring to mind when readdressing your notes. Develop your own shorthand for brevity. But beware! Do not omit words that offer the correct sense or you may experience confusion later over a notation you have not made clear.

For example, in paragraph 2, last point above, you may have made the note: 'Brain no ox. long enough → posbl. stroke/death.' The correct notation for absolute clarity must be: 'Brain no ox. long enough → posbl. stroke *or* death.' When you leave out the word 'or', you change the possible meaning to 'stroke *and* death' which would be incorrect.

Another example, paragraph 2, penultimate line: if you wrote: 'Retardatn. if infants deprived ox./birth', this would be incorrect. You should have written: '*Posbl*. retardatn. if infants deprived ox./birth'. The words 'may result' in the original text means retardation is possible, not definite.

By now, senior students will begin to see how this note-taking skill will greatly aid their essays. Younger students, too, can benefit significantly by developing the same skill. When required to research material for class projects, using the Internet, scan a few relevant texts for Main Ideas. Print out the ones you think you may want and then adopt the Smart Note-taking method to continue your assignment.

For pupils grade five and upwards, here is an important message.

Just because you are not shown, in class, the skills we are discussing, is no excuse for not practising and using them. Claiming ignorance is a poor defence. If you continue with bad habits such as copying large blocks of text from research notes, word-for-word, you are creating a rod for your back. So work smart: correct problems now and you will avoid them later. Believe me, saving time and effort today will increase the savings in your later secondary and tertiary years many fold.

If you want to be ahead of the game, whether for essays or class projects, identify the Main Ideas and Supporting Details in your chosen texts before you start. Then simply select those Main Ideas you wish to include in your assignment. Following the same format as your notes, *each paragraph* in the body of your work should contain a Main Idea followed by Supporting Details.

For seniors facing exams, I cannot overemphasise the importance of this.

It means that when you are under pressure, you won't be in a state wondering how you are going to put your ideas into a structured format.

On the next page, you will find another exercise. Employing the same strategies, make notes on the following three continuous paragraphs. Avoid checking our suggested notes on page 63, until you have completed the exercise:

'A diet low in fat can give you amazing health benefits: it will allow your blood to begin to flow freely and cleanly to every nook and cranny in your body—carrying oxygen to service and revitalise your tissues.

PARAGRAPH 1
MAIN IDEA:
SUPPORTING DETAILS:

For greatest impact, your diet should also be low in refined sugars, white flour and salt, as these can also hamper oxygen's vital role. In other words, a sensible, low fat diet will help to give you back what you should have had in the first place: a healthy cardiovascular system.

PARAGRAPH 2
MAIN IDEA:
SUPPORTING DETAILS:

Of course, as you're no doubt aware, you can rev things up even more to increase your lung capacity and improve your oxygen uptake. If you're feeling harassed, ill tempered, exhausted or just plain stressed, your life could become amazing, simply through re-scheduling your daily routine to include one more vital factor: *exercise!*'

PARAGRAPH 3
MAIN IDEA:
SUPPORTING DETAILS:

Our suggested notes are on the opposite page.

'A diet low in fat can give you amazing health benefits: it will allow your blood to begin to flow freely and cleanly to every nook and cranny in your body—carrying oxygen to service and revitalise your tissues.

↓

PARAGRAPH 1
MAIN IDEA:
Low fat diet → advantages → glowing health
SUPPORTING DETAILS:
Blood reaches tiny recesses/body
Carries ox. → replenishes cells/tissues

For greatest impact, your diet should also be low in refined sugars, white flour and salt, as these can also hamper oxygen's vital role. In other words, a sensible, low fat diet will help to give you back what you should have had in the first place: a healthy cardiovascular system.

↓

PARAGRAPH 2
MAIN IDEA:
Sensible low fat diet → healthy cardiovascular system
SUPPORTING DETAILS:
Best results → also low sugar/wh. flour/salt
Wrong foods hinder ox. role

Of course, as you're no doubt aware, you can rev things up even more to increase your lung capacity and improve your oxygen uptake. If you're feeling harassed, ill tempered, exhausted or just plain stressed, your life could become amazing, simply through re-scheduling your daily routine to include one more vital factor: *exercise!*'

↓

PARAGRAPH 3
MAIN IDEA:
Exercise → greater ox. uptake → better life
SUPPORTING DETAILS:
Ex. improves lung function → more ox. in body
Ox. transforms → tired, bad tempered, stressed,
O'whelmed
1 crucial change → include daily exercise → life ↑☺

Remember, the Main Idea in a paragraph is *usually* in the first sentence—but not always. Did you notice something different in paragraph 2 of the previous passage? In scanning the paragraph you would have found that the Main Idea is that 'a sensible low fat diet means a healthier cardiovascular system'. (That is, healthier blood vessels of the heart: cardio = heart; vascular = vessels.) However, these details don't occur until the last sentence.

Similarly, in paragraph 3, the Main Idea is that 'exercise can deliver more oxygen to the body'. Yet, 'exercise' is the very last word. Don't therefore fall into the trap of believing the first sentence will *always* give you the Main Idea. The whole paragraph has to be quickly scanned first, for its full meaning.

Following, is an example of how you might have presented the previous three paragraphs in your final essay. Having researched from other sources and by injecting a little personality your finished text might read:

'Glowing good health is the reward of a low fat diet. It allows for a clean bloodstream where oxygen can be carried to cells in every corner of the body.

A strong cardiovascular system is essential for good health. Poor food choices such as fast food, for example—rich in fats, salt, sugars and white flour—can hinder oxygen's role and threaten well-being.

However, a sound diet is not the only factor in staying fit. The quality of living can be vastly uplifted by simply adding exercise to your day. Exercise greatly improves deep breathing and lung function, allowing more oxygen-rich blood to flow through your tissues. How can you be irritable or stressed if you're playing basketball or jogging around a park? So put on your cross-trainers and step out into the air. Oxygen. It can change your life!'

Finally, it is vital when transcribing text to notes and in writing your essay, that you use *the information* only—not the author's words. By this I mean: put your personal stamp on your work. Plagiarising, or copying someone else, verbatim (word-for-word), is a big no-no in the world of literature, punishable by law. So any hint that you have copied an author's work, presenting entire passages as your own, will not only lose you marks. It may result in a fail.

Also avoid using the same clichés or specific words that point directly to the author's text. If you wish to make a direct quote of someone else's work to support an argument or offer validity to your discussion, make sure that it is clearly referenced in the appropriate manner. (This applies to senior students who learn this referencing requirement in class.) In summary, to become a smart note-taker, the main points are worth revisiting:

1. Read your assignment question *thoroughly*. Do not proceed until you are certain you understand it. (Note: a chair has four legs, but so have a good many other things.)

2. The Internet doesn't make you smart! You get smart by learning how to use it effectively. Scan the text for Main Ideas. Print out what you need and then highlight the Main Ideas and Supporting Details with two different colours.

3. Make notes using *your own words*. Keep each detail brief, but don't leave out important words that will be needed to ensure clarity later. Develop your own shorthand.

4. Never copy slabs of text verbatim. It's okay, though, to use single words or terms from the text that deliver the correct meaning or sense of a passage. For example, 'cardiovascular system'; 'low fat diet'; 'oxygen'; 'lungs'; 'refined sugars', and so on.

However, referring to paragraph 1 in the text, page 63, were you to make the notation: 'Low fat diet → amazing health benefits' or (paragraph 3) 'Rev things up → increase lung capacity → improve ox. uptake', this would be copying the author's personal description.

In other words, you are expected to use your own brainpower; to stand on your own two feet and not use someone else's work as a crutch. If you do, an examiner will quickly see what is happening and you won't have a leg to stand on.

Keep up your practice

Once you have begun to master note-taking, you will find essay writing so much easier to address. Nevertheless, there are some smart skills to be acquired there, too. Keep reading. There's more fun ahead!

The next four chapters are devoted more to upper primary students and contain some effective writing strategies that might be used as a platform on which to build skills for later years. Chapters 25 to 39, after that, are designed more specifically for seniors, rather than those who are yet to face the rigors of full-on study and exams.

Nonetheless, it would pay all age groups to scan the texts of all chapters and read the areas that will assist them. Younger students at both secondary and primary level can learn a great deal by reading at least some of these latter chapters in preparation for their more challenging senior years ahead. You'll find some suggestions in the next chapter, page 67.

The final chapter, 'Reach for the sky', should not be missed by anyone.

21

Upper primary: Transition to secondary school

Your secondary years are not that far away.

In fact, before you can say 'Bob's your uncle' you'll have shed the mantle of senior student at primary school and be a brand new student again at secondary school. Then, a great deal of the information in this book, designed to support you during those challenging years, will become applicable.

It makes sense to do all you can now to prepare for the time ahead, doesn't it? I recommend to senior students that they put time in on a *routine basis* to gain that all-important edge when it comes to exam time. In a sense, the same advice can apply to you: being one or two steps ahead of your peers as you approach and enter the next phase of your schooling, may not seem much. However, think about this for a moment:

Do you hope to begin secondary school from a position of ignorance or awareness? That is, do you want to be that ostrich with his head in the sand, or will you be happier knowing what your up-and-coming academic demands are likely to be? To be so happy will give you that edge I mentioned. This means not only developing useful skills for your senior years, but being able to put some of them into practice from the moment you step up to secondary school. In other words, getting a *head start* at working smart.

Your head start to secondary school

At the moment, of course, you are still enjoying your formative years. There are many wonderful childhood experiences left in store before you reach the threshold of adulthood that will place greater demands on your time. However, let's say you are interested in knowing how to get that head start. Beyond the next four chapters, 21 to 24, there are chapters you could explore to sharpen up your awareness and skills.

If you'd rather check them later, put a marker at this page.

- Chapter 25: Pressing the right buttons (page 105)
- Chapter 26: What you will learn (page 107)
- Chapter 27: Creative essays (page 111)
- Chapter 28: Descriptive and personal essays (page 120)
- Chapter 33: Skill 5: Brainstorming (page 159)
- Chapter 35: Skill 7: Planning your essay (pages 172-6 only)
- Chapter 38: Skill 9: Editing your essay (page 202)
- Chapter 40: Reach for the sky (page 209)

At secondary level, *formal* essay writing will not feature in your curriculum for some time. However, you will certainly be writing a great deal on different subjects: English, history, geography, art history, and so on. To be a smart note-taker, capable of efficiently converting your notes into text, will give you an outstanding advantage. You can measure this, simply by your performance and the time you will save compared to your classmates.

Later, as essays become a part of your schedule, you will already have those valuable skills up your sleeve—or in your bag of skills as we've said. When you revisit this book more in depth as you progress in your secondary years, your grasp of essay requirements will be well in place. You will already know how to take notes efficiently, how to identify the *whys and wherefores* of an author's intentions, and to produce essays that reflect imagination and your understanding of an issue.

Don't wait!

But you don't have to wait until secondary school!

If you are in upper primary, note-taking is an important skill you can acquire and use *right now.*

Remember Zak's note-taking problem, page 54? His experience is typical of those encountered by secondary students of all ages who come to us. Recently, I spoke to a parent whose son, Kairus, is in Year 10. During class discussions, Kairus began busily copying notes from the board afraid of running out of time. His teacher admonished him for not paying attention. 'Listen to the discussion, first,' she said. When given time to write, Kairus was so stressed, his notes ended up a scribbled mess that he couldn't understand. He began dreading class and didn't know what to do. He thought it was his fault and his confidence began to plummet.

Actually, it wasn't Kairus's fault at all. Well-intentioned as his teacher was, a critical process in the teaching method had been overlooked: showing him a skill that would have solved the problem.

Transition Program

One of our innovations is a Transition Program for upper primary and junior secondary students, designed to catch potential problems before they arise or develop.

The happy result is that student self-esteem and confidence is improved, not diminished. It was not until Kairus joined us that his confidence was restored. He had travelled a pretty rough road during his early secondary years. He was so relieved to realise he didn't have a problem; that it wasn't lack of ability that had been holding him back, but simply a lack of *awareness* and the skills to match.

At school Kairus had only been shown one side of the coin: what *not* to do. But importantly, his busy teacher forgot the other side: *what* to do, and *how* to do it. Showing Kairus the most effective and time-saving approach to his tasks, we were soon able to turn that around.

Smart note-taking

Look back now, at the note-taking problems Zak had, and how he solved them using 'Skill 4: Smart note-taking', on page 54.

Read the chapter again. Then, next time you find yourself on the Internet, or studying the encyclopaedia looking for information for a classroom project, use the skills described.

Keeping to our note-taking guidelines, look for the Main Ideas and Supporting Details. Jot them down and then develop them in your own words and style. This will not only provide excellent practice, it will mean your school project will be well structured and deserving of a good mark.

Remember: move well away from relying on nice headings and borders and copying slabs from books to get you through. These points and the 'how' of smart note-taking are advice, like Kairus, you may not receive in class.

You may already have tried the smart note-taking exercises beginning on pages 58 and 62. If so, well done! However, here is another text, along the same guidelines, just for you. Try it out. It's about meteors and meteorites. Do you know the difference?

Read on and you'll find out:

'Have you ever seen a falling star? Chances are, it was probably a piece of extraterrestrial (ET) matter, otherwise known as a "meteor", burning fiercely as it plummeted towards Earth. Some meteors, however, don't burn up. If large enough, they can withstand the extreme heat caused by friction, as they charge to Earth. In reaching the Earth's surface, they become known as "meteorites". Due to their mysterious origins, coming from some unknown place in our universe, meteorites are a source of great interest to scientists from the fields of physics, chemistry, mineralogy and metallurgy.

PARAGRAPH 1
MAIN IDEA:
SUPPORTING DETAILS:

However, this was not always the case. Up until the nineteenth century, due to scepticism, astronomers were not much interested in meteors. Then, in 1803 in L'Aigle, France, hundreds of stones fell to earth. This forced the conservative French Academy to acknowledge a fact: the matter was of ET origin. Some ET matter is known to have originated from solar-system dust and fine particles from comets. However, it is the larger ET meteorites in the form of pieces of rock or metal that scientists are better able to study.

PARAGRAPH 2
MAIN IDEA:
SUPPORTING DETAILS:

Meteors come in all shapes and sizes. Our planet's surface offers us clues about larger meteorites that have crashed to Earth, causing substantial damage. The great speed with which Earth's gravity pulls meteorites towards it, means they often cause craters many times larger than their actual size. One such crater is the Arizona Meteorite Crater, 1,400 metres in diameter and 200 metres deep. It is surprising to know that the meteorite itself was relatively small, being only 17 metres in diameter. Scientists think that the extinction of dinosaurs was due to a meteorite, ten kilometres in width, colliding with Earth; that this caused immense heat and a massive cloud of black dust; that the black cloud encircled the earth, destroying the lush plant life on which the dinosaurs depended for life.'

PARAGRAPH 3
MAIN IDEA:
SUPPORTING DETAILS:

How did you go? Here is our version of note-taking for the meteor piece. Some words are in full for your understanding but you are encouraged to create your own shorthand. Clearly understanding your notes is most important here. Remember, the keys to good note-taking are:

1. Record enough detail to allow you to write an accurate account.
2. Keep each detail clear but as brief as possible.

Notice we have used our own words in our notes to describe the text. For practice, look up different words to use from your thesaurus.

'Have you ever seen a falling star? Chances are, it was probably a piece of extraterrestrial (ET) matter, otherwise known as a "meteor", burning fiercely as it plummeted towards Earth. Some meteors, however, don't burn up. If large enough, they can withstand the extreme heat caused by friction, as they charge to Earth. In reaching the Earth's surface, they become known as "meteorites". Due to their mysterious origins, coming from some unknown place in our universe, meteorites are a source of great interest to scientists from the fields of physics, chemistry, mineralogy and metallurgy.

↓

PARAGRAPH 1
MAIN IDEA:
Meteorite = ET matter ↓ space. Studied by science.
SUPPORTING DETAILS:
Meteors resemble falling stars. Combust as ↓ to Earth.
Meteor<u>ites</u> survive due to size. (Don't incinerate.)
(NB Meteorite = reaches Earth. Meteor = burns up)
Scientists: mineralogy/metallurgy/physics/chem.

However, this was not always the case. Up until the nineteenth century, due to scepticism, astronomers were not much interested in meteors. Then, in 1803 in L'Aigle, France, hundreds of stones fell to earth. This forced the conservative French Academy to acknowledge a fact: the matter was of ET origin. Some ET matter is known to have originated from solar-system dust and fine particles from comets. However, it is the larger ET meteorites in the form of pieces of rock or metal, which scientists are better able to study.

↓

PARAGRAPH 2
MAIN IDEA:
French Academy first to recognise ET matter 1803
SUPPORTING DETAILS:
Before, astronomers doubted ET existence.
1803 → stones hailed over L'Aigle, France. Scientists
realised stones ↓ outer space. ET dust/comet debris—too small
to study. Meteorites (rocks, metal) can be studied.

Meteors come in all shapes and sizes. Our planet's surface offers us clues about larger meteorites that have crashed to Earth, causing substantial damage. The great speed with which Earth's gravity pulls meteorites towards it, means they often cause craters many times larger than their actual size. One such crater is the Arizona Meteorite Crater, 1,400 metres in diameter and 200 metres deep. It is surprising to know that the meteorite itself was relatively small, being only 17 metres in diameter. Scientists think that the extinction of dinosaurs was due to a meteorite, ten kilometres in width, colliding with Earth; that this caused immense heat and a massive cloud of black dust; that the black cloud encircled the earth, destroying the lush plant life on which the dinosaurs depended for life.'

↓

PARAGRAPH 3
MAIN IDEA:
Earth surface damage reveals nature/meteorites; speed of crash → huge craters Earth's surface.
SUPPORTING DETAILS: Arizona Meteorite Crater—
1,400M wide/200M deep. Yet meteorite only 17M wide.
Sci. belief → dinosaurs wiped out ↓ meteorite 10Km wide.
Collision gen. intense heat/gigantic bl cloud engulfed Earth
destroyed dino. plant food → extinction.

Acronyms and other abbreviations

You may not need the following information for some time. However, it's handy to know. Also, it should be explained, due to the use of 'ET' in the text.

Note, instead of 'extraterrestrial', we used 'ET' for short. You can do this, too. However, if you used 'ET' in your essay, you'd need to give the reader its meaning. So use the full version *the first time* you mention the word, followed by the letters in brackets, as appears in the original text. The letters can then be used alone in the rest of the story/text. This also applies where you want to use a shortened version of say, an organisation or government body.

For example, in writing about the World Health Organization you might say: 'The World Health Organization (WHO) raised concerns about the issue in March. A spokesperson for the WHO, Ms. Helga Schmidt, told delegates that . . .' and so on. Watch out for initials that start with a vowel in your text: take the 'Absolutely Brilliant Writers' Association (ABWA)'. Once you've mentioned it, you might then say: '<u>An</u> ABWA member said . . .' So don't forget to use the correct definite article directly before vowels.

By the way, words created from the first letters of other words are called 'acronyms' (pronounced 'acro-nims'). The above WHO example is one. You might have heard about NATO on the news. This stands for the <u>N</u>orth <u>A</u>tlantic <u>T</u>reaty <u>O</u>rganization. NASA means the <u>N</u>ational <u>A</u>eronautics and <u>S</u>pace <u>A</u>d-ministration. Sometimes when an acronym is really well known, like NATO and NASA, writers or reporters might use it without using the words in full.

If in doubt, it's best to mention the full version first, then put the initials in brackets, as just explained.

Writing a creative story

For advice that may help you to write a better creative story in class today, check out Chapter 27, 'Creative essays', page 111. In this chapter you will find the opening paragraph examples of two of our Grade 5 pupils, Harrie and Az. It shows how they *pressed the reader's buttons* (See 'Pressing the right buttons', page 105) by using their imagination and some effective, direct speech to make the reader want to read more.

Using action or dialogue or perhaps a person's thoughts, as Harrie and Az have done, is a great attention grabber for beginning a story. Another handy option you might like to try is what I call the 'Funnel Approach'.

The Funnel Approach

When asked to write a story about a particular subject in class, many pupils around your age resort to a common habit: they use the title of the story to begin their essay. We talk about this on page 194, in our 'first draft' chapter. The example of the story or essay discussed is entitled, 'What concerns me most about growing old'.

An average, Grade 5 student might begin: 'What concerns me most about growing old is . . .' We show senior students, and you can learn this now, too, how they might start their essays, using the Funnel Approach to overcome this problem.

FUNNEL APPROACH
TO INTRODUCTIONS

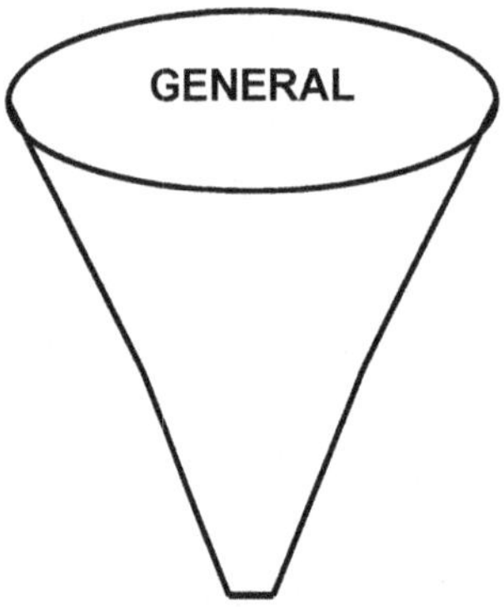

SPECIFIC

The Funnel Approach encourages students to view essay introductions like a funnel: broad at the top and narrow at the bottom. This means beginning your essay by generally discussing broader issues. Research for your story might be obtained, for example, by talking to an elderly family member; or you could look up the Internet or ask your parents or guardians for their comments. Having written your general overview, (the broad part of the funnel), you then become more specific (like the narrow end of the funnel). When you do this, you might mention the essay topic as the Main Idea. This could happen in or near the final sentence of the introduction.

Then as with *any* essay, the idea/s in the last sentence or two of your introduction should link to the idea/s in the first sentence or two of the next paragraph—or directly to the topic. Linking sentences or words can then occur in each paragraph. In the first paragraph below, we have underlined the words that do this. Let's look at these and what we mean about the Funnel Approach. Tips on linking the remaining paragraphs are then over the page.

Your introduction
Essay title: 'What concerns me most about growing old'
Essay type: Personal

Until about a century ago, many people didn't live very long. Diseases and deaths in childbirth were largely to blame for this. In those times good hygiene was almost unknown and living conditions were very poor. Today, some people live to be a hundred. Many are in their seventies or eighties. This is largely due to advances in medicine and greatly improved standards of living. But what does growing old really mean? I wouldn't want to be 90 if I were bedridden or very ill. It would concern me if <u>I couldn't be with friends</u> or do everyday things like playing music or even taking the dog to the park for a game of catch.

Let's now put the introductory paragraph into a funnel to see its shape:

G E N E R A L

Until about a century ago, many people didn't live very
long. Diseases and deaths in childbirth were largely
to blame for this. In those times good hygiene was
almost unknown and living conditions were very
poor. Today, some people live to be a hundred.
Many are in their seventies or eighties. This
is largely due to advances in medicine and
greatly improved standards of living.

S P E C I F I C

But, what does growing old really
mean? I wouldn't want to be 90
if I were bedridden or very ill.
It would concern me if I
<u>couldn't be with friends</u>
or do everyday things
like playing music or
even taking the
dog to the park
for a game
of catch.

Linking your paragraphs

Next, we need a linking sentence to connect paragraph 1 with paragraph 2, which follows:

Friends are an important part of growing old. I would hate to be without them. My grandmother, who is 72, is always doing things with her friends like playing Scrabble and going to golf. My grandfather (Papou) really loves his friends. He can often be seen with one or two of his cronies chatting in Greek over coffee in High Street. Sadly, two of his best friends have died which means there are fewer people whose company he can enjoy. That's the part I would hate about growing old. Papou always says he never wants to be a burden to his family, but what happens when all your friends have gone? Loneliness can be a terrible thing. It becomes a big issue as you get older. That's really when you need your friends the most.

Can you find the Main Idea in the introductory paragraph? Connected to the topic, 'What concerns me most about growing old', it is this: the writer would hate to be about 90 if it meant being bedridden or ill and unable to enjoy friends and activities such as playing music and taking the dog to the park. The part of the Main Idea about friends ('It would concern me if I couldn't be with friends . . .') has been picked up and neatly linked to the next paragraph with the use of the sentence: 'Friends are an important part of growing old.' Get the idea?

On another point, the end part of the Main Idea mentions perhaps not being able to enjoy two things. What are they? Yes, that's right:

1. 'friends'
2. 'everyday things' (like playing music and playing catch with the dog)

These two subjects are now nicely set up as the Main Ideas for your following paragraphs.

In paragraph 2, we discussed the Main Idea about 'friends'. We developed the theme by adding some Supporting Details about friends and what they mean in old age. In the third paragraph which you can check out in due course in the Appendix, page 256, we address the Main Idea about 'everyday things' and then add the Supporting Details about playing music and taking the dog to the park for a game.

We linked the first two paragraphs, using the Main Idea of 'friends' as the theme. You will notice that at the end of paragraph 2, there is a point made about loneliness becoming a big issue as you get older which is when you really need friends the most. This temporarily completes the discussion about friends.

In our third paragraph, we introduce and discuss the idea that it would be a concern if everyday things couldn't be enjoyed. This becomes the Main Idea for paragraph 3, which begins: 'Another issue, I know, is that everyday things become more difficult as you get older.' (We refer to it as 'another issue' so that there is a flow-on effect from the previous paragraph.)

Test your skills

Why not test your writing skills right now, with the following short exercise? Continue writing the third paragraph yourself. Remember, you need to include the Supporting Details that have already been suggested: 'playing music and playing games with the dog in the park'.

Take a spare piece of paper and rewrite the first two paragraphs we have shown you. This will put you into the swing of things. Then rewrite the first sentence of paragraph 3, (see third line down, at the top of this page) and continue with your own version of the suggested Supporting Details.

Give it some thought.

Write the paragraph and then finish off the entire piece with a concluding paragraph. When you write your last paragraph, keep the topic in mind and bring the threads of the essay together.

Try to think of some good ideas that will make your writing stand out. We've thought of some. Create your two paragraphs as suggested. Then, you can check out how we finished the piece by turning to the Appendix, pages 256-7, where the entire essay and further comments are presented.

Fluency Links

Before we leave the subject of linking sentences—on page 188, Chapter 36, you will find a list of 'Fluency Links'. Fluency Links are one or two words that link the ideas contained in one sentence or clause, to the ideas contained in the next sentence or clause (for example: *however* or *nonetheless,* etc.). Read more about them on pages 187-8.

Fluency Links are a very handy writing tool to have around. Use them just when you need a special word/s that will allow two sentences, where one thought flows on to the next, to hang nicely together. In other words, they alert your reader to the connection between one idea that you have just made, to one that you are about to make.

Why not also attempt some introductory paragraphs on your own, using the following topic ideas?

Do a little research or some detective work, if necessary, to get some background information. Remember, information means you can write from a position of knowledge. So research is very important if you are to write a convincing story. You could begin your introduction with action and dialogue, as explained in 'Creative essays', page 111—or you could use the Funnel Approach just mentioned.

Some of the essays below are purely creative; others invite the descriptive or personal approach.

For example, the first topic, 'My favourite holiday', would generally be expected to be a personal or descriptive essay. However, what if you decided your favourite holiday was a trip to the moon? You couldn't write that one from a personal point of view, could you? It would be a creative essay. But this would be an exception rather than the rule. Just ask yourself, 'what is the main point of view from which I want to write my story?' and that will help you decide its type.

We have offered our suggestions as to each essay type, as your guide. Remember, these all come under the creative *style* of essay. See 'What you will learn', page 107, and the suggested pages in the 'essay planning' chapter, 172-176, for more helpful hints. 'Descriptive and personal essays' (page 120) will also be of some value.

Read these areas before you start. Then, see if you can write at least one or two full pages.

- My favourite holiday *(personal or descriptive)*
- My life as a pet cat, pet dog, duck, hamster or other pet *(creative)*
- The best thing that has even happened to me *(personal)*
- The mystery of the giant oak *(creative)*
- Number 9, Cloud Hill, Paradise *(creative)*
- The clock struck midnight and my life changed forever *(creative)*
- The best thing about summer holidays *(personal or descriptive)*
- I am a hundred dollar bill *(creative)*
- The clairvoyant looked deep into the crystal ball *(creative)*
- My favourite past-time *(personal)*

In our next chapter for upper primary, we will begin to address a key difference between primary and secondary school—and what it may mean for you.

Do you know what it is?

22

Upper primary: Exciting changes

They say a change is as good as a holiday!

For many, going to a new school will be just as exciting, with new people to meet, new friends to make, new rules to follow. Entering the second phase of your school career means there'll be many changes in your new life—and one of them is the way you will be expected to approach tasks.

With this thought and your future success in mind, ask yourself this: what are at least two basic skills you will need as you progress in your secondary years? Many pupils are not made aware of their importance—yet they are major stepping stones to achievement:

1. Reading and understanding a question.
2. Writing clearly and concisely while addressing a topic.

This may seem logical. Yet many students from both government and private schools are sent into uncharted waters totally unprepared and unskilled for the challenges ahead. Consequently, many do not to reach their potential. Since we are creatures of habit, this is a disturbing thought: there is every chance the unskilled student will carry the same poor habits into adulthood.

Whether it be Year 7 English, Year 12 Politics, or Media Studies at university—your knowledge of the subject won't matter a stitch—if you do not know *how to communicate!*

The ability to communicate at secondary and tertiary level is central to student success—then, and in life. This brings us to a significant difference between primary and secondary school: you will be expected to *think more* and so learn how to shape and discuss your ideas and opinions. Most importantly, you will have to know how to justify those opinions.

That is, you have to show by giving examples that your point of view is valid, or believable. The higher aim is to do it so well, you win an audience or reader over to your point of view. Actually, it's quite a fun exercise once you learn how. So don't fret, in a moment we will offer some topics and advice to help you get started.

When you were in Grades 2 up to 5, many tasks involved you or your teacher reading and presenting the teacher's and other people's ideas. However, as you move into your secondary years, that will all change: you will be expected to read, research, and weigh up the ideas of others, and *then form your own opinions* about them. So, you will no longer be only writing creative or personal stories. You will be expected to write essays about issues. You will be expected to read and examine novels and plays; to probe and discuss writers' motives—their reasons for writing something—behind their works. Your writing will therefore need to have quite a mature level of structure, planning and purpose.

In a recent news article, a 13-year-old, Year 8 student complained he could not cope with school. The problem? Things had changed since primary school. His teachers were now seeking his *opinions* on a variety of issues and topics. Trouble was, he didn't have any opinions! More importantly, eight years at school had not prepared him for this stage of his education.

> 'Essay' is the name given to any short piece of writing about a particular subject, or topic. It is therefore used to describe the many different topics that students are expected to write about during their secondary and tertiary years.
>
> You can learn more about essays, or texts, in 'Pressing the right buttons', page 105, 'What you will learn', page 107, and, if you want to tackle some parts, 'Text analysis essays', page 135.

This media article highlights findings at our tutoring centres. In fact, one of our principal activities is assisting pupils to regain their confidence and self-esteem by alerting them to skills they were somehow never taught.

Then we teach them the skills.

In less time than it takes to peel and eat a juicy orange we can take students from a state of ignorance to a state of awareness. In less than a term, we sow the seeds of understanding and then watch as their confidence springs up like bean shoots responding to the light. Within a few months, most of our pupils mature and flourish.

With newly learned skills they can take a topic, turn it upside-down, inside out, research it, plan it and present a clear soundly developed essay well within the given time-frame.

Luckily, you are reading this book. You, too, can start learning the skills for working smart *before* you head off to secondary school.

The art of persuasion

Understanding how to write an essay where you adopt a particular point of view, then put up a good argument for it, is an excellent way to begin. This is called a 'persuasive' type of essay. You persuade readers towards your opinion. (An 'argumentative' essay takes things further: firstly, you adopt a point of view. You support your viewpoint using some convincing arguments. But you also introduce *the opposite view* and discuss the reasons you think they are not as good as your view. In other words, you discuss two sides of the issue—an argument 'for' and an argument 'against'. Or put another way, the 'pros and cons' of the matter.)

Topics don't necessarily have to be dead serious like the arguments presented in a court of law. You may possibly have seen these depicted in shows on TV. The lighter side of presenting an argument is often reflected in popular TV debates: they are tongue-in-cheek and the audiences love them.

The essay topic can be anything taken from everyday life. For example, our first essay topic suggestion on page 81 is entitled, 'Should the school canteen sell junk food?' This gives you a chance to think through and tackle something you are familiar with—and then to develop your line of reasoning. Using familiar topics like this means we can soon teach you how to *develop an opinion* and to *justify your stand.*

No wrong or right of it

Remember, in choosing to adopt a point of view, there is not necessarily a right or wrong answer. It may be simply a matter of opinion.

For example, the French eat snails called 'escargots' (pronounced *escargo*). Many people love them. Others from different cultures who have not been brought up eating snails think they are disgusting. Devouring a juicy hamburger may be your idea of heaven. A vegetarian would probably think the opposite. Who is right? No one, of course. In the end, it is only a point of view.

Likewise, there is no wrong or right of the school canteen selling junk food (although some arguments against it may be quite strong). For example, an argument 'for' the case may be this: if it did not sell junk food, canteen sales may drop. This could mean less profit to provide much needed sporting equipment for the school. Sporting equipment offers opportunities for exercise and social activities that help to boost health.

So whether you choose to adopt an argument 'for' the school canteen selling junk food or 'against' the practice, *it is still only your opinion.* As you get older you will begin to realise that issues are seldom seen as purely black or white, wrong or right. There can be many shades of grey in between—rendered simply by how people *see an issue.* **Of course, this is not the same as the difference between wrong and right, according to the laws of a country.**

The key to a good argument is how smart you are at persuasion; how convincing you are. If you present a viewpoint and make people believe it's a really *good* idea—perhaps the best they've heard, you can count on it: your argument has been a rollicking success. Here are some topics that require you to develop reasoned contentions. So think them through, and create some sound arguments that can be supported with a good dose of logic.

- Should the school canteen sell junk food?
- Is television a waste of time?
- Should every child have a mobile phone?
- May I please have a raise? [Write a thoughtful letter to your parents/ guardians suggesting the reason/s your pocket money should be doubled. (Check the 'Win-win' section that follows, first.)]
- May we have longer holidays, please? [Write to your principal suggesting the reason/s your school should have two weeks more holidays each year. (Again, check the 'Win-win' section, first.)]

Win-win

When you write a persuasive essay, you must remember to keep your eye on something important: the need for a win-win situation. By that is meant, the outcome will not only be good for *you*—the reasons you present must also be good for the reader/s whom you are attempting to persuade, or win over. Importantly, it is not only *what* you say; it is *how* you say it (the tone of your writing voice) that may convince an otherwise reluctant reader to at least consider your suggestion.

The tone of your writing voice can perhaps be best illustrated this way: you wouldn't expect to convince an adult to allow you to have something special if you said crossly: 'Give it to me!' would you? Instead you might bring them their favourite slippers, a cup of tea or a cool drink and then ask in a pleasant voice: 'May I have it, please?' (See more on 'Tone', page 189, and check out *The Tone Zone* lists at edworksglobal.com; click on 'Checklists and Templates'.)

That's over-simplifying things, of course. You may still be a long way from getting the nod. So if a person really needs convincing, being as sweet as apple pie may not be enough, and if your argument is a weak one, your chances of success will be practically zero! You will therefore need to learn more about the art of persuasion through presenting strong arguments. In fact, understanding the power of win-win and the art of persuasion go hand in hand.

Take, for example, the essay suggested about doubling your pocket money. Your persuasive argument has a greater chance of success if you offer something in return. The person you are asking needs to get something out of it too; needs a good reason for granting your request. You might therefore offer to do the dinner dishes or wash the family car for a while or offer a 15-minute neck massage every Friday night—that sort of thing. Even an upheld promise to be nice to everyone could bring its rewards. The adults might consider that a real win for them!

These are simple ideas, easy to think up. In a moment, we will look at other more thoughtful arguments you might pose, were you to write the persuasive letter just discussed. In the meantime, it will assist your understanding if you first read:

1. The 'brainstorming' chapter, page 159, and
2. The 'essay planning' chapter, page 172—to the end of the 'G-Plan for Essay Writing Example', page 176 (five pages)

If you prefer, you could come back to do the letter exercise after finishing the parts of the book that interest you at this stage.

Using the working smart guidelines, let's look at how you would go about writing the persuasive letter, 'May I please have a raise?'

When you're ready!

23

Upper primary: Learning to think

Whether writing a letter or an essay, before you put pen to paper you should brainstorm your ideas. Then plan your piece using the best *Plan* to suit. We'll show you how to do this shortly.

The 'brainstorming' chapter shows a checklist for senior students to brainstorm ideas for an issue-based essay. Incidentally, don't be concerned about the term 'issue-based'. All it means is *any matter or topic for discussion.* (Whether you cleaned your teeth last night before bed or did your homework may be an issue for discussion at breakfast.) There's also a checklist for upper primary students to practise brainstorming and writing about issues. A copy for enlarging and photocopying is in the Appendix, page 237, but for easy access, templates and checklists for working smart practice can be printed from our website, edworksglobal.com; see the 'Checklists and Templates' tab. Why not keep a few spare copies in a special folder?

As mentioned on page 159 ('Brainstorming'), a common criticism of student writers is that they don't probe the issues that they write about deeply enough. Our brainstorming checklist helps pupils to consider all the likely angles (perspectives) of an issue. It's designed to trigger ideas and make you think. You will see there are at least six angles (in column A) to check. Each angle has two perspectives: the 'Small Picture' and the 'Big Picture', making 12 different angles altogether. You might think of others.

Some angles may not apply to the topic (issue) you are writing about. That's fine. But importantly, the checklist will give you the chance to at least ask the questions: 'Does this angle apply? Will it help my argument?' If it doesn't apply, you go on to check the next one. If it does, you make a note in column B, the Small Picture, or C, the Big Picture (or both columns). To support your argument, the notes should describe the outcome, or effect, you think the issue would have on those angles.

The Small Picture relates to individuals, like you or your friends or family members. The Big Picture relates to communities (including school communities) or wider society—(in other words, big groups of people working or living together and sharing the same issues.)

Remember, this is just the ideas phase of your writing exercise. You might use all the ideas you jot down. You may leave one or two out when you sit down to write your piece. You weigh that up at the time of writing.

For a ready understanding, let's use the letter, 'May I please have a raise?' as an example. We will check out each angle as we go to see whether it applies or not. Then we can make our notes in the B and C columns, looking at the Small Picture (the impact on individuals) and the Big Picture (the impacts on groups or society). We'll guide you through it, so don't worry.

Here's the situation: There has been quite a bit of disharmony in your household, lately. This has been largely due to arguments about the use of the telephone. Many week nights and especially on weekends, you are always on the phone to your friends. The phone is always tied up and mum and dad are beside themselves. Dad can never make a call without hearing your chatting voice and mum, the main family breadwinner, can never get through from work to tell dad she's coming home. It's becoming unbearable for all parties.

So—you've had a brilliant idea! A simple solution to the family problems: your own mobile phone. This would achieve two things: It would free up the family telephone, and you could talk endlessly to your friends without your parents constantly knocking on your door, telling you to get off the line.

You decide the only way you will ever get your own phone is to fund it yourself. So you'll need to save up for it. You already get good pocket money. But with your new goal in mind, you know it will take an age to achieve it . . . unless you can persuade the adults to *double your pocket money.*

That's a pretty big request for most adults to be asked to consider. So, how do you go about it? The very first thing you should think about is this: if you want to persuade anyone, you will have to be fair and reasonable. You will need to offer some incentives; some nice rewards in return for their generosity: in other words, offer a win-win situation. Double the pocket money is a 100 per cent increase. So the oldies will certainly need some convincing. Here's where brainstorming comes in.

The brainstorming checklist will help to spark off a few good ideas for your persuasive letter. Remember! Your request needs to be handled very carefully. You will need to give it a thoughtful touch that will impress your reader/s; impress them so much, they will want to sit up and listen to what you have to say. So—let's have a look.

Are your checklist copies ready?

BRAINSTORMING ISSUE-BASED ESSAYS CHECKLIST FOR UPPER PRIMARY STUDENTS

Essay title:

Essay type: Argumentative or Persuasive

Essay's aim/s:		
A. ANGLE (Perspective) **Ask: Can the issue or outcome be seen from this angle?**	**B. SMALL PICTURE** (Micro View) **Would/does the issue affect individuals? How?**	**C. BIG PICTURE** (Macro View) **Does the issue affect the community or society? How?**
1. MONEY (ECONOMIC)		
2. GROUP (SOCIAL) (Family, school, club, society, etc.)		
3. RIGHT OR WRONG (MORAL) (According to law)		
4. STATE OF MIND (PSYCHOLOGICAL) (Happy, sad, angry, worried, etc.)		
5. ENVIRONMENTAL		
6. OTHER		

Although you intend writing a letter, we may use the term 'essay', as well. We will also use 'parents' and 'mum and dad', although we are aware that someone other than a parent may care for you. Each time you address one of the boxes in Column B on the checklist, ask yourself: 'Does this Angle apply to the Small Picture?' Each time you address one of the boxes in Column C on the checklist, ask yourself: 'Does this Angle apply to the Big Picture?'

Don't forget to also think about short-term and long-term effects for each box. You will see what we mean as we develop your letter. Here are the steps you would take starting from the top of the checklist:

1. On your photocopied checklist, fill in the essay title. In this case it's: 'May I please have a raise?' Next, highlight the essay 'type', whether it's an argumentative essay (offering two sides of an argument) or a persuasive essay (trying to convince a person to see your point of view). In this case it's a persuasive essay: you want to *persuade* your parents to double your pocket money.

2. In the very first row of the table, ask, what is/are the essay's aims? You should write: 'To persuade my parents to double my pocket money to fund my own mobile phone'.

   By the way, consider for a moment that you are writing the essay suggested on page 81, 'Is television a waste of time?' When you think about it, the topic asks you to form an opinion by answering 'yes' or 'no'. To persuade the reader that your opinion has merit, you have to go one step beyond just persuading. You have to present arguments 'for' as well as arguments 'against' the issue to show both sides. To be convincing, your arguments 'for' must be sound, the arguments 'against' showing weaknesses in that opposite view, which make your argument even stronger. So for that essay, at 'Essay's Aims' depending on your opinion, you might write something like: 'To argue that television is not a waste of time'. That's the issue. Are you beginning to see the difference between the two essay types? Let's look at the checklist boxes.

Each time you check Column A, say the word 'angle' to yourself after each box heading—for example money *angle,* group *angle,* and so on. This is a good way to quickly grasp what the words mean.

Box 1/B Money Angle (economic)—Small Picture

This is about the Money Angle of an issue, as it relates to individuals. Do we have something to fill in here? How does the issue affect you or your parents, as individuals? You might want to persuade your parents that if you had double pocket money, it would teach you the value of money and how to manage it. That may convince them. In the box, jot down a brief note: 'Teach me value/money; learn how save/manage'. When making notes, as in note-taking exercises, remember to keep them short. They are only a reminder for writing your letter. It should therefore be detailed, but each detail kept brief.

Another idea on the economic front (the Money Angle) is that you could offer to wash your dad's car on a regular basis. Your persuasive argument might be that doing work in return for a raise would *also* teach you the value of money. Working for money through having a job or business is how society operates. To learn this early could motivate you to do well in your studies: good results mean greater job opportunities in life; less chance of having to rely on the Government for support. So your note might say: 'Work for raise: wash d/car → apprec. value $. Study smart/raise chances good job & future'.

Box 1/C Money Angle (economic)—Big Picture

This covers the Money Angle, as it relates to the community or society.

Think it through!

If more kids learned how to save and manage money from an early age, it would not only help the community; in the long-term, it would help the entire country. Many people would have the saving habit. They would know how to look after their money so they could invest for the future.

'So what?' you might think. 'How does *that* help the community or the country, for that matter?'

Let's investigate this one further for a moment. It might help you to understand how parts of the economy can operate.

People invest their savings in a lump sum to gain a nice profit from the investment, right? This provides a nest egg for special times, or security later in life. But how is the profit made? Just as banks give 'interest' on savings accounts, money invested can earn interest or 'dividends'. These are payments to investors for the use of their money. Large companies can then use this money for research or development.

When you invest your lump sum, your money really goes to work. It works not only for you, the investor. It works for the whole economy of a region. This happens because *many* people are investing at the same time. So large pools of money can be put into projects big and small—and this can have what is called a 'flow-down effect', reaching out to all corners of a community, a country or even the world. Next time you toss one small pebble into a pond, watch how the ripple effect spreads wider and wider across the water.

The entire economy is stimulated when people invest and this provides growth in commerce and industry. That means more jobs can be created, people can be trained, new businesses can spring up to provide the goods or services needed and established businesses can expand and flourish. Let's take an example of how investment helps the economy:

Building a hotel from investors' money

Let's say a hotel is built from investors' money. To begin, how many different kinds of people or businesses would this affect? Try: architects, drafts people, building materials manufacturers, an array of trades people, designers and suppliers of furniture-bathroom-and-kitchen equipment; then there's interior designers and decorators, wool and cotton growers for carpets and fabrics and their makers, factory hands, crockery and cutlery manufacturers; managers, swimming pool merchants, landscape gardeners and suppliers, plastic pot-plant makers, the scientists who create plastics, cleaners, accountants, advertising agencies, printers, stationers, waiters, valets, chefs, cooks, washer-uppers—well, dishwasher stackers then—and of course, there's all the food that nourishes these people and the hotel guests to come, so that's another chain of participants. That adds farmers (and their suppliers of machinery, fertilisers, seeds and animals and the scientists involved), market personnel plus suppliers of the goods needed to run the stores. As you can see, we could go on, *ad infinitum:* choose any *one* of the above and we could create chain upon chain of workers; even dishwasher stackers presumably use cars or public transport for work. How many more would that link to our list? Quite a few people. All kept in jobs and helping the economy along.

So—when the hotel is complete, guests will arrive and pay for the services. A well-managed hotel will attract many customers and make good money (have a high turnover). Some of the turnover goes towards hotel maintenance, staff wages, taxes and so on and what's left, hopefully, is a nice sound profit.

The hotel management can then take the profit and become investors themselves, ploughing the profit back into the economy through more investment. So the cycle goes, stimulating opportunities for further growth. Now that's progress!

Okay, discussion over. Let's get back to the drawing board.

Remember, we were looking at different aspects of what it would mean to have a strong saving habit. Here's another point: having a strong saving habit means fewer people might gamble. (Gambling opens a large can of worms as far as the Big Picture is concerned, as you will see on page 160 of our 'brainstorming' chapter.) Fewer people would be in debt. The saving habit could carry people through to old age, reducing those needing the pension. Government money could therefore be spent on schools and hospitals.

Obviously, these things wouldn't happen *just because* you suddenly got a raise and started saving. However, remember the aim of the letter is to show your parents you are serious. You have given it some thought, including the *ideal* situation just mentioned. Let's record the points for good measure. We can decide whether to use them later if they fit well in our letter. Something like: 'If people saved/invested → help growth/dev & economy. Less gambling/ debt. No eld/pensions → more govt $ for schools/hospitals', will do the trick.

Box 2/B Group Angle (social)—Small Picture

This is the Group Angle; or another way of saying it, the Social Angle. That is, it simply relates to life and issues within a group or society. The group may be your family group, your school, a club or church group that you belong to—or it might just mean your community or the society in which we all live.

The nature of your topic means we would be considering everyday life in your family group. Let's say you'd like to offer something to your mum (or another carer) in return for the raise. At the same time, this could actually contribute to your family's well-being: if you make mum happy, with a bit of luck, it might rub off on everyone. So, why not offer to give your mum a relaxing 15 minute neck massage every Friday night, for example, while watching television?

If you presented it in a generous caring way rather than a chore, it may be something she would look forward to. Seeing mum happy, your siblings might follow your lead. This would make everyone feel good, doing things for one another. Your little neck massage could therefore do a good deal towards drawing the family closer together.

When members of society do caring things for each other that draw them together, it's called 'social cohesion' (people sticking together). To make the note in Box 2/B, therefore, you might write: 'Fridays → neck massage/mum → family well-being'. When writing your letter, this note will remind you about the idea of the massage and the likely result (a happier mum and family).

Box 2/C Group Angle (social)—Big Picture

The issue of receiving double pocket money would not have any long- or short-term impact on the Big Picture that I can think of. Can you think of something? If so, make a note. Otherwise, let's move on to Box 3/B

Boxes 3/B and 3/C Right or Wrong Angle (moral)—Both Pictures

I can't think of anything for these columns either. On the other hand, were you brainstorming for, 'Is television a waste of time?' you might argue 'yes', it is a waste of time. To support this view you might say nothing good comes from TV, leading you to think about crimes that might be committed through some people getting ideas from TV crime programs. So you see the nature of the topic can dictate whether the Box applies. For now, let's skip to the next one:

Box 4/B State of Mind Angle (psychological)—Small Picture

Is there a State of Mind Angle to your persuasive letter to your parents? Remember, there have been a lot of arguments over your constant use of the family telephone. Having your own phone should solve this problem altogether and stop the conflict. Everyone's state of mind would be calmer and more content. You could even offer the use of your phone to another family member at certain times. All in all, your new mobile would give everyone a bit of a psychological lift and be a relief to the adults. So write in, say: 'Own phone → free up fam/phone → fam/happy/ relieved. Stops arguing (avoids conflict)'.

Box 4/C State of Mind Angle (psychological)—Big Picture

No relevance that I can see. What about you? Nope? Okay—to the next one.

Boxes 5/B Environmental Angle—Small Picture

Nothing leaps out for the Environmental Angle from the Small Picture point of view. Surely doubling your pocket money to save for your own phone has no connection to the environment. But wait, what about this next idea; we wouldn't have thought of this without the checklist:

Box 5/C Environmental Angle—Big Picture

Apart from 'please, get off the phone,' let's say your parents are always telling you not to hog the bathroom in the mornings; to get out of the shower and make way for someone else. Your persuasive letter could therefore suggest to your parents that in return for double pocket money, you would take shorter showers. This will (i) contribute to family well-being through your co-operation (for Box 2/B), but (ii) shorter showers will save precious water and reduce greenhouse gases (for Box 5/C—the Big Picture). You didn't think of that, did you?

This could have been something you saw on TV in a government ad or while surfing the Net for a school project. (Check www.climatechange.gov.au for more about global warming and reducing greenhouse gases and www.ypte.org.uk for great A-Z fact sheets on a range of environmental issues.) Although the idea came to us when we checked the issue against the Environmental Angle, it has two different possible effects:

At the individual level, as mentioned, it aims to help family well-being (group or social relations). Having realised where it should go, you would put a note in Box 2/B that might say: 'Short/showers → co-operation → fam/well-being'. As with giving your mum a neck massage on Friday nights, when you write your letter later, it will remind you about the point.

From the environmental point of view, shorter showers would have an impact on the Environmental Big Picture. It would be a small impact if you were the only one doing it. But if everyone did it, the effects would be huge. When you sit down to write your letter, you will probably impress your parents if you include details you may have researched (for example, each minute you cut down on showers saves litres of water and up to half a kilogram in greenhouse gases). Your note in Box 5/C might therefore say: 'Short/showers → save water; cut greenh/gas (saves up to ½ kg per min.)'

Boxes 6/B Other Angle—Small Picture

Our last row of boxes is there for any other angles that an issue may raise. In this case, perhaps we could reserve Box 6 for the 'Personal Growth' Angle. Then in Box 6/B, the Small Picture, you could write that being given more pocket money would allow you to set higher goals for yourself, such as the new phone—but other things, too. It would help to make you more independent and contribute to your personal growth. Your note there could be: 'Raise p/money → achieve goals/independence → pers/growth'.

Box 6/C Other Angle—Big Picture

Here you might write that learning to be independent and to set goals would make you a more responsible adult, leading to you being more productive and not a burden on society. You would therefore be less likely to need social welfare (be on the dole). You could jot in this box: 'Raise p/money → learn goal setting/independence → reliable adult/not burden/society'.

As you can see, having a checklist in front of you as you plan your letter can prompt some really great ideas. Our completed checklist of brainstormed notes is over the page.

In the next chapter we will show you how your persuasive points can be transferred from the checklist in order of importance to the paragraphs of your Plan and then into your letter.

BRAINSTORMING ISSUE-BASED ESSAYS CHECKLIST FOR UPPER PRIMARY STUDENTS

Essay title: 'May I please have a raise?'
Essay type: Argumentative or Persuasive

Essay's aim/s: *To persuade my parents to double my pocket money to fund my own mobile phone.*

A. **ANGLE** (Perspective) **Ask: Can the issue or outcome be seen from this angle?**	B. **SMALL PICTURE** (Micro View) **Would/does the issue affect individuals? How?**	C. **BIG PICTURE** (Macro View) **Does the issue affect the community or society? How?**
1. MONEY (ECONOMIC)	*1.Teach me value/money. Learn how save/manage. 2. Work for raise → wash d/car → apprec. value $. Study smart/raise chances good job & future.*	*If everyone saved/invested → help growth/dev & national economy. Also less gambling/debt. No eld/pensions → more Govt $ for schools/hospitals.*
2. GROUP (SOCIAL) (Family, school, club, society, etc.)	*1. Fridays → Neck massage/mum → family well-being. 2. Short/showers → co-operation → fam/well-being.*	
3. RIGHT OR WRONG (MORAL) (According to law)		
4. STATE OF MIND (PSYCHOLOGICAL) (Happy, sad, angry, worried, etc.)	*Own phone → free up fam/phone → fam/happy/relieved. Stops arguing (avoids conflict).*	
5. ENVIRONMENTAL		*Short/showers → save water; cut greenh/gas (saves up to ½ kg per min.).*
6. OTHER	*Raise p/money → achieve goals/independence → pers/growth.*	*Raise p/money → learn goal/setting/ independence → reliable adult/no burden/society.*

Remember, next time you are asked to write about an issue in class such as the topics already suggested, you will now have a much better understanding of what to look for. It means you will be able to tackle the topic in a more active and structured way, rather than snoozing on the job and just hoping for the best. The checklist will stir your mind. It will teach you how to create sound ideas.

In the years ahead, using the format will guide your thinking and ensure all bases are covered. With a little practice, thoughts will spring to mind and you won't be able to jot them down fast enough. In fact, our Grade 5 pupils in preparing for scholarship exams soon learn how to brainstorm and plan persuasive essays in less than five minutes! Active learning like this is a part of working smart.

Now that our ideas are done, it's time to do our Plan and write our letter.

24

Upper primary: Planning your persuasive letter

Planning is absolutely vital for the success of your writing.

What would books be like if writers didn't plan their ideas on paper, first? Unpublishable? Probably! We've already advised you read pages 172-176 in the 'essay planning' chapter to learn more about planning. You will see four types of Plans that can be used for different essay types. You won't have to worry about the seniors A-Plan, the T-Plan or the L-Plan for some years yet. However, the A-Plan and G-Plan for juniors (below and next page) are designed for the topics we have been discussing.

Below is the basic structure of the A-Plan for argumentative writing. (We touched on this essay type, page 86, point 2, for the essay about TV.)

SKELETON A-PLAN (ARGUMENTATIVE): PARAGRAPHS FOR AN ESSAY TOPIC

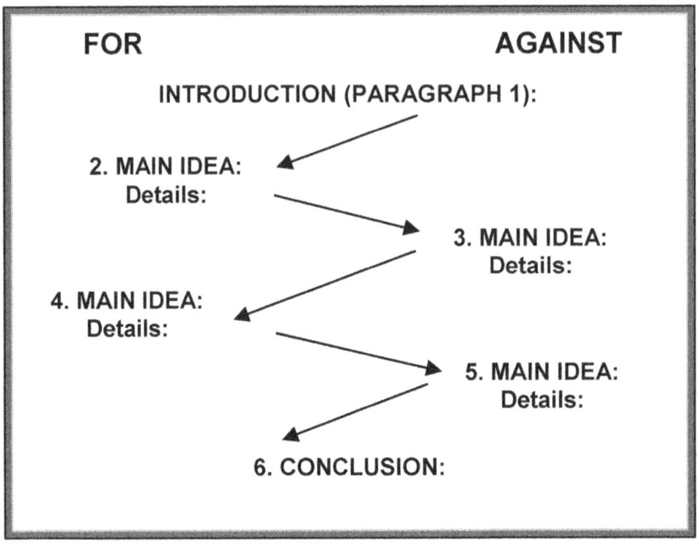

The A-Plan is different to other Plans due to the need for arguments 'for' and 'against'. As mentioned, you could use this one for, 'Is television a waste of time?' in the previous chapter. The six paragraphs shown are only an example. You may have more or less, depending on the length of your written piece. Also, introductions and conclusions may consist of more than one paragraph, depending on the length and type of essay.

For now, let's consider the G-Plan (General Plan).

You will remember this from page 56 in our 'note-taking' chapter: the G-Plan is suitable for planning many types of essays and is ideal for your persuasive piece.

**SKELETON G-PLAN (GENERAL)
PARAGRAPHS FOR AN ESSAY**

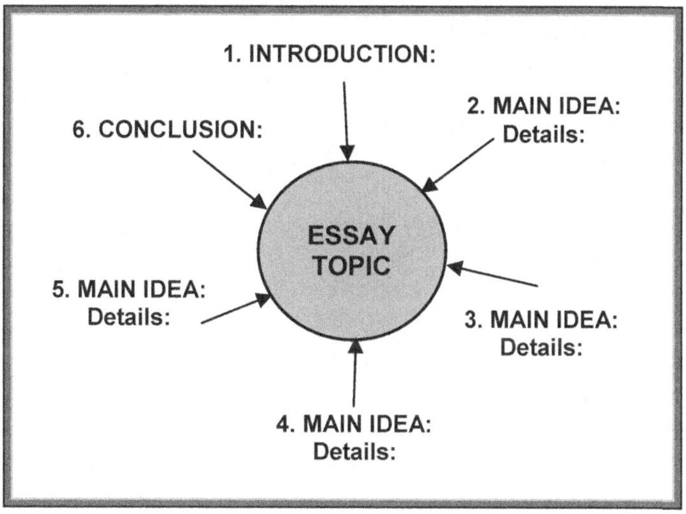

The G-Plan above represents a text also comprised of six paragraphs: an introduction, four main body paragraphs and a conclusion. Again, this is only a simple guide. It shows when we remove the words of the essay, leaving the bare bones or skeleton, we can see how experienced writers structure their texts.

Our next step is to put flesh on the bones of our G-Plan as we plan our persuasive letter using the ideas from our brainstorming checklist. We've completed the Plan over the page, to demonstrate how it might be done.

When planning later without our help, place your completed brainstorming checklist beside you to keep track of your ideas. You would also need a spare sheet of paper for mapping out your paragraphs on your own G-Plan (or A-Plan) as the case may be, just as we will show you. Now turn the page to see how we've arranged the brainstorming notes that we made together in the last chapter, on our G-Plan:

G-PLAN (GENERAL): EXAMPLE UPPER PRIMARY STUDENTS

Essay title: 'May I please have a raise?'

Essay type: Persuasive letter

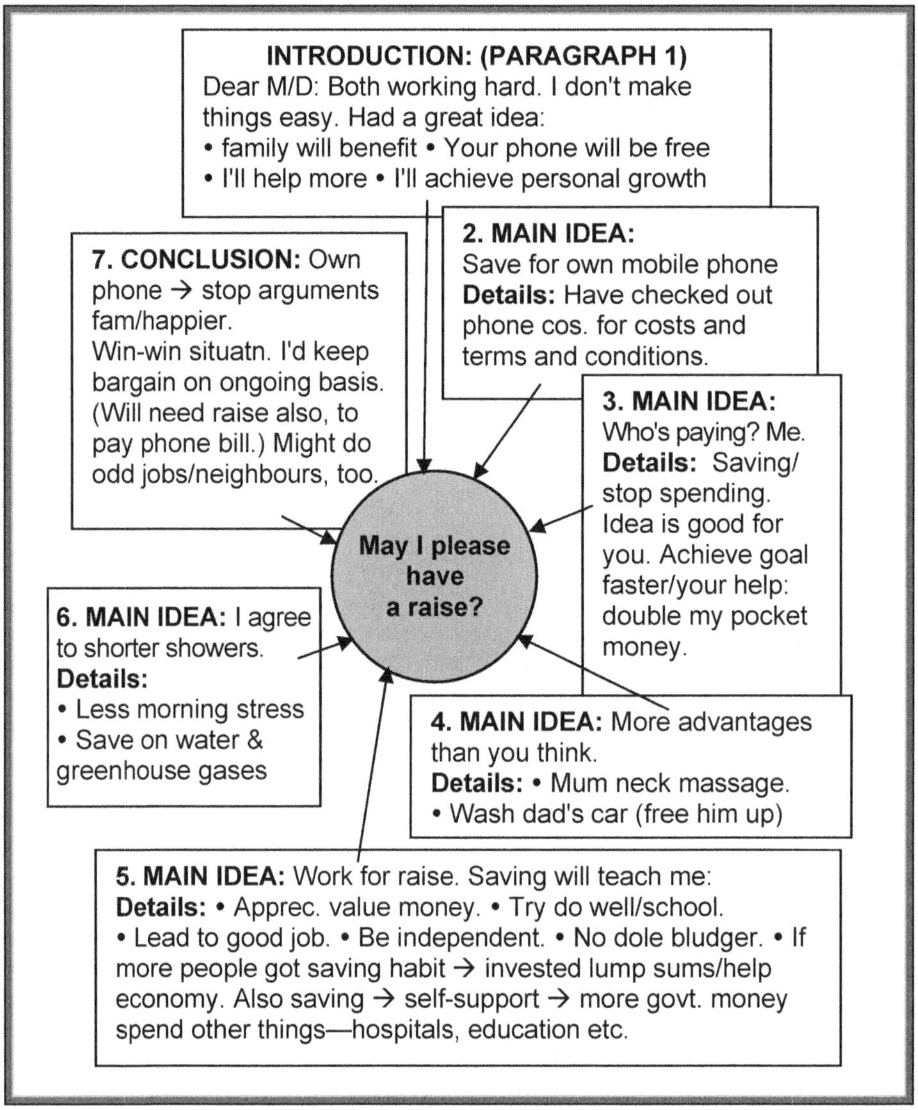

Our notes are written more fully than needed, to aid your understanding. However, a quickly written, but clear Plan using shorthand notes will serve you best in learning to practise quickly. (Fine liners are neat and handy pens, producing slender clean lines.) *Regular practice* is again the key to working smart and achieving a good result.

Although the Main Idea of the letter is to persuade your parents that you need a raise, notice we haven't mentioned that until paragraph 3. Why? Well, it would be silly to throw your chances of success out the window by blurting out the reason for the letter straight away, wouldn't it? You've already spent some time in the ideas department. It would be a pity to spoil things now.

Carrots and parsnips

The goal of a persuasive piece is to make your readers responsive and open to your suggestions. You need to *butter their parsnips* a little, first, by offering some flattering words that will make them feel good. Not only that, you have to dangle a carrot or two that offer attractive benefits as well. With this in mind, you would therefore use some of your better persuasive points *before* you put in your major request for a pocket money raise.

Now, if we use this ploy with mum and dad, *you* know that *they* know you are perhaps doing this with an ulterior motive in mind. That's not such a bad thing. They may exchange secret smiles and be quite proud of you for the thought you have put into your request. But remember, a little harmless flattery when you want something is one thing. What's important, however, is this: if you make any promises, you should keep them. This is what builds a person's good character and makes them known and respected for being trustworthy and reliable. In life, that counts for a great deal and is a valuable lesson to learn early.

Take a little time now to study the completed Plan. Check it against the ideas on the brainstorming checklist and you will see we have used all the points, except at 1/C (We thought that could be better used for a class essay on the topic, rather than a personal family letter.) In a moment, you can read our persuasive letter example. This was accomplished by referring to the notes on the Plan. When you plan in this way, it means you won't lose good ideas. You could even plan one day and write an essay the next.

As we have said, you may not use all your brainstormed notes. In fact, you should always be prepared to perhaps have new and sometimes better ideas as you write. Or you may change things later to enhance your writing. This means it may end up being a little different to what you thought it would be when you started out. That's the very nature of writing. Good writers always prune and polish (redraft) their work to produce the very best they can. One famous writer did 30 redrafts of her recent novel before she was satisfied it was ready for publication. Her dedication paid off: the book was a best-seller!

By the way, we have set out the letter in much the same way you will be expected to set out your essays as you progress during your secondary years. It's not such a bad thing to be aware of this now.

Persuasive letter (essay)—example

Essay title: 'May I please have a raise?'

Essay type: Persuasive letter

Essay's aims (Statement of Intention):

The following letter will attempt to persuade my parents to double my pocket money to fund my own mobile phone:

At home.

Saturday, 13th October

Dear Mum and Dad,

I know you are both working very hard at the moment. I also realise that when I get on the phone or stay in the shower too long, I don't make things easier for you. I'm sorry this happens; I don't mean to be a nuisance. Anyway, mum and dad, hopefully, that's all going to change. I've had a great idea and with your help, I think the whole family can share in the benefits. It means you will be able to use your phone whenever you like. My idea also means I will start helping around the place more and will also learn things that will make me a better person.

It is because you are always so open and willing to do what is best for me, that I am excited to tell you my plan: I am going to save up for my own phone. You know, a mobile. I checked out several phone companies and they gave me all their data on costs and terms and conditions and so on, which I can discuss with you later.

Of course, you will be wondering who is going to pay for this great idea. Well, don't worry, I have that already worked out. Instead of spending my pocket money at weekends, I'm going to open a bank account and start saving. It would take quite a long time, but there is a faster way and this is where you might like to come in. My idea has some good things in it for you as well as for me. Basically, I am hoping you might agree to doubling my pocket money to help this plan along.

There are more advantages for you than you might expect. I have thought about it a lot. I would promise to do certain things to make life happier for you both in return for your help: mum, for you, on Friday nights, I would like to give you a 15 minute neck massage after your week at the office—for as long as you want. And dad, I'd like very much to take over the chore of washing your car. This would free you up. But it would also teach me the following good lesson:

You are always telling me money doesn't grow on trees. I believe that working for my raise and learning to save will really make me appreciate the value of money; perhaps invest a little later on. It has already made me think about doing well at school: If I can then get a good job that will make me successful and independent, I will be able to become a responsible adult and not bludge on the dole and so on. I guess if more young people got the idea, the economy would benefit and the Government would have more money to spread around.

Oh, I almost forgot—I would also promise to take shorter showers so the mornings wouldn't be so stressful. You know, dad, looking at the big picture, that would even save on the greenhouse gases you are always talking about. Up to half a kilogram is saved, you know, for every minute cut down. I think I could cut a good 3 minutes off my time ☺.

Anyway, mum and dad, I hope you will give my idea some thought. One of the main things is I think that it would stop the arguing and we'd all be a lot happier. You would have your phone back. I'd have my phone and we'd all get many advantages. You could even use my phone if you ever wanted to. I would be happy to keep up my side of the bargain on an ongoing basis. Of course, I will also need the extra pocket money to top up my phone card. I might do some odd jobs in the neighbourhood as well.

I would be happy to discuss this whole issue with you once you've talked it over. Hope to hear from you soon.

With love,
(Signed)

Now that you've been shown how to write a persuasive piece, perhaps you may wish to try something on your own. Have fun with it and remember, keep copies of checklists always on hand as your guide.

It is not intended that these last four chapters for upper primary students be substituted for the ensuing Parts for older students. Indeed, I encourage you as a fifth- or sixth-grader to learn as much as you can from the following chapters, particularly those already suggested at the top of page 67.

Especially, you should read the last chapter, 'Reach for the sky', page 209, which is directed at all students. There you will find our 'Time Out 15' exercises that you might put into practice when ready. Also check out the Appendix for information including our 'Grammar and Punctuation Tips', page 238, in case you need to brush up; they may come in handy.

In the meantime, for the following chapters, arm yourself with a highlighter and some tags. Then you can easily flip back to the pages you may want to check again later. Above all, don't forget the meaning of 'working smart'—*less time and effort for better results!*

That's the key to your ultimate success.

PART 3

Get set . . .

CHAPTERS 25 - 40

SECONDARY AND SENIORS, AND STUDENTS IN GENERAL

Understanding essay writing

Dear Student,

Although Part 3 is predominantly directed at secondary, and particularly, senior secondary students, younger pupils have already been encouraged to read several chapters to enhance their understanding of essay writing. Please refer back to page 67 for the recommended texts for younger readers that occur in the chapters that follow.

Tertiary students:
As has been noted by Dr. McKeown and Professor Vajda in the Foreword, tertiary students may also find certain chapters in Part 3 very useful in preparation of their written assignments.

25

Pressing the right buttons

In my broad experience as a psychologist and educator, the skill of written communication has always been the greatest predictor of student success.

In a class of say, 25, where most may have a full *grasp* of an issue, it is only the student who can *communicate* the issue in writing, who excels. The significance of this vital skill will become more evident as the next chapters unfold. Note them, follow our advice, and you will be well on the way to gaining higher grades.

It looks simple enough on the surface: producing an essay requires knowing how to write a short piece about a particular subject. An obvious statement perhaps. Yet many secondary students *do not know how* to produce a good essay.

In tackling the job, they flounder. They use no guidelines; are unaware of brainstorming. They know nothing of essay structure, Main Ideas and Supporting or Substantiating Details; nothing of developing a personal style; of how to analyse, persuade, inform or entertain. They've never heard of emotional accord, identifying issues and evaluating ideas.

This flies in the face of logic. How can one achieve a creditable mark for an essay with so few skills? If you are shrugging silently to yourself, the ensuing chapters are designed with you in mind. Even if you have some bases already covered, you may wish to fine-tune your skills in other areas. So don't worry. We'll soon have you ship-shape and in the know. After all, it's the *knowing how* of essay writing that determines an essay's ultimate worth: the value, or mark, an examiner will place on *how well you are able to communicate your subject.*

Look at it this way: why would judges at a cake-making contest nibble on the cakes? Because they are hungry? One would hope not. As judges, they are using certain criteria to assess each entry: its presentation, its structure, flavour, aroma, texture, and so on. In short, the cake-nibbling judges are measuring *the skill* of the contestant as a cake maker.

So why do examiners read examination essays? For literary entertainment? The question is just as absurd! No—as examiners, they are using certain criteria to assess the worthiness of each essay: its presentation, its structure, content, validity, personal style, imagery, and so on. In short, the essay-reading examiners are measuring skill: the skill of the student to communicate a given subject, via the written word.

Let's return to cakes for a moment. Take Janet, queen of all cake-makers. As a smart cake-making contestant, Janet has done her research. She knows what the judges are looking for and creates her cakes accordingly. She's learned what inspires a delighted patting of the stomach, a smacking of the lips, a rapturous roll of the eyes. She knows what sets her cakes apart, what finishing touches turn a judge's head.

In short, Janet knows how to press a judge's button!

Writing has its parallels. Like the judges in the cake-making contest, the examiners are hoping to be impressed. They are looking for something that transcends the run of the mill; something with special qualities. You have to be aware of what those qualities might be, and learn how to capture and instil them in your writing. In other words, as an essay writer, you too, you must learn how to press buttons.

In making this point to pupils, our staff will draw a quick circle on paper. Pointing at areas away from the circle, they will ask: 'Why would you press here, or here,' and then (placing a finger on the circle) continue, 'when you know the right button is *here*?' It is an image, pupils say, which sticks in their minds. It is a vivid reminder to them to *address the issues that will elicit the desired responses* to their writing—and result in a commendable mark.

Such issues will be addressed in the coming chapters. However, be aware it is beyond the scope of this book to include all the guidelines and ideas we can impart to our students during our tutoring sessions. Nonetheless, it will seek to raise an awareness of the *knowing how* of essay writing and offers important tools (clear strategies, exercises and 'Brain-booster' checklists) so that pupils can readily and successfully develop the skills for working smart in preparation for their assignments and exams.

Let's find out what you will learn.

26

What you will learn

Some of you will be poised precariously on new ground.

To give you the confidence, support and knowledge you will need to write accomplished essays, let's start at the beginning.

An essay can be about any topic under the sun.

However, the essays you are likely to encounter generally conform to several main types. This allows us to label and put them into pigeonholes. We can then define how each essay should be approached and handled.

We should firstly establish clear terms for ready understanding of our discussion. The term, essay 'type', will therefore be used throughout these chapters to describe the specific nature of an essay: 'creative', 'argumentative', 'informative', 'descriptive' essays, and so on. While each essay type has different writing requirements, some are linked by a certain common feature or features. We have therefore grouped the nine essay types to be outlined, into four main 'styles'. They are, as follows:

ESSAY STYLE	ESSAY TYPE
1. CREATIVE	Creative Descriptive Personal
2. ISSUE-BASED	Argumentative Persuasive
3. ANALYTICAL	Text analysis Language analysis
4. INFORMATIVE	Informative Instructional

Note that as shown in the preceding table, issue-based and analytical essays are separated into two styles. Although a key requirement of issue-based essays is *analysis* of an issue, analysis of *text* and analysis of *language* require different approaches in the essay planning and writing.

In describing whether a text is an editorial, Letter to the Editor, media article, review and so on, the term 'format' is used—eg editorial format.

You have met the term, 'text structure' in our discussion on smart note-taking in Chapter 19, page 93. In this context, 'text structure' or 'essay structure' describes the manner in which writers structure their texts using Main Ideas and Supporting/Substantiating Details.

Essay writing features to be covered in this, and the next 14 chapters are:

- Reading the essay question
- Essay styles and types (includes description of type, introductory paragraphs and examples)
- Brainstorming (includes issue-based checklist and creative methods)
- Doing your research (includes a 'Text Analysis Checklist')
- Planning your essay (includes Plan examples and guidelines, exercises and checklists)
- First draft (includes exercises)
- Editing your work to final copy
- Sitting for exams
- Practice exercises (includes ten-week sample of 15 minute exercises to develop and refine your skills for working smart)

Before we go on, your pocket book could do with an indelible entry:

'The purpose of the written word is effective communication.'

We'll put flesh on the bones of each point, as we go. However, keep this pearl of wisdom about the purpose of writing well to the fore where you can see it, as we proceed. That and of course, 'pressing buttons'.

Reading the essay question

On examining this issue, hearken back to our previous chapter on smart note-taking and re-read pages 57-8. These remind you to read the question carefully. Read it several times, or you will be letting yourself down.

As you address an essay writing question, you should make brief notes. Importantly, these notes should be used as a checklist when reviewing your essay, to ensure you have covered all the criteria. Ask yourself the following:

1. What 'type' of essay is it? Argumentative? Creative? Instructional? And so on. (Essay types are covered in more detail in a moment.)

2. Who are my target readers? Here, the examiner is not the target reader. The examiner judges the work from the *viewpoint* of the target reader to whom your essay is directed.

3. What elements or issues, if any, need to be discussed? For example, political, economic, social, etc. (This will be discussed further in our 'brainstorming' and 'essay planning' chapters.)

4. Have I interpreted the question correctly? (Carefully check again.)

Essay styles and types

For our purposes, *the style* of an essay describes a significant feature (or features). This feature is shared by certain *types* of essays, which allows us to place them into groups. Grouping is not meant to constrain your approach to a topic, or to place it into one particular category for all time. We are not saying this way is set in concrete. Indeed, you will find that some topics overlap and could be written from various points of view across different styles.

For example, an argumentative essay could be written as a persuasive essay and vice versa; or given a different slant, an informative topic could become an issue-based one. Usually your guidelines are clear, but your teacher is again your point of reference when you are not sure.

1. Creative style:

Essay types: 'creative', 'descriptive' and 'personal'

Key elements in creative writing are imagination, free thought, escapism and novelty. Depending on the type of essay, these factors can be included in varying degrees: creative essays, *per se,* should predominantly or wholly contain these components. Descriptive and personal essays are well served by the injection of personality and some creative flair when recording personal comments and reflecting upon experiences based on reality. That is, remember your reader, and impart your information imaginatively. We provide examples later, when each essay type is discussed. Other chapters will guide you in writing your own.

2. Issue-based style:

Essay types: 'argumentative', 'persuasive'

These types require research and an evaluation of the pros and cons of a topic, proposal or issue. Students are required to adopt a critical stance and to argue their points of view employing Supporting/Substantiating Details. These essay types are expounded in Chapter 29 and guidelines for essay writing are also given in the chapters that follow.

3. Analytical style:

Essay types: 'text analysis' and 'language analysis'

Text analysis provides opportunities for exploring our own value systems, the mores (pronounced 'mor-aze', and meaning the accepted moral customs) of societies and the strategies used by authors to evoke reader responses to issues. The essay requires your response to a text from your own point of view while reflecting your comprehension of the issues it contains; or a response that conveys your understanding of an author's stance. This requires not only identification and substantiation of time-old, human Motivators (love, hate, betrayal, etc.) and Belief Systems, but an understanding of the impact of the Motivators used in the text, and an insight into the author's intentions.

The approach to language analysis is quite different, given that student responses are non-critical rather than polemic. The use of language in the media can be subtle or strong. Either way, its impact on readers and audiences can be profound. Language analysis requires the collection of a cross-section of views about a topic. The language employed to express those views is then analysed for its use of strategies to influence reader/audience responses and issue outcomes.

4. Informative style:

Essay types: 'informative' and 'instructional'

The role of these types of essays is to inform the reader about a particular subject. Research will be required for informative essays and depending on the topic, for many instructional essays. Further explanations and assistance are available in later chapters.

Creative essay writing is an interesting place to begin.

Let's investigate!

27

Creative essays

By its very nature, creative writing is original.

It is words brought into existence for the very first time by their writer; hallmarked by a personal style and imagination, sprung from a myriad electrical impulses inside the brain. Even if an idea is as old as time, the creative manner in which it is expressed, is what gives it its stamp of originality.

Naturally enough, a creative essay is an exciting opportunity to showcase your skills as an imaginative writer. Creative writing is a broad ranging genre: it may comprise just a paragraph or two, or be a short story or poem. Alternatively, it may take the form of a novel, play or screenplay, containing plots, sub-plots, drama, comedy, romance, mystery, intrigue, and so on. Whether it's a two-page creative essay, a short story or a novel, the goal of the writer should always be *to entertain* the reader. Your writing must draw the reader into your story and allow them to experience any, or all, of a gamut of emotions made possible through your choice of words and your ability to communicate language.

Examples in film and television

We are surrounded every day by creative writing—especially when we go to the cinema or watch television. Next time you sit down to view a drama or comedy at home, keep a notepad beside you and make notes on what you observe. You'll find: main characters (the protagonists), the supporting characters, the good, the bad, a storyline, a main plot with a climax and usually, sub-plots linked to the main plot. (Sub-plots are often resolved before the main plot reaches its climax.) Sometimes the writer or director has chosen to weave strong or subtle messages into the story. They might be of a moral or humanitarian nature, for example, intended to make the audience think.

Observe how the film opens and closes. Note how the plot is developed. When is the main character/s introduced? What conflict or problems does s/he face that need solving? From whose viewpoint is the story being told?

How does the writer establish the background to the story? How is atmosphere created? How is the main climax reached? (There may be more than one climax.) How does the story end?

If the writer has written a good script, emotions will run high during the climax/es of the story. Jot down the emotions you feel as the story unfolds and the climaxes are reached. What emotive tools, or means, are used to create these emotions? For example:

Emotive tools		**Emotion/s felt**
suspense	→	excitement, nervousness, fear
humour	→	happiness, excitement, delight
violence	→	horror, disgust, fear
romance	→	happiness, empathy, longing
action	→	elation, admiration, envy, awe
adventure	→	exhilaration, wonder, yearning

Plots, sub-plots and climaxes

The plot is the main story. *Sub-plots,* or side stories—if used—are connected to, and developed along with, the plot. This is often achieved by switching from one to the other and is a clever way to create tension. *The main climax* occurs when the threads of a story are brought together in one revealing or thrilling moment. It is the highest or most exciting point of the story.

For example, the plot of your story may be about a war correspondent, the hero, who sets out to rescue an orphan from certain oppression and poverty from inside a war zone. He seeks to smuggle the child across a war-ravaged border to the safety of a peaceful country. A sub-plot developed may be a potential love-interest between the hero and a nurse who helps him in his plight. Now we need an antagonist (a scoundrel opposing the hero). So a second sub-plot may be about a spy for the other side who plots to uncover the hero's escape plan and bring him to a ghastly end.

One sub-plot is resolved before the story's climax when there is a struggle between the antagonist and the hero who (as usually happens) wins the day. The suspenseful climax occurs at the war torn border as the hero, nurse and child approach enemy lines and attempt to cross, undetected. The second sub-plot is resolved to reader satisfaction in a smaller climax at the end. Once in the safety of the friendly zone, the hero and nurse, faced with going their separate ways, are forced at last to declare their undying love for one another. Incidentally, there is no rule about sub-plots. You may have none. You may have three or four. Too many sub-plots, however, may confuse both writer and reader.

Now that we understand some of the basic terms of creative writing, let's look at how you should go about producing your essay.

Your introduction

The introductory paragraph/s offers you a powerful opportunity! You only get it once. Embrace it therefore with enthusiasm, and bring all the knowledge, creativity and skill you can, to its writing. Why?

Imagine this scene: your teacher's classroom (or examiner's study); a desk on which sit piles of essay assignments waiting to be marked. It's 7.30 Friday, on a warm summer's evening, and your teacher's spouse is out with the two kids taking in a popular movie. Is your teacher having a good time? Does he want to be there? Is he bored to distraction having to wade through page after page of well-intentioned, but often, puerile, prose?

The answer, of course, is no, no and (probably) yes!

That is, until he picks up your creative essay and reads the opening lines:

'Kirby dropped the phone back into its cradle, his stomach in a knot. His heart punched at his chest like an iron fist. What would happen next? Would Suzette call the police, now she knew the truth? He threw back the bedclothes and walked out onto the balcony, barefooted, into the New York night air. Only a miracle could save him now and, what do you know? He didn't believe in miracles.'

You have just pressed your first button! Your reader is instantly intrigued. What has Kirby done? Who is Suzette? His colleague, wife, love-interest, his daughter? What 'truth' is he referring to and how will he resolve his problem? Is it life-threatening? What crime, if any, has he committed? Already atmosphere is created; the plot is thickening. The reader is curious and wants more.

For your introduction, most people respond well to writing that begins with action and/or thoughts or dialogue. Curiosity aroused, it motivates the reader to delve further. Incidentally, a reminder here: creative writing, as inferred earlier, is not all drama. Comedy or adventure may well be your forte. Nonetheless, this should not prevent usage of either action or dialogue (or both) in your opening paragraph/s.

On page 241, in the Appendix, you will find a list of verbs we call, 'Verb-Speak', compiled for use with dialogue in your texts. Most of the verbs describe the speaking *tone* (the manner in which something is said or communicated) eg 'I won't let it beat me,' she *whispered.* (Or, she *cried,* she *growled,* etc.) You'll find them handy when grasping for an atmospheric verb. But, don't overdo it; s/he *said,* often works best. The 'Verb-Speak' list can also be found at edworksglobal.com, Checklists and Templates/The Tone Zone.

Here's one way of structuring your creative essay: outline your intended story on paper (during the planning stage, to be discussed) then choose a dramatic moment as your introductory paragraph, using the action/dialogue techniques mentioned. Once done, leave the action or drama and go back to an earlier point in the story where it begins to unfold—achieved with something like: 'It all began . . .' or 'I remember well that cold Friday last year.' That is, proceed to tell your story in flashback, bringing it to the point in the first paragraph. Then go on to resolve your protagonist's dilemma, including a powerful climax, perhaps with a twist or a surprise at the end.

In fiction or creative writing, avoid weaving lengthy unwieldy sentences into long paragraphs. Keep them short and to the point (or relatively so, depending on the mood) and especially in the opening stages. Keep your reader enthralled. Long heavy paragraphs may induce sleep or plain loss of interest for your story. A good way of remembering this is to look at the white spaces around your paragraphs. Short paragraphs make your work easier to read.

By the way, how do you like this for the first line of a novel? *I Capture the Castle,* by Dodie Smith, was published in 1948: 'I write this sitting in the kitchen sink.' Do you think author, Ms Smith, knew how to press buttons?

Adding punch to your creative style with short sentences

Short sentences within your short paragraphs in creative writing can have an impact that longer sentences often can't produce. Putting a handful of words together just before direct speech, for instance, can add personality, atmosphere, and sometimes a sense of urgency or drama to the scene you are creating. They are quite easy to generate. Just 'step into your scene' and the brain sparks will start flying. Here are some examples:

- I made a quick decision.
- Marsh adjusted her glasses.
- Sangster hesitated.
- She drummed her fingers.
- I shot him a brief glance.
- I grinned at Franklyn.
- They fell silent.
- The African was late.
- Ken-ichi beamed.
- Her mind raced.
- York gave a cynical laugh.
- Mrs. Peabody stood firm.
- His cheeks coloured.
- She dreaded his reply.
- Chandler turned to him.

Check out the following sentence and see how we might improve it, as discussed. Instead of writing, 'He said he was looking for Hollingsworth, so I decided to tell him that I was Hollingsworth,' try this:

'Truth is,' drawled the stranger, 'I'm after a man called Hollingsworth.'

I made a quick decision. 'You're looking at him,' I said evenly, putting out my hand.

Emotional accord and your thesaurus

Remember, too, that when someone begins to read your essay, the reader's mind is blank. They are relying on you to fill in the details by creating colourful images and characters in your essay. Your words are powerful tools. Use them to paint a canvas across your reader's mind.

But importantly, the words you choose to project emotions such as fear, excitement, anger, joy and so on, should be in *accord* (agreement) with the emotion you wish to create in each scene. We call this 'emotional accord'.

So consider your words carefully. Weigh them against similar words and see which one fits best. For example, 'he muttered to himself' or 'he cursed inwardly' are milder than 'he raged'. Which one suits your context? Similarly, the word 'crash', creates a stronger image than 'bump'. Which is better suited to your scene? A thesaurus will help you to develop a wider vocabulary and provide you with a number of possibilities. Always keep it handy.

Creative writing examples

Following are samples of creative writing from two of our grade 5 pupils. Harrie is just coming to grips with using adjectives and adverbs to colour his writing. He avoids the predictable formats of pupils of his age, and uses direct speech, action and imagery as bait to hook the reader's attention. Overall, we think he does a good job.

However, note that as just discussed, some of his word choices are perhaps a little strong for the emotion he seeks to convey. Harrie's dad loves fishing. Guess where Harrie found his inspiration?

'The gentle rippling of the waves against the sea-green sides of the skipper's Mary-Lou was the captain's idea of paradise. He soon noticed though, that no fish had come near either his rod or boat. "Damned fish!" he raged. It became clear that all the flat-head had made their way to deeper waters. With a tiring groan, the skipper went to the bridge and skilfully steered the Mary-Lou towards the horizon. It was then that fish of all shapes and types could be seen, as their blackened shadows glided through the water.'

Az, also grade 5, captures a scene of adventure, family life and good imagery, in just three brief lines. Yep, we're goin' fishin' again:

' "I've got one!" We all glanced over as Cody, my brother, tugged frantically on his fishing line. The new rod strained so far forward I thought it was going to snap. In an instant the line flicked back and dangled lifelessly.'

We think year 10 student, Yolandé, may be published some time in the future with a little more practice. Her writing is starting to show great promise. Here are some excerpts from her creative writing essay titled, 'Visions', which offers a good measure of excitement, fear, suspense, curiosity, atmosphere—and watch out for a surprise twist at the end.

Remember! Your storyline must naturally relate to the essay topic. However, a good writer will always have an ear or an eye for new ideas, even when not on the job.
Jotting thoughts into your pocket book may provide you with just the starting point you need if you are later asked to write a creative essay. Your world is full of everyday things that can trigger new ideas. They might be inspired by seeing a film or a play, by a personal experience or a dream, reading a news item or magazine, overhearing a conversation, or by a favourite hobby or sport.

'Visions

Kate's footsteps echoed off the hard wet concrete as she walked along the deserted street. The chill of the cold night air made her bones ache and she longed to be at home. She imagined sitting in front of her large open fire as it hissed and crackled, devouring the wood. She thought of Marmalade, her cat, lying gently on her lap, purring with contentment. She hurried on, her fantasy slipping to the back of her mind.

Suddenly, a bright luminescent light flashed before Kate's eyes. She saw a vision that deeply disturbed her. A woman lay, apparently unconscious, in a bath. Kate shuddered with fright that her imagination should create such real life clarity.

Forcing herself to hum a tune, she gradually forgot what she had seen in her mind, and continued her long walk home.

(Kate gets home and lets her cat in.)
The darkness bothered her tonight; she had never noticed just how black it was before. She wasn't usually this nervous; after all, she had lived independently for almost six years. To ease her thoughts Kate quickly went around the apartment flicking on all the lights. The kitchen's warm glow seemed comforting and for the first time that night she felt the growls of hunger from deep inside her. While preparing her dinner Kate took out a large knife to slice the carrots. Suddenly, without warning, the bright luminescent light flashed again before her eyes. She saw a woman, the same woman from her eerie vision earlier that night, making two cups of coffee and cutting two slices of chocolate cake. The vision then faded as quickly as it had come. Kate felt uneasy as she continued slicing the carrots. She didn't understand what was happening. She had never seen this woman before in her life, and yet this was the second time tonight she had visualised her.

(Kate goes to bed but, in the middle of the night ...)
Suddenly, Kate was awake again. She had had a disturbing dream. It was like the one she had visualised in her waking hours the day before. This time, the woman was screaming as a tall blonde man in a dark suit, came menacingly towards her holding a long, silk scarf. Kate lay rigid in her bed, afraid to move as she felt the presence of someone standing in her bedroom, watching her. Marmalade began to mew, breaking the silence and fear that had trapped her. She heard herself saying, "It was only a dream, don't be ridiculous!" She pushed the bedcovers aside, slid quickly out of bed and put Marmalade outside.

(Kate makes hot milk and goes back to bed. But she wakes in the early morning drenched in perspiration from a nightmare.)
The image of her nightmare returned to haunt her. This time the tall, blonde man in a dark suit was busy disposing of evidence. The lifeless form of the woman in her visions lay in the bath. As he washed his hands, Kate saw the man's reflection in the mirror and it shocked her. He was very handsome. Why would anyone want to do something so horrific? Somehow, his good looks belied the evil deed.

(Kate rises and sets off to catch a train to work, trying to shake off a feeling of foreboding. She checks out the news while waiting for the train.
Kate couldn't believe what she was reading. Was this some kind of a joke? No, it couldn't be. It was her secret. As the train pulled into the station she continued to scan the news item in utter disbelief. But it had to be true; there it was in black and white right before her eyes.

(On the train, Kate suddenly decides to report her visions to the police.)
Entering the Darlington police station, Kate asked to see the homicide detectives in charge of the *Julie* murder case as it had been named in the news report.

She was told to wait in the visitors' lounge. A wave of nervousness swept over her. What if they didn't believe her? What if they laughed at her talk of visions and nightmares? Worst of all, what if they accused her of the murder? With all the detailed information she could provide would they possibly think she was capable of such a horrendous deed? Could they? Surely not! They couldn't believe that *she* was responsible.

The officer who had told her to wait approached Kate and told her that Detective Nichols was able to see her now. She walked into the cold, grey interview room and shuddered involuntarily, feeling apprehensive. At the back of the room a door opened and Kate swung around. She stood, transfixed, unable to believe what she saw! Entering the room, a smile on his handsome face and dressed in a dark suit, was the tall blonde man from her nightmare.'

Some creative writing topics

Once you have completed reading the book's guidelines, you could select from among the following titles to practise your essay writing skills.

- Eight famous, historical figures attend a dinner party
- I was taken hostage
- I am Houdini's reincarnation
- 'Shhh!' whispered Elvis. 'May I come in?'
- I survived a shipwreck
- My two hundred year life as a violin
- I was Sir David Attenborough's cameraman
- Without a sound, he raised the window
- I was born in 1790
- Letters from my aunt/uncle

Establishing a story's background

In establishing a background to your story, make sure to weave it neatly into the main body of your text. Don't simply make a bald statement of the facts. There are ways of doing this, perhaps by using dialogue or thoughts, and emotive language, again, to draw your reader in. A good story, well told, should hold a reader captive. Ideally, they shouldn't want to put it down.

For example, perhaps our friend, Kirby, mentioned earlier, is a stock broker, working on the floor of the New York Stock Exchange. Perhaps, also, over time, he has daringly and secretly skimmed funds from a wealthy client's shares portfolio. He intends putting the money back after speculating in high risk options for himself, where he dreams of making a big bag of money.

This would be very boring reported as I have just done. However, what if you were to write the following, instead:

'The noise as he entered the trading floor on Wall Street was running at a fever pitch but Kirby thrived on it. He strode immediately to his desk and looked at the screen. Blue Star Mines was up by a full dollar on yesterday's closing. *Thank you very much.* He grinned inwardly. He'd just made himself another ten grand using his client's money. How he loved this job! It was like taking candy from a baby. Of course, he was going to give the candy back, just as soon as he'd grabbed a giant all-day sucker for himself. What a sucker that would be! He chuckled, pleased at his own little joke.'

We have used the strategy of describing the main character's thoughts here, instead of using dialogue to help depict the situation. This not only works well to impart information, but adds light and shade to your writing by varying the dialogue format.

Descriptive essay writing and personal essay writing will be defined in the next chapter. These have elements of creativity, but may use personal experiences, introspection and observation to elicit subject detail.

Have you had an FMB, lately? I'll be ready when you are.

28

Descriptive and personal essays

Descriptive and personal essays provide further opportunities for imagery and creative flair. However, rather than flights of fancy, they generally reflect real life situations.

Descriptive essay writing

Descriptive writing is just that: it describes things. In that it relies on memory, introspection or observation to provide the subject matter, it is not creative writing. That is, phenomena and events already exist or have already occurred; you do not bring them into existence. However, placing it under the heading of a creative writing 'style' reminds us to record subject details using imagination and personality. That is, *be creative* in your delivery of words.

A descriptive narrative may include: past or present events, reflections or reminiscences, or descriptions of people, scenery, responses or feelings. Like a personal essay, some descriptive pieces may be introspective: the exploration of thoughts and impressions that you or the person whose experiences you are recording, experienced at a particular time of life.

As discussed in 'Creative essays—Establishing a story's background', page 118, merely stating bald facts is boring and unimaginative. So tap into your creative side. Be imaginative. Use evocative language to record your descriptive details. Employ colour and highlights to paint vivid pictures for your readers. However, it is important to keep your writing well balanced.

By this I mean: avoid the trap of seasoning your text with an over-supply of adjectives and/or adverbs. A surfeit of rich prose can cause a reader's loss of appetite for any essay. It's like using herbs and spices in food to add interest and flavour: too much can spoil the dish. So keep an eye to balance. Use powerful language when needed, but remember the light and shade. Introductions, conclusions (and climaxes when writing creative essays) are good places to flex your creative muscle. But refrain from showing off—your examiner is far too sharp to be fooled by it.

In some descriptive writing, you might reflect upon events, situations or experiences in your life, as your sources of inspiration. Picture them in your mind. Imagine you have returned to a scene from your recent or distant past. What do you see and hear? What do you smell? Include any of these: the setting, people, scenery, objects, impressions, responses and feelings. Similarly, you could recount the experiences of others.

My remarkable friend, Hilda, believe it or not, was 111 years of age when she died recently. In spite of a slowness of step towards the end, on good days, Hilda's eyes burned brightly, her mind as sharp as a tack. At 93, this feisty old lady committed her memories to a book, transcribed and bound by a friend into 34 short descriptive essays. They richly depict events, memories and observations—from her childish pranks at six years of age when Queen Victoria was still on the throne, to her 100th birthday.

To have the privilege of reading some of Hilda's descriptive work is, indeed, a treat—and one that seems fitting to share with you now. It is rare for any of us to have the opportunity to glimpse the past through the eyes of someone who has witnessed not only three centuries, but immense technological and social change: from candles to the electric light, from phaetons (horse drawn carriages) to the modern motor car, and from the world of family entertainment—a sing-song around a 19th century piano—to the cinematographic wonders of the big screen.

Following, I have chosen two descriptive pieces from Hilda's book. They eloquently reflect many of the elements discussed at the beginning of this chapter of recollections, personal impressions and descriptive sequences about settings and people. The first is the introductory paragraph from her Story 6, entitled, 'Melbourne in the early 1900's'.

Remember, this grand old lady was born in 1893!

'Melbourne in the early days had a charm and elegance about it; an air of refinement. It was a town of wide streets and fine buildings enhanced by beautiful churches and gardens, like the Fitzroy and Treasury. Prancing horses with long tails and flowing manes drew phaetons and other carriages, while trams rattled down the centre of the streets. These always fascinated me as a child. Mother and I loved going to town; it was quite an event! The shops had island windows just inside their entrances. Attendants in top hats and pale grey uniforms adorned with silver buttons stood outside the shops and opened the glass doors for lady customers. A black-suited floorwalker then conducted them to various departments. The sales ladies behind the counters wore tight-fitting bodices and long, full black skirts. These young women gave service with a smile. If madam required a pair of gloves, a small cushion was placed on the counter under her arm, while the sales lady carefully moulded the glove to her customer's hand. Tall stools were placed along the counters for the customer to rest upon while being served. Life was leisurely in those early days.'

Next, Hilda gives us a glimpse of life at the close of the nineteenth century with her narrative from Story 17, 'The Little Toyshop':

'How many remember, a very long time ago, the tiny old-fashioned shops scattered around the suburbs of Melbourne? There were four in Burnley where I lived: a grocer, a greengrocer, a smallgoods shop and the fourth, a little toyshop. These old shops were usually painted black and situated on a corner of a side street. Each was like a small three-roomed house. A wall was knocked out for a door to the entrance of the shop, and the house window served to display the goods. Given that I was only a child, the one of most interest to me was the tiny toyshop run by the elderly Miss Wilson.

Everyone knew Miss Wilson and her famous toyshop. It had a long window with a gas light overhead. In the centre of the window sat a medium-sized doll with a smiling, china face and flaxen curls. She was dressed as a fairy, the white, filmy skirt of the dress spread around her. A gold crown was on her head; a wand with a gold star was in her hand. Crowded around her on the floor were dozens and dozens of small figures in various, brightly coloured costumes: soldiers, sailors, milkmaids and peasants. The floor was completely covered with these little dolls and an assortment of toys. There wasn't room to put a pin between them.'

Here are some descriptive essay titles for your consideration:

- Favourite celebrations (eg Christmas, Hanukkah, Chinese New Year, Eid, Diwali, birthdays, etc.)
- A day on the river
- My bedroom
- Weekend in the snow
- My family
- My house was burgled
- My favourite holiday
- School
- I come from afar; *or,* S/he came from afar

A reminder that descriptive essays just describe things. They neither persuade nor argue the point; these are the roles of issue-based essays. Once you have read all the essay chapters, why not come back and try some of the descriptive titles suggested? Do you want to tag this page?

Personal essay writing

Personal essays are, of course, written from a personal perspective. In fact, they may not always be essays, but take the form of a diary, postcards, letters and so on. You can make this choice once the topic is decided upon, and you know your teacher approves.

Personal writing embraces any of the human issues and experiences we encounter through life, from the day we recall our conscious thoughts as a child, to the day we draw our last breath. It may be expressed through reflection, the sharing of views and opinions, the describing of events, experiences and people.

Your personal writing should avoid the prosaic—always venture beyond the mere recording of phenomena. A good personal essay will probe, expose issues and feelings, evaluate, and reach conclusions. Above all, personal writing should always be individualistic and peppered with descriptive imagery and thoughtful, well-selected prose to capture and hold the reader. Keep the following points in mind for writing your personal piece:

1. Whether you are recounting your distant or immediate past, or projecting your hopes for the future, you should not only describe the situation you remember, or aspire to, but also examine feelings and responses. Gently stir your reader's emotions, but take care not to slip into melodrama.

2. If you are writing about a past event, did these feelings motivate you to make decisions that affect you now?

3. In recalling events or memories, evaluate the thoughts and experiences you had then, and compare them to how you might react in the present with the wisdom of hindsight.

Here are some personal essay writing topics that may help to put these comments into perspective. Select a title or two when you have finished reading the essay writing chapters and try your hand at composing two or three pages. The more you practice what you learn, the easier the process will become. In fact, just knowing what to do isn't enough if you want to improve your grades. Remember when you first learned to roller blade or ride a bike? Becoming skilled didn't mean just understanding the drill, did it? It was getting on those wheels and going for a practice ride!

- My greatest ambition
- My pet and I
- A day I'd rather forget
- The day I met . . .
- A celebration to remember
- I love (TV, the theatre, the cinema, the country, the beach)
- My (mother, father or other relative) and I

Let's look at how a personal essay, 'My father and I', might begin:

My father was old, even before I was born—older, than my maternal grandfather in fact. Although mother was 35 when I burst into the world, my father was 28 years her senior. I secretly read letters they had exchanged when I was two. Clearly, mum, who probably married him more out of fear than anything else, held little true affection for him, then. That came later. But dad—dad had worshipped the ground she walked on. He'd had her on a pedestal for as long as I can recall. As for me, I was his only child. Dad must have thought all his birthdays had come at once when I was born. Until I was 12, anyway, I felt he loved me more than life. Then the unthinkable happened and it changed everything:

This opening paragraph has evoked a number of issues that the reader expects to be developed and satisfied in the course of the essay. These Main Ideas provide the backbone for the development of the essay:

1. What was the 'unthinkable' event that took place? You *could* use a handy strategy here. To keep your readers interested, reveal the event later in your essay. The second paragraph might therefore begin: 'However, I am ahead of myself.' Then begin to reflect on life much earlier. What were life and the love of a father like, before the event? What experiences were shared with him? Did his being older add richness to these experiences due to his wisdom?

2. Why was the mother acting out of fear when she married the father? Remembering the topic is not about the mother, per se, we could explain this point by briefly describing the mother's background and reflecting upon the possible reasons that gave rise to her fear. (Perhaps she had been a very plain, only child who lacked self-esteem. Perhaps when she married at 33, the father had been her only suitor and she had been afraid of being left on the shelf.)

3. Why were her feelings later developed for the father? This question could be answered with moving and/or funny anecdotes. What kind of man was he? (This gives an excellent opening for the writer to sketch a cameo of the father: his characteristics, ideals, nature and how they may have affected the writer.)

4. Once revealed, why and how did the unthinkable event change everything? What effect did it have on the writer's relationship and life with his father? How are the issues seen, now, with the advantage of maturity and experience? Has the event and its outcomes had a negative or positive impact on how the writer now views life?

In the next chapter, the style changes as we look at issue-based essays. This makes them challenging on a different level. Let's explore them.

29

Issue-based essays: arguments and persuasion

Recently, a major international cigarette corporation made a big boo-boo.

Represented by a company spokesman in an eastern European country, it caused a global uproar. The Government of the eastern European nation was about to action a plan to limit the country's cigarette advertising, due to its high smoking rate and associated cancer incidence. In a counter attempt, the cigarette company put forward an argument. This said, in effect, that the Government would save more money if people smoked the company's cigarettes, than if they didn't. That is, the sales of its cigarettes would kill more people off earlier, and save money. (Fewer old people would mean fewer pension pay-outs.)

The cigarette corporation's head office could not have been pleased. Not only had its representative played neatly into the hands of its adversaries (the anti-smoking lobbyists), it had presented the company's already tarnished image, in a confronting, cold and calculating light. What an act of folly! If the cigarette company's spokesman had been sitting for a Year 7, argumentative essay exam, he would have been given a big fat fail.

Argumentative essay writing

There are argumentative essays. There are persuasive essays. You may be asked to write either or both, depending on your teacher. Many teachers prefer a debate format (argumentative): views are presented and opposing views argued against. Others believe presenting opposing ideas exposes the weaknesses of one's views. Thus, they prefer the persuasive format.

My personal belief is that if you are confident and skilled enough (qualities this book aims to help you develop), you should be capable of highlighting and identifying the weaknesses of possible alternatives without undermining your stance. However, be guided by your teacher here.

The word 'argument' may conjure an immediate sense of wrangling and fierce debate. However, an argumentative essay shouldn't reflect the type of arguments you may have at home or at school—the fiery, irrational, blow-your-top sort of argument. In an argumentative essay, your argument should be logical, justifiable and therefore convincing. It should stick to the topic and be supported by statistical or other evidence and examples.

Short quotations from expert and historical figures add colour and persuasion to your point of view. The points you present to support your stand should be clear, sequential, uncomplicated and intended to win your reader over. Conversely, the opposing argument should be outlined with equal clarity and intended to add greater support and conviction to your own viewpoint.

As you research and gather material, note and prioritise the strengths of your argument while highlighting the main weaknesses in the opposing stance: your argumentative piece will benefit greatly from a climactic, cleanly delivered, knockout punch. However, having said this, be aware it is the *weight* of your argument that wins the day. Therefore, opposing arguments should be presented calmly and moderately and without the need for verbal histrionics. Be careful, too, not to offend a reader's sensibilities with rash generalisations or extreme political or religious statements.

We will show you the smart way to plan for your argumentative essay and the issues you need to address, in the 'planning' chapter, page 177.

In the meantime, here are some argumentative essay topics at which to try your hand, when you are ready. You could also write these from a persuasive point of view:

- Fashion is manipulated to take advantage of the vanity in us all
- Youth unemployment wouldn't be a problem if the kids stayed at school instead of living off welfare
- Should heroin injecting rooms be legalised?
- Domestic cars should be banned in big cities
- Television violence should be more strictly censored
- Couples should have only one child
- Should medical health care be free?
- Amnesty should be available to all illegal boat people
- Poker machines should be banned

Essay writing conventions

Don't forget to check an essay's convention! You will find as you advance through school to university that essay writing is influenced by certain rules. What is appropriate for your senior school years becomes inappropriate at tertiary level, and even among subjects at both levels, the conventions differ.

It is your job to ensure you are complying with the required conventions.

We can demonstrate this in our introduction, by using two different conventions in addressing the same topic for a formal, argumentative essay. Example one, suited to a convention at tertiary level, is presented in a more general format. The second example, suited to senior school, contains a more structured format: the essay topic question is repeated, and the Main Ideas of the essay are recorded so that they can be substantiated in the main body of the essay. The tertiary example contains a first and second paragraph, incidentally, to give you a broader appreciation of the argument. (In fact, note that for longer essays of more than approximately 750 words where an in depth demonstration of background knowledge is required, two or more introductory as well as concluding paragraphs may be appropriate.)

Incidentally, for guidelines also on the convention that may be required by your teacher for the citing of research articles, please see page 148, third paragraph, 'Language analysis essays' chapter.

Example 1—Tertiary level:

Introduction

Essay title: 'Does the Internet serve democracy?'

Essay type: Argumentative

Statement of Intention:

The following essay will attempt to argue that the Internet serves democracy.

Political history is littered with examples of democracy being thwarted, due to knowledge and information being in the hands of a few. The Internet, however, puts knowledge and information into the hands of the masses, thereby aiding and nurturing the democratic process: individuals are able to announce, publish and disseminate their information and ideas through the internet medium. Democracy is further enhanced through websites, Facebook, Twitter, emailing, and other forms of computer-mediated communication. These so-called 'virtual communities' have been described as global communities where people are no longer parochially classed as citizens, but global 'netizens'. Rheingold (1993) warns, however, that their use may pose some threat to privacy or freedom of speech through censorship by service providers. The Internet notwithstanding, 'big brother' already impinges upon our privacy and right to choose through credit rating checks, mailing lists, reverse telephone directories, and so on.

Virtual communities have also led some to argue that individual cultures and people's democratic rights to preserve them are threatened by the phenomenon of cultural globalisation. A fusion of world cultures is not conceivable, however. Although the Internet may foster a global community, it is one where individuals enjoy and share the *diversity* of their cultures, and, as Warfield (1998) comments, where 'pride and enthusiasm for local cultures is retained'.

Example 2—Senior secondary level:

Introduction

Essay title: 'Does the Internet serve democracy?'

Essay type: Argumentative

Statement of Intention:

The following essay will attempt to argue that the Internet serves democracy.

Political history is littered with examples of democracy being thwarted due to knowledge and information being in the hands of a few. The Internet, however, puts knowledge and information into the hands of the masses, thereby assisting to serve the democratic process: individuals are able to announce, publish and disseminate their information and ideas through the internet medium. Democracy is further enhanced through websites, Facebook, Twitter, emailing, and other forms of computer-mediated communication. These so-called 'virtual communities' have been described as global communities where people are no longer parochially classed as citizens, but global 'netizens'. Rheingold (1993) warns, however, that their use may pose some threat to privacy or freedom of speech through censorship by service providers. Critically, however, the Internet serves democracy through its very transparency. Others may also argue the 'information-rich/information-poor' debate. Nonetheless, for the majority, democracy is allowed to flourish, unrestrained by economic, political, religious or geographic boundaries. Most importantly, the Internet has proven to be a powerful tool in the hands of oppressed peoples.

Note: for an opening paragraph, the convention requires the topic to be clearly acknowledged and the essay's Main Ideas recorded for development in the main body of the essay (not shown here). The Main Ideas are that:

1. The Internet serves democracy. *(For)*
2. It serves democracy by putting knowledge and information into the hands of the masses: *(For)*
3. Use of *virtual communities* may pose a threat to privacy or freedom of speech [censorship by service providers, as warned by Rheingold (1993)]. *(Against)*
4. However—the Internet serves democracy due to its transparency, where there can be no hidden agendas. *(For)*
5. Some may argue the 'information-rich/poor' debate. *(Against)*
6. Even so, for most, democracy is allowed to flourish, unrestrained by economic, political, religious or geographic boundaries that may otherwise be imposed by individual nations or creeds. *(For)*

7. The Internet gives power to oppressed groups that would otherwise remain powerless. (This Main Idea is supported in the essay's conclusion with this example: in our recent era, through a war of words the East Timorese, the Libyans and the Egyptians, for example, were able to awaken the world to the oppression and often, atrocities, occurring behind their closed borders, resulting in the withdrawal or overthrow of their powerful military governments and moves towards democracy. Their examples have given inspiration to other oppressed communities.) *(For)*

This concluding paragraph in complete form can be found in our 'First draft' chapter, page 201. Although not shown in its entirety, the essay is also used to demonstrate how to plan an argumentative essay, (page 177).

Persuasive essay writing

A persuasive piece is more a one-sided view of an issue, rather than a presentation of both sides. As with argumentative essays, the aim is to persuade your reader to share your opinion. Here are some persuasive essay titles. (Note that these could just as well be approached from an argumentative viewpoint, where both sides of the argument are posed.)

- Eating disorders in young girls are influenced by thin models
- An HIV test should be mandatory for people undergoing surgery
- Welfare benefits should not be available to smokers
- Zoos should be banned
- Fast food is gradually killing us
- Beauty is more important than brains
- Governments should fully fund university placements
- Police should receive higher salaries
- Alcohol should have similar health warnings to cigarettes
- All mothers should be awarded medals for gallantry

Introduction

Our following introductory paragraph for a formal, persuasive essay was written by Genevieve, our Year 12 student:

'Essay title: "Is the information technology revolution friend or foe of community and urban citizenship? Is there anything governments can do to maximise its potential for community well-being?"

Essay type: Persuasive

Statement of Intention:
The following essay will attempt to show that the information technology revolution is a friend of the community and urban citizenship. It will also suggest what governments can do to maximise the potential of information technology for community well-being.

All new technology creates controversy and fear when it first appears. When radio and television were first invented, they were blamed for the fragmentation of community and family ideals such as socialisation and intellectual interaction, and, later, violence. However, overall, negative impacts have been minimal. Society adjusts and comes up with new checks and balances. Information technology is not a force that will mean the demise of citizenship. Nor, however, as some theorists suggest, will it solve all of society's ills. Information technology simply enhances urban living, and helps to further community-mindedness. By governments ensuring that all sectors have equal access to computer-related technology, community well-being will be further aided. The information technology revolution should therefore be seen as a friend of the community and urban citizenship, and not a foe.'

Note that in her opening paragraph, Genevieve has adhered to the convention of the formal essay, requiring the topic to be clearly acknowledged (see her last two lines, underlined, for your attention). She has also presented the Main Ideas of the essay in the introduction, for further development in the main body of the essay. The Main Ideas are that:

1. Information technology enhances urban living.
2. Information technology helps to further community mindedness.
3. Governments can maximise the potential of information technology for community well-being by ensuring that all sectors have equal access to computer-related technology.

A persuasive speech or editorial: vignette introduction example
You will notice the formality required for the previous, argumentative and persuasive essays. However, you may have call at some time to write a more emotive, informal persuasive piece on a human issue for say, a speech or an editorial. Here you might use a vignette or anecdote in your introduction. Whilst observing the importance of the topic, this allows the use of imagery and emotive language to attract attention to the piece and to highlight the issues from a human perspective. (For added tips, see reference to our 'Language Analysis Checklist', pages 132, 146 and 242.) Nonetheless, the convention still prevails: the topic is acknowledged (underlined for you in the piece, following) and the Main Ideas are established.

Here is the example:

Introduction

Essay title: 'Is homelessness a self-inflicted condition? Should the Government be spending more to fight a growing problem?'

Essay type: Persuasive

Statement of Intention:

The following essay will attempt to persuade the reader that homelessness is not a self-inflicted condition and that government fiscal policy is failing to adequately address a growing problem.

Icy beams of first light push back the night sky over Acland Street as they find him.

Beads of frost cling to his unkempt beard. His eyes are wide open, staring, their haunting look of fear a mirror to the last moments of his life. His pockets are empty. A beer bottle lies shattered on the wet ground. They later hear that this John Doe of no fixed address was once a war hero—but homeless for the 12 years before his senseless death.

Why did he die? Because four drunken youths took their Friday night *frolic* too far? No. Because he was homeless—unsafe, unconnected, vulnerable. A watery stew had been his last meal from the soup kitchen. But hopelessness had been his daily bread, the road to nowhere his daily path.

What government policies for the homeless are in place that would have given John Doe, and others like him, a safe harbour from which to repair a shattered life? Where are the structures that help to rebuild a sense of worth, that revive faith and pride? Where is the funding that delivers the rights of all to live in a house; that allows the return of the homeless to the family fold and community? Homelessness is not a self-inflicted condition. It is a disadvantaged human state conferred by circumstances some call 'fate' and sustained by a grossly inadequate, government fiscal policy. Yes, the Government can spend a lot more to fight this growing problem.

The Main Ideas are:

1. A homeless man is found, accidentally killed by drunken youths.
2. He has been homeless for 12 years. The point is raised that his cause of death was not the youths, but rather his state of homelessness that disconnected him from society and made him vulnerable.
3. His homelessness is conferred by circumstances some call 'fate'. It is not self-inflicted. This offers the opportunity in the main body of the essay to briefly show that as a war veteran, John Doe was unsupported by the Government after returning from Vietnam. He received no counselling, no rehabilitation, no financial support. That he had heroically fought to serve his country was ignored. He had felt a second class citizen. The essay cites the domino effect: his disillusionment, the loss of self-esteem, of jobs he tried to hold and ultimately, his family.

4. In the main body of the essay, other case studies paint alarming stories of destitution and growing poverty among families, single men, the elderly, and among women and children: Andrew, 46, was a working father of four before losing his full-time factory job. He had a mortgage and couldn't find sufficient work to sustain the payments. He began drinking. He lost everything: his home, his wife and his four children.
5. What government funding policies address the problem of homelessness? The last of the introductory paragraphs asks several questions to be answered in the main body of the essay, finishing with a statement reflecting the topic title. This indicates the writer's clear stance and intention to persuade the reader towards that line of argument.

Letters to the Editor

At some time you may be asked to write a letter to a news editor. For this informal style, start by checking, 'Letters to the Editor' in the media. Presentation is important: your language should be tailored to persuade or argue an issue in a well-informed, concise and cogent manner. Whilst clever headings using alliteration or metaphors have a role to play, your understanding of persuasive language and how it can be used will be your key to success.

In Chapter 31, we explore language analysis. Once able to identify the language and tone of other writers, you will be better equipped to employ similar strategies when writing your own material. You may have a logical argument with a good deal of merit. However, if you are unable to present your views using your tools of persuasion, you may as well have no argument at all.

An argument can be presented from two primary stances: the 'objective' stance where you offer logic and reasoning and points of fact to build and strengthen your case, and the 'subjective' stance where strategies are used to evoke a personal emotive response from your reader. Remember, people are seldom swayed by the objective side or cold hard facts alone. It is human nature to seek reassurance at a personal (subjective) level. In presenting a persuasive argument, it is not only *what* you say, but *how* you say it that will elevate your stance from the prosaic to the powerful.

Language Analysis Checklist

Read Chapter 31 to learn how language is used to advantage. A handy resource in identifying writers' language is our 'Language Analysis Checklist' in the Appendix, page 242. Many positive strategies on this checklist can be used as effective tools to craft your own informal persuasive works such as letters, scripts, editorials or speeches and may prove useful in the years to come. For recognising tone of voice, 'Identifying Tone' is on page 247. Both checklists can also be printed at edworksglobal.com. Click Checklists and Templates.

Meanwhile, you can also learn from Daniel, our senior secondary student, who proposed this persuasive piece, a 'Letter to the Editor', in response to the passing of government legislation banning smoking in enclosed public places. It will also help you identify the conventional format.

Read it first.

Then review it and check the underlined words where we identify the use of different stances. (See 'Objective stance' and 'Subjective stance' on the following page.)

' "Government legislates to butt out smoking in enclosed public places"

Congratulations to the Government; it has finally made the right move!

The banning of smoking in enclosed, public places will ensure a safer and healthier environment for all. It will also mean that non-smokers, like me, will not be forced to endure the offensive odour of toxic cigarette smoke in restaurants, bars and other public venues.

The real breakthrough, of course, lies in the health benefits for smokers. Research has shown that over 20,000 Australians die each year from smoking related illnesses. That is more than cancer, AIDS, suicide, road trauma and homicide combined. If this legislation can prompt smokers to kick the habit, then it has been a success.

As we know, smokers aren't the only ones to suffer. Passive smoking has been long recognised as just as deadly. Research suggests that people subjected to ongoing passive smoke have a 30 per cent increased risk of lung cancer. This courageous stance against the cigarette lobby has sent a strong message to tobacco companies that the Government values the health and well-being of non-smokers over and above any revenues.

Asthma sufferers can also breathe a deep sigh of relief! With the staggering increase in asthma amongst the general population, the Government could no longer ignore the health of those whose lives were not only made miserable, but threatened, whenever they entered an enclosed, public venue.

While I am sure that some hotels, casinos and restaurants may cry foul, it seems crystal clear they will also benefit from this new legislation. A smoke-free environment will surely attract those customers who had previously refused to subject their bodies to air bound carcinogens. The legislation will also protect these businesses from the possibility of lawsuits from employees or customers who would otherwise have been exposed to unwanted tobacco smoke.

As stated by oncologist, Dr. David Bernstein, the fact that 300,000 Australian teenagers take up cigarettes each year means that we should not rest on our laurels. We need to foster a greater association between good times and a smoke-free environment to deter our young from being seduced by these noxious *cancer sticks.* We need to do all we can to help them say *no* to that first offer of a cigarette. The new government legislation is a step in the right direction.

I applaud the Government once more, for its strength of character in maintaining its conviction to *butt out* this most deadly of habits.'

Before reading on, study the foregoing text and see if you can identify at least some of the persuasive strategies that Daniel has used.

Objective stance

Our student's use of statistics (objective stance) offered in a non-threatening, reader-friendly tone, gives the argument substance and validity while the figure of authority, 'oncologist, Dr. David Bernstein', offers elements of both the objective and subjective by combining credibility with a sense of reassurance.

Subjective stance

You will note that the piece begins and ends in a personal (subjective) vein ('Congratulations to the Government' and 'I applaud the Government'), whilst puns and imagery are used to strong emotive effect to also elicit a personal reader response. For example, 'This courageous stance' (imagery); Asthma sufferers can also 'breathe a sigh of relief' (pun); 'cry foul' and 'crystal clear' (imagery and a play on the idea of toxic versus clean environment); 'noxious cancer sticks' (imagery) and 'butt out' (pun). The use of, 'As we know', in paragraph 3, is a strategy employed to align the reader with the writer.

In the next chapter, we offer valuable pointers for analysing text. If you are unaware of how to prepare for such essay questions, you will find it very helpful. You will also learn, in nearby chapters how to address issue-based essays using a construct I designed for our pupils. This valuable tool will enable you to develop your line of reasoning in a comprehensive manner by examining the various perspectives: social, moral or political, and so on. (See 'Twelve perspectives', page 159, and our checklist, page 160, of our 'brain-storming' chapter.)

But—all work and no play . . . So grab an FMB.

Then I'll show you how to go about it!

30

Text analysis essays

Sticks and stones: these were our first pens; our paper, the bare earth. The genesis of the written word came about as Homo sapiens scratched symbols of survival in the primeval dirt and etched tribal rites in slabs of stone.

Just think how impoverished we'd be today if our writing modes had failed to flourish from these primitive beginnings. Where would we all be without books or computers at our disposal? Our self-expression would be repressed, our knowledge exchanged by word of mouth and wild gesticulation.

The written word allows us to enjoy literature and share information on a global scale. We can communicate ideas, raise awareness, expose issues, persuade, dissuade, argue, inform, educate, sing and tell stories. Writing enables us to reflect on our pasts, to guide the young, comfort the elderly, to entertain, to provoke, shock, woo, censure, praise, and offer thanks and apology. In short, there is virtually nothing in the human experience that the written word cannot express.

Hold this last thought as we begin to talk about the written words, or *texts,* that you are asked to study and respond to in your senior years.

The human experience

Time after time, I chat to pupils about analysing texts and discover they are in the dark as to what to look for when they are reading. In fact, many don't realise they *should* be looking for something. They read passively, as they might the Sunday paper: scan a bit here, a bit there. No purpose. No structure. Not much read in depth.

When quizzed about classroom instructions prior to reading a text, it becomes clear that part of the reason students' fail to read actively and with purpose is that they are simply told: *read the text, then we'll discuss it.* That's like going on a scavenger hunt without being told what to bring back.

If you pay attention, now, it will change the way you look at text analysis forever. You will not only work smart by saving time; your new insight will bring greater enjoyment to your reading. In fact, you may even become a bit of a bookworm. What joy that would bring to your English teacher!

Text can be any words used to write or print something: a short extract or the main body of words in a book, news item or other media. It embodies a wide number of different, fictitious or non-fiction written forms in *print,* from news, autobiographical and biographical works, diaries and journals, poetry, short stories and novels—to *non-print* forms such as film and video, radio and television, oral history and the performed play.

Broad sweeping as these literary modes may be, they have a common feature: they reflect the human experience. Even stories of wildlife and nature are written by humans who consciously or unconsciously leave imprints on their work: these provide us with clues about their philosophies, personal ideals or value systems. The very fact that a work exists tells us about human challenge, passion and endeavour.

Probing the novel

We cannot address every mode here. However, if we examine the novel and its text analysis requirements, it will also give you a good background when studying other text forms. The novel, of course, is regarded as a work of fiction (size being anything bigger than about 40,000 words). Fiction nonetheless draws on the human experience for its substance. Authors use characters, plots and sub-plots to reflect or recreate in fiction-form the dreams, emotions, actions, challenges, conflicts, tragedies and triumphs that have befallen human beings throughout the history of humankind.

Students generally recognise this reflective nature of the novel. But many fail to appreciate a significant, inherent process that occurs in its writing: the deliberate manipulation of the plot and characters of the story by the author, so that when a novel is read, its issues can be explored and interpreted by the reader.

What do we mean by 'manipulation of the plot'? This is the very innate nature of the novel. The author is like the director of a movie, *pulling the strings* of every word planted on the page, manoeuvring the characters from one place to another, controlling their actions, thoughts and words. With this thought in mind, once the main characters are written in, good novelists will usually set up certain challenges to be met. This is designed to maintain reader interest in the story line. They then conceive how they want their characters to respond to the challenges. In turn, the reader responds to the novel, using a personal set of values and experiences against which they can interpret, measure and judge the issues depicted.

Personal life experiences allow readers to appreciate or identify with, characters in a novel. For example, we all face adversity in life, be it large or small. Such times often reveal truths about our own character that may surprise us, or give us pause for thought. When we are in the comfort zones of our familiar daily routines or socialising with close friends and family, it's very easy to believe we are the world's ideal sort of person. Right? However, imagine suddenly being confronted by a harsher reality of life: a run of financial bad luck, a change of environment from the city to the country or from one country to another, or the necessity to respond to a person in need. Now we really find out about ourselves—about our strengths and weaknesses. Now we are forced to confront our true identities and perhaps to experience personal growth, or to come to terms with our frailties.

These confronting issues equip us to interpret text with the insight of experience, allow us to empathise with or judge characters we read about.

Strategies of the author

When we peel back the fictitious layers of a novel and look more deeply at an author's intentions, certain interesting strategies emerge. For example, pitting challenges against a novel's protagonist by placing him or her in difficult or testing conditions allows the author to probe the very same moral, social, political or emotional dilemmas that human beings have grappled with for centuries. In turn, readers are invited on a subconscious level, to explore and identify with, the issues depicted—and perhaps to compare or *question* their own value systems against those of the characters in the story.

Authors are always seeking to explore human nature through their works. One way of doing this is to pluck their characters from their normal environments and comfort zones, and place them in unfamiliar surroundings. For example, characters may have to face a transition from country to city life or from one culture to another. When this happens, they are likely to be confronted by value systems and mindsets that conflict with those they have left behind. You have only to look at the often extreme views that exist on issues like politics, deforestation, gun control, climate change and so on, between cities and conservative rural belts across the nations of the world. The strategy of moving key characters to contrasting environs therefore enables authors to highlight and explore differing morals or beliefs: white on white will never offer a clear perspective. However, put a city dweller in a country town and immediately the contrasts are thrown up in sharp relief.

For example, a city protagonist with what she believes is a 'normal' view on deforestation (ie stop the logging), is attacked as a 'radical' in the country (given that farmers in the past have relied heavily on logging and clearing land to maintain their livelihoods).

The views are all relative. The city character is therefore forced to re-evaluate and question her views and to reaffirm or change them. The reader goes through the same process. In this mainstream-to-marginalised scenario, the author has opportunities to further portray human nature: the strengths and weaknesses of the character in struggling emotionally (and physically) to justify her beliefs. As readers, we can then evaluate and form opinions about the aptness of the character's thoughts and actions.

Science fiction: an author's tool

Another effective means of exploring human nature is through the genre of science fiction. Authors can use this as a valuable tool to highlight complex global issues that may otherwise be difficult to evaluate. For example, genetic engineering is a highly sensitive moral issue. However, society struggles to objectively judge its likely long-term impact. This is due to the inherent, step-by-step nature of its evolution over many years. To witness only *one* or *two* such evolutionary steps in an entire lifetime means our perspective about likely outcomes may be distorted. This is where a science fiction author enables us to travel to a future century. Here we can be confronted with the full ramifications of genetic engineering at that time. This assists us to examine and question the possible aftermath of society's present-day decisions.

By now, if you were previously in the dark, the light should be dawning: as students of the novel, firstly, you need to recognise an author's deliberate manipulation of the plot and its characters. It is only then that you will be equipped to advance beyond descriptive prose, to analysis.

Text analysis

Analysing a text requires you to develop your own objective line of reasoning in very much the same way you would an argumentative or persuasive essay; or to identify and substantiate the stance of an author whose work you are analysing. (You will see how an author's stance on issues is identified and substantiated when we present a complete text analysis essay example on George Orwell's, 'Animal Farm', page 141 of this chapter.)

Unlike mathematics which incorporates convergent thinking (involving only one answer), text analysis is oriented towards divergent thinking: this leads to no, one answer, but a number of possible answers, verified through substantiation. In an examination or classroom environment, the aim of text analysis therefore is to *demonstrate your ability to present a coherent contention,* be it yours or that of an author. The strength of your substantiation provides an insight into your grasp of the text. The format for writing a text response is not difficult: one simply presents a reasonable point of view, or argument, and supports it.

At the end of the last chapter, we mentioned the construct containing 12 perspectives for brainstorming issue-based essays that will assist you to develop a coherent line of reasoning (see page 160 of our 'brainstorming' chapter). Similarly, we have a 'Text Analysis Checklist' through which you can read and analyse a text. You will find this later in our 'research' chapter on page 169. The great advantage is, by learning to analyse and reason, you will not only be working smart, you will acquire life long independent analytical skills.

The importance of planning

There is absolutely no doubt that learning how to plan establishes the foundation of a good essay. Many teachers see pupils who have a good grasp of a text, but who under-perform in written exercises. Planning ensures that your ideas are presented in a coherent and fluent structure. Planning also enables you to evaluate the validity of your argument and to determine whether that argument addresses the essay topic effectively, *before* you commit yourself to print. Therefore an important key to successful text analysis is: *always plan!* We will show you how to do this on page 172.

How to effectively read a text

Remember, you are not about to flip through the weekend media for a bit of light entertainment. Reading a novel for text analysis means you will have to identify, and then respond to, the issues that the work presents. This is achieved by developing or identifying a coherent point of view that demonstrates your understanding of the text.

So passive reading is out! You must be aware of the exercise's aim. This means reading in an active, in depth sense, probing beyond a superficial glance and questioning the ploys and strategies of the author. This logically leads to the formation of your personal views, (how *you* interpret the issues)—or to your identifying the views of the author. These options then allow you to present a line of reasoning or argument. Therefore, before you even begin to read a novel, you must acknowledge *the purpose of the task!*

The first stage of analysing a text is to understand a fact of human nature: since time immemorial, human beings have been inherently compelled to maintain balance in their lives. Psychologically, this is called 'homeostasis'. For example, if criticised, we quickly seek to justify ourselves; if we knock something over, we seek to put it upright; if guilty of something, we seek to assuage the guilt; if hurt, we seek to lick our wounds, and so on.

Motivators and Belief Systems

When the stress of imbalance occurs, the human states we experience such as guilt, fear, jealousy, hate, joy, and so on, can all be seen as 'Motivators'.

Motivators fuel our need for a response to restore balance, or homeostasis. In turn, the nature of our responses (how we go about things) is influenced by our 'Belief Systems': are we fatalists, or non-fatalists? Do we believe fate rules our lives, or that we have relative control over our own destinies?

Nothing has changed. Today's modern world reflects the same human Motivators, the same basic Belief Systems of ancient times. Given that the human characters in a book are drawn from reality, authors naturally use these same Motivators to flesh out character personalities. As a result, these human Motivators occur not only in the novel, but in all of literature. Thus, Shakespeare is as relevant today as he was 400 hundred years ago.

Consequently, most essay questions on text analysis encourage you to explore issues within the context of Motivators that influence all human behaviour. As characters in literature struggle with their personal demons to restore homeostasis—or indeed, restore homeostasis through triumph over adversity, authors are encouraging you to form opinions and evaluate the morality of the characters' responses. They are holding up a mirror to their readers and asking: *What do you see?* That is, in terms of your personal morals and value systems and your experience as a thinking, feeling, fellow human being, what do you perceive is happening here?

As a pupil, however, your role must go beyond just recognising the human Motivators where you think, *that's lust; that's greed;* or *that's courage!* Within the context of the topic question you must clearly *demonstrate* your grasp of the text. So—in writing your text analysis essay, your job is to:

1. Identify the Motivators by quoting dialogue or citing examples from the text.
2. Clearly explain the impacts these human Motivators have upon the characters that in turn, affect story outcomes.
3. Reveal and explain the author's intentions.

Naturally, these issues are not expressed as, for example, 'the motivators are . . .' or 'the author's intentions are . . .', and so on. Rather, it is the evidence of these factors that needs to be discussed by incorporating such evidence into your essay. Remember, you are not giving a précis of the novel. The purpose of the essay exercise is for you to demonstrate your understanding of the text.

When you see text analysis, the above points should jump to mind. This is what analysis is all about. Subsequent chapters offer further insight on planning and writing text analysis essays. However, the following complete text analysis essay on George Orwell's popular senior year novel, 'Animal Farm', offers sound guidelines on how such essays may be structured.

Text analysis essay—example

Essay title: 'In "Animal Farm", George Orwell explores the process of revolution and clearly indicates the importance of leadership. Without Snowball, the revolution failed.' Discuss.

Essay type: Text analysis

Statement of Intention:

The following essay will attempt to demonstrate Orwell's negative stance on revolutionary processes and his view that when leadership is corrupted by power, its role in successful revolution is rendered ineffective. It will also seek to show how Snowball's self-interest and willingness to compromise his values to achieve power, rendered him a potentially impotent force in the revolution.

Set in the English countryside, George Orwell's timeless novel, 'Animal Farm', is a political satire on Stalinism and the Russian Revolution. The satirical nature of the novel, with pigs depicted as the ruling caste, clearly reflects Orwell's contempt for the revolutionary and leadership processes. Importantly, it also offers a critical insight into the inherent weaknesses of the revolutionary process. Orwell explores key issues to demonstrate his contention: the inability to transfer ideals into reality and the difficulties in sharing power equally to create lasting, true democracies. He also underscores the role of vigilance by the masses in safeguarding democratic processes against self-serving interests. In his exploration, Orwell dismisses the significance of the potential leadership of the ambitious pig, Snowball, in establishing due democratic process.

The rebellion of the farm animals against the intemperate and cruel Mr. Jones and the subsequent corruption of the pigs serve as a vehicle for Orwell to indirectly denounce the Russian Revolution. Rather than focussing on leadership as an integral part of revolution, he centres our attention on the inevitable corruption of characters that are in positions of power. Orwell contends that, irrespective of who the leader is, the outcome will always be the same. He attributes this largely to the processes of power and the concept of equality being inherently flawed. This is clearly depicted when the animals, including the pigs, overthrow and expel Mr. Jones. While their chant, 'four legs good, two legs bad', serves as a rally cry against Mr. Jones and reflects their initial contempt, the pigs soon take on human characteristics. Ultimately, having lived in Jones's house, taken his food and set up a brewery for their own ends, they walk on two legs. Orwell's vivid reminder that history repeats itself highlights the ineffectiveness of leadership when, in the absence of public scrutiny and accountability, leaders readily succumb to the seductive influences of power.

Orwell clearly argues that the revolutionary process, per se, is doomed to failure, illustrating that old orders are simply replaced by new which soon imitate their forerunners. He attributes this to revolutions being built on abstract ideals that are too rigid and impractical to be transferred into reality. Orwell uses Old Major, the Seven Commandments and the gradual erosion of all ideals to illustrate that a violent overthrow based on self-interest is unlikely to result in a peaceful and prosperous society where equality and justice prevail.

This idea is succinctly portrayed when the dogs are unable to resist their basic instincts in wanting to kill the rats, as they nonetheless attend a meeting to hear Old Major's idealistic plea for socialism and equality. Further, Orwell does not mention Napoleon or Snowball during Old Major's great speech. This is intended to show that the pigs simply feed off Old Major's socialist views, reshaping them to their own self-serving advantage; that Old Major's ideals are seen by Napoleon and Snowball as no more than a vehicle for domination. Moreover, there is not a time when all the animals experience equality, reflecting the innate weakness of the revolutionary process; its inability to separate itself from the uncontrollable sins of human nature where power seduces all.

Power, a key element of revolutionary processes, is not a commodity that can be shared equally. 'Animal Farm' explores the difficulties surrounding the need for all members of a society to have a voice and some control over their lives. Jones's dictatorial nature, however, clearly exemplifies the worst aspects of power where the interests of society are circumvented for the self-serving goals of a few. Orwell's exploration delves into the processes of decision-making and accountability whereby power begets power, which in turn leads to corruption and instability. The animals are unable to share power equally because, as they rapidly realise, leaders are required to make decisions. Napoleon and Snowball consequently compete for leadership, but both have hidden agendas and obvious failings that become more evident as their power increases.

In the early stages of the novel, Orwell describes Snowball as a pig similar to Napoleon. Snowball is party to Napoleon's decision that the pigs, only, should get all the milk and apples, thereby critically emphasising the inherent inequality within the revolutionary process. However, in this 'new' economic and political system that contradicts the essence of equality, both pigs want to be leader. Orwell later portrays their growing dissention: 'Snowball and Napoleon were by far the most active in the debates. But it was noticed that these two were never in agreement: whatever suggestion either of them made, the other could be counted to oppose it.' Orwell again highlights the pigs' self-centred unwillingness to set differences aside for the sake of the others when he later recounts: 'These two disagreed at every point disagreement was possible.' In pursuit of leadership, Snowball's schemes become increasingly grandiose and differences escalate: 'Within a few weeks Snowball's plans for the windmill were fully worked out. . . . Only Napoleon held aloof. . . . One day, however, he arrived unexpectedly to examine the plans. He . . . stood for a little while contemplating them out of the corner of his eye; then suddenly he lifted his leg, urinated over the plans and walked out without uttering a word.'

Orwell argues that the key to achieving and maintaining true democracy lies in the masses and not leadership. The majority, however, need to be vigilant, to remain fully involved in the political process and to hold their leaders accountable for the decisions made. Orwell contends that, if the masses cease to actively partake in the process and become passive, democracy becomes nothing more than a hollow promise where the self-interests of leaders are left unchallenged. The sheep serve to illustrate Orwell's contention as they mindlessly and passively follow, allowing Napoleon's dictatorship to become stronger.

Orwell explores many aspects of revolution in 'Animal Farm'. He evaluates the degree to which ideals set up revolutions to fail. The difficulty in fair and equitable power sharing is examined, as well as the need for active participation by the masses in the political process. As an allegory, Orwell's novel reflects that due to the innate flaws of human nature where power breeds corruption causing democratic ideals to falter, leadership plays a minor role. Thus, Snowball's self-interest and compromised values in his quest for power, and the apathy of the general farm animals and their inability to accept responsibility to safeguard society, render Snowball an ineffective participant in the revolutionary process and its outcome.

Note that the normal conventions are followed in the essay's introduction. The Statement of Intention firstly offers a clear explanation of what the essay writer is setting out to achieve. In the introduction, the reader is then offered a brief overview of the novel's setting, its nature and, cutting straight to the essence of the essay topic, the negative stances of the author, George Orwell, in (i) revolutionary processes and (ii) leadership processes; and (iii) Snowball's potential impact on the uprising. The three primary elements of the topic discussion are therefore acknowledged at the first opportunity.

These acknowledgements are substantiated in the following manner: Orwell's stance on revolutionary and leadership processes is distinctly expressed when the essay writer notes: 'The satirical nature of the novel, with pigs depicted as the ruling caste, clearly reflects Orwell's contempt for the revolutionary and leadership processes.' The essay writer then identifies factors behind Orwell's critical view of leadership, linking these to Snowball's potential impact upon the success of the rebellion when it is stated that '. . . Orwell dismisses the significance of the potential leadership of the ambitious pig, Snowball, in establishing due democratic process'.

The Main Ideas of the essay are then developed through further discussion in the main body. (Note that the essay writer has kept faithfully to the topic throughout the essay.) The Main Ideas are:

1. That the Russian Revolution is an example where the history of corruption repeats itself.

2. That incongruence exists between ideals and reality.

3. The difficulties of power sharing and their impact upon leadership roles, specifically in relation to Snowball.

4. The need for ongoing vigilance by the masses, rather than leadership, to safeguard democracy.

Motivators identified and supported with examples

You will note that the Motivators of power, greed and selfishness are thoroughly aired and well supported by examples in the essay. For instance, the concept of 'power' is depicted through the uprising of the farm animals to wrench control from the clutches of the insidious Mr. Jones. However, the egalitarian nature of this power, where all the farm animals were to have enjoyed equality and democracy, is soon undermined through the pursuits of self-power by the aspiring leaders, Napoleon and Snowball.

Impact of Motivators on the story's characters—example

In turn, the impact that the Motivators, *power* and *greed* have on the characters in the story is also well defined by the essay writer: when, for example, having lived in Jones's house and taken over his food, the pigs ultimately are seen walking about on two legs. By discussing the *selfishness* and *greed* of the pigs, Napoleon and Snowball, in deciding that the pigs should have the best foods—the milk and the apples—the essay writer highlights the critical point of the novel that underscores the inequality of the revolutionary process.

Author's intentions well explained

Orwell's *intentions* are also clearly revealed by the essay writer. They are:

1. To demonstrate his criticism and contempt for revolutionary and leadership processes through the use of farm animals in a political satire.
2. To demonstrate that the human Motivators, power, greed, and selfishness mar these processes and cause democratic ideals to falter.
3. To alert the masses that they must remain active and watchful, holding their leaders fully accountable for their actions, if democracy is to be achieved and maintained.

In the conclusion, the essay writer keeps *steadfastly to the essay topic* and reaffirms Orwell's contention that it is the impact of unattainable ideals and the corruptive influences of power, self-interest and apathy that undermine the revolutionary process. As such, leadership and Snowball are seen as having little bearing.

Our chapter on language analysis essay writing comes next. This also offers plenty of assistance if you need guidance on how to go about it. You may just want to scan the pages and come back to them later to read them in greater depth when you need the guidelines.

31

Language analysis essays

Developing a skill for analysing language can be exciting.

As a student, your main focus will be on analysing the *written* word. But in so doing, you will also gain a knack for analysing people's language in general, like that of politicians or other players in the public forum. Analysing the language of adversaries in a polemic, or debate, requires plenty of information gathering, reading and critical investigative thinking. So be prepared for it! Importantly, it requires the ability to *analyse the strategies* used by commentators—writers, cartoonists or politicians, for example—as they seek to elicit certain reader or audience responses to their views.

Many students don't see this. They miss the point of *language* analysis, and make the mistake of merely describing the issue itself. Language analysis, however, requires much more than producing a descriptive essay.

Interpreting the language of debate for your language analysis essay demands that you must firstly understand both the issue and the nature of the argument. Investigating the response in the media therefore requires solid background research to establish a wide sample of convergent and divergent opinions that might be expressed through different media formats such as editorials, cartoons, Letters to the Editor, and so on. The selected articles are then examined, dissected and analysed so that the issue can be evaluated and writer performances scrutinised and assessed. This calls for introspection and probing beneath the surface of the arguments, to uncover the motivation and strategies of the polemicists, and to reveal their intentions.

The word, *perspicacity,* means 'keen perception or discernment'. That is the skill you must develop and bring into play when analysis of language is required. The articles you gather should allow you to compare and contrast the dynamics of at least two, or several, lines of thinking. *Your role is not to express an opinion, but to analyse the strategies and intentions behind the language of those who do.*

Language Analysis Checklist

To assist your essay writing, the earlier mentioned, 'Language Analysis Checklist', with 27 listed strategies, is now available to you for the analysis of language. This checklist will help you to identify the many ploys used by writers or commentators to influence reader or audience points of view.

Some strategies are used so cleverly that we are unaware of being coaxed or coerced into accepting a line of argument. Recently, in discussing the need for higher salaries for Parliament's top jobs with the media, a politician used the old cliché, 'If you pay peanuts, you'll get monkeys.'

Here is a clever strategy at work: we all see the logic of the argument (you get what you pay for). But simultaneously, the comment is dosed with a subtle warning: a fear tactic to strengthen the argument: *do we want to entrust our welfare and the future of our country to a group of monkeys?*

On the opposite page, the following sample of four strategies from the checklist will give you an idea of its value. A full checklist is in the Appendix, page 242, and on the Edworks website, edworksglobal.com. Remember, once you have learned the skill of identifying and analysing language, you can employ some of the positive strategies in your own issue-based essays.

Look at item 1 on the checklist for a moment. Identifying writers' intentions offers clues to their strategies and vice versa: writers with an *intention,* say, to shield readers from reality, may use euphemistic language as a *strategy,* where mild rather than offensive or upsetting words describe a situation. Consider here the death of the great Australian cricketer, Sir Donald Bradman.

LANGUAGE ANALYSIS CHECKLIST (SAMPLE)

STRATEGY	DEFINITION	INTENTION
1. Euphemism	A mild or indirect expression in lieu of one which may upset or offend. eg *passed away = died.*	Shields reader from reality. Aims to assuage impact.
2. False analogy	Comparison of two totally different things. eg *Environmentalists are just like hippies as they don't see the value of progress.*	To benefit the contention by imposing a false relationship, often to instil fear.
3. Rationalism	Where politicians, for example, 'rationalise' a salary increase on the premise such salaries are key for political parties to attract top people. Reality is they want more money.	To justify an action in the eyes of readers/audience when it is not accurate or correct.
4. Appeals to tradition	The past is cited to excuse future or current behaviour. eg *When I was young, we learnt by rote and it didn't do us any harm.*	Aim is to offer an excuse to prevent change or protect own interests.

Although the cold harsh fact was 'Bradman dies', the media reported his death in euphemisms that rested more gently on the mind, reflecting the general warmth with which this sporting hero was held. News items typically declared: 'Our Don departs' and 'Farewell to The Don'.

On the other hand, a writer may use the *strategy* of 'selective evidence' to support a case with the *intention* to present an argument that would otherwise lack strong support were all the evidence made known. For example, a cigarette company may restrict its use of data to achieve this end.

As discussed in 'Letters to the Editor', page 132, in presenting convincing arguments, writers adopt *objective* and *subjective* stances to gain a positive reader response. An objective stance presents facts and logic to substantiate the writer's point of view. A subjective stance seeks to foster reassurance and well-being to gain reader support, or conversely, dissuade the reader from an opposing view by creating concern. Thus, strategies may be used to instil comfort or fear, to justify one's actions, to gain credibility by association, to establish authority or to confuse or distract the reader from an issue that might otherwise undermine the writer's argument—and so on.

Note that not all strategies are laudable. Therefore, where you might identify them in the writings of others, you would be expected to avoid such tactics in your own works—for example, the use of false analogies or the misuse of statistics is simply misleading. Such deception is unethical and wrong.

Another negative device is *emotional blackmail*. It seeks to exert influence by casting guilt or fear into a reader. For example: 'Every child deserves the best education money can buy.' The statement aims to evoke insecurity, so that readers accept a writer's line of argument, uncritically.

If you're still feeling a bit lost, don't worry. Our 'planning' chapter contains a language analysis Plan, pages 180 and 182, and point-by-point essay tips.

But before commencing, be sure to check the convention your teacher wants you to follow regarding the format and structure of your essay as well as the citing of research articles. Requirements between schools can differ. In your final school year, some teachers may prefer the Harvard system of tertiary level, where the author is credited in, or at the end of, the sentence in which research is quoted, for example, (Arndt, B. 25.02.1997, p.17). However, a bibliography at the end of an essay should have more data, including both the title and publication of the research piece. For example: 1. Arndt, B. Without the needle the damage is done. *The Age,* 25.02.1997, p.17.

To help you better grasp language analysis essay writing requirements, we present, below, a complete and insightful essay on the subject of climate change, written by our final year student, Emily. Comments follow the essay.

Language analysis essay writing—example

'Essay title: "An analysis of media reports on climate change"
Essay type: Language analysis

Statement of Intention:

The following essay will attempt to analyse and elucidate the language used in arguments presented on the issue of climate change in two media articles.

The opinion piece of columnist, Andrew Bolt, "Hysteria heats up", published in the Herald Sun, 28th September, and a second, October 5th, 2005, attack both the credibility of climate change claims and those who proselytise pro-climate change views within a scientific and media context. Employing an aggressive and sarcastic tone, Bolt contends the climate change argument is merely hysteria, alleging that a new book on the subject by scientist, Tim Flannery, preaches unscientific falsehoods. In direct response, Tim Flannery stoked the fire of debate with his own opinion piece entitled, "Here are the facts, Bolt", featured in The Age, 8th October, 2005. In an authoritative manner, Flannery counters Bolt's accusations, asserting the scientific validity of his book. He implies that those such as Bolt who dispute the existence of climate change are in denial. Fulfilling the expectations of their disparate readerships, Bolt and Flannery adopt strong stances in defending their opposing contentions. Bolt employs a variety of emotive devices incorporating sarcasm, loaded language, inclusive pronouns and personal slight. Flannery counters Bolt's criticisms with an equally dismissive stance, employing a more considered and didactic approach, displaying disdain for Bolt's charged attack. Flannery's use of personal pronouns, in conjunction with a forceful rebuttal, is intended to assert his authority as he counters Bolt's "whoppers".

In, "Hysteria heats up", Bolt uses sardonic language and ridicule to attack Flannery's stance and sway the reader to dually discount Flannery and the climate change debate. He intersperses a diatribe with loaded terms, declaring global warming claims as statistical "tricks" and "more booga-booga" to render banal Flannery's environmental concerns, rejecting them as not the findings of a "climate" scientist, but the histrionic scare-mongering of an academic "bones" expert. Bolt further employs a cynical tone, mocking the idea that "the end of the world is nigh", not only to evoke doubt, but contempt, among Bolt's readership for someone who is so out of touch with their views. In addition, the writer seeks to undermine Flannery's authority, declaring his climate change theories, "lavish" and inferring they bare closer critical scrutiny. Bolt interlaces his personal criticisms of Flannery with what he presents as the truth or "fact". Such strategies are designed to reinforce an undercurrent of climate change doubt in the reader's mind and the notion that Flannery has embellished and fabricated the findings in his book to his own ends. Indeed, while maintaining his controversialist stance throughout the article, Bolt goes so far as to suggest Flannery seems to have lost his reason "to our new green gods", using the hyperbole to further personalise his attack and disparage the scientist in the reader's eyes.

Bolt couples his assault with selective quotations from Flannery's book, asserting his own polemic and matching Flannery's quotes—which he derogatively labels, "wild claims" to further fuel scepticism—with experts' counter quotes. This device implies that aside from Flannery having distorted the truth, "Hysteria heats up" is well researched. The use of substantiation is also intended to ferry readers closer to Bolt's contention, encouraging them to believe—albeit, through such highly selective quotes—that they, themselves, oppose Flannery's theories, and in so doing join Bolt's point of view. Having positioned his readers accordingly, and having accused the scientist of making "many other errors", Bolt pilots them to collectively condemn Flannery and the notion that when "myths rule men's minds", the belief in climate change, itself, is a threat and "danger" to society.

The provocative headline of Tim Flannery's measured response, "Here are the facts, Bolt", designed to alert readers to a contest worth observing, is reinforced by the scientist's opening riposte, "A writer named Andrew Bolt . . .", pejoratively denying Bolt's bona fide status. In manipulating his readers' perceptions, Flannery creates a decisive dichotomy between himself and Bolt as he seeks to secure the intellectual high ground. He employs alternating tones of reason and sceptical derision in a move to defend himself against Bolt's personal attack, and to reaffirm the authority of his stance on the importance of acknowledging climate change. Flannery, like the columnist, utilises quotations from his adversary's articles to discredit him in the eyes of the readers. The manner in which these quotes are embedded within his polemic, surrounded as they are by derisive calls of "whopper" and "howler", presents Bolt as petty and infantile; a hot-headed amateur who is "infuriated" that Flannery "has ignored him and refused to say sorry." In so doing, Flannery seeks to cement his reputation by asserting himself as the reasoned, unruffled expert who makes clear point-by-point arguments to ensure the irrational and misinformed journalist can understand them.

He then proceeds to pour scorn on Bolt's credibility, accusing him not only of being misinformed, but, "lying through his teeth".

In contrast to Bolt's use of the collective pronoun, where the reader is implicated in the argument, Flannery employs an opposing strategy. In making frequent use of the personal pronoun, "I", throughout the opinion piece, Flannery stamps his authority and position as an expert author and leading scientist on the subject matter. Having established his credibility, Flannery aims to further accentuate a self-assured stance in his readers' minds by maintaining the use of the personal pronoun throughout his letter. This confident posture is a technique designed to elevate and reaffirm Flannery's status in the face of Bolt's accusations, and to inspire trust in Flannery as a person and reputable scientist. In so doing, Flannery's language is comparatively restrained, which heightens its impact. Rather than manipulating emotions, he uses the strength of evidence in facts, figures and expert opinion of those such as British environmentalist, George Monbiot, to reassure the reader he is well-informed and educated on the topic. Flannery concludes his letter, aligning Bolt with a "shrinking and discredited minority", to establish with his readers that Bolt is irrelevant and offers no credibility to the environmental debate.

Although Bolt and Flannery represent opposing positions, the manner in which they employ language techniques to appeal to their respective readerships is comparable. As has been discussed, each writer makes frequent use of personal attacks to discredit the opinion and integrity of the other. This is achieved through the use of selective quotations and evidence on the part of both writers. Nevertheless, there are significant differences in the tones adopted by the authors. Bolt aims to hook the attention of his readers through greater inflammatory and argumentative language than Flannery who presents a carefully constructed response in which he focuses more on appeals to reason. There is also a discrepancy between the two writers regarding the complexity and form of language used. In keeping with the two discrete reader demographics of the Herald Sun and The Age, Bolt chooses to employ simpler, more emotive language than Flannery, who instead commands a sophisticated, scholarly vocabulary and sentence structure. Thus, Bolt and Flannery implicitly acknowledge that their readerships and corresponding media ultimately influence the manner in which they use language.

The contest between Andrew Bolt and Tim Flannery portrayed respectively in "Hysteria heats up" and "Here are the facts, Bolt", reflect highly divergent stances on the controversial issue of climate change. While Bolt believes Flannery employs "exaggeration" and "untruths" in his new book, *The Weather Makers: The History and Future Impact of Climate Change,* "to 'prove' man-made climate change is a menace", Flannery himself is incensed that Bolt questions his scientific credibility while choosing to ignore the wealth of science on the subject. In so doing, the writers employ a disparate range of persuasive techniques. Irrespective of the truth, both men stand strong in their convictions, and choose to persuade their readers through assertive and forceful language while accommodating the contrasting natures of their reader demographic.'

Points of discussion are:

1. In her introductory paragraph, Emily immediately introduces Bolt's article, providing a brief overview and contention and identifying his tone. Similarly, she offers the same details with respect to Flannery's response. She then offers an insight into the targeted readers and a preview of the language strategies she has detected and expounded in her essay.

2. In the main body of the essay, Emily proceeds to identify a key device employed by Bolt, citing his sardonic, loaded and mocking use of language (statistical 'tricks' and 'booga-booga') (*strategy*) and demonstrates how he turns to his advantage his condemnation of Flannery's allegedly spurious statements. She refers again to the tone, and cites its use: 'Bolt employs a cynical tone, mocking the idea that "the end of the world is nigh" ' (*strategy*). Emily underscores that Bolt's use of personal attack is to heighten reader doubt and reinforce that Flannery is an opportunist. She contends Bolt's derision is to pilot his readers 'to collectively condemn' both Flannery and the notion that when 'myths rule men's minds' the belief in climate change, itself, is a danger to us all *(intention)*.

3. Contrasting Bolt's emotive and controversial piece with Flannery's measured rebuttal in, 'Here are the facts, Bolt' (The Age), Emily identifies the scientist's denial of Bolt's status with, 'A writer named Andrew Bolt . . .' (*strategy*) which speaks to weaken Bolt's credibility (*intention*). She illustrates that, rather than manipulating emotions, he uses 'alternating tones of reason and sceptical derision' *(strategy)* 'in a move to defend himself against Bolt's personal attack' *(intention)*. She points out that Flannery seeks to differentiate himself from Bolt 'to depict himself as the reasoned, unruffled expert' (*intention*). Emily notes Flannery's strong and forceful language where he accuses Bolt of 'lying through his teeth' (*strategy*), designed, she advises us, to 'pour scorn on Bolt's credibility' (*intention*).

4. Emily compares the opponents' use of the different pronouns: Bolt, the inclusive, collective 'we', and Flannery, the authoritative, personal 'I' (*strategy*), each to buttress readership support and gain a sharper opposing edge (*intention*). She cites Flannery's use of restrained language as a means of reaffirming his integrity (*intention*) and detects that his use of the expert opinion of George Monbiot (*strategy*) is to 'reassure the reader he is well-informed and educated on the topic' (*strategy*). Emily further notes Flannery's attempt to marginalise Bolt (*intention*) by referring to him as part of a 'shrinking and discredited minority' (*strategy*).

5. In concluding her essay, Emily restates the relative positions of both Bolt and Flannery and gives an overview of the tone and key language strategies employed. She reiterates that the authors' contrasting socio-economic readerships influence their approaches, each seeking to assert his authority by tailoring his words to accommodate and persuade his readers.

Note that Emily has correctly followed the convention of language analysis and has not adopted a stance or simply *described* the articles' issue. The key has been language *analysis:* what strategies are brought to bear and what intentions to influence the reader lie behind them. In identifying these elements, also observe Emily's skill in seamlessly integrating quotes from the articles to demonstrate her recognition and understanding of the techniques adopted by the writers. Quotes bring a 'showing the examiner' quality to your writing, not just the 'telling'; several quotes and their interpretation should therefore play evidential roles in your essays.

Incidentally, do not label such examples with 'strategy' or 'intention' in brackets; this was just to help you in the discussion on this and the previous page. You could however use the words in a sentence, if appropriate, by commenting, for example, 'The writer's intention, here, is to alert his readers to the issue by employing several strategies.'

The next chapter completes our descriptions of the main essay types you are likely to meet in your final senior years. Following our last two essay types, 'informative' and 'instructional', coming up next, we will get down to some brainstorming ideas. Then we'll look at planning, possibly the most important aspect of working smart when you are writing an essay of any type.

Before leaving this chapter, however, remember that language analysis is a skill that will come with practise—you won't crack the codes of controversialists overnight. So prick up your ears when a worthy polemic hits the airwaves and watch, read, listen and learn from media reports: how an issue is couched and what postures and language are adopted by commentators. There's plenty of grist for your mill out there: humankind has thrived on conflict and debate probably since Neanderthals and modern humans met eyeball to eyeball on the frontiers of time.

If you need to brush up, investigate an issue and experiment! Think about it, analyse it, evaluate it; jot down your findings: what terms are used, what tones are used? What strategies, and to what end? And when you come to write an essay, think like a sculptor. Your essay is your art, conceived, assembled and honed with skill by your hand to be traded with your examiner for a grade worth its value. So read on and when ready, gather your tools (page 199) and practise your craft. When it comes to the crunch of exams, chances are, your vibrant and intelligent showcase essay will not only tick all the boxes, but bring a quiet smile to your examiner's face.

32

Informative and instructional essays

The media contains a stack of hints about informative writing. Browse through the pages of a popular magazine for young women and you'll find plenty of instructional writing on how to survive the romantic adventures of womanhood.

Informative essay writing

If you want to get an idea of what informative writing is all about, you can't go wrong with a weekend news magazine for its articles. In fact, it's a good way to get a feel for the writer's approach to language, tone and personal style.

Naturally enough, informative essay writing seeks to enlighten the reader about an issue or topic. As suggested, the format could be a news article or report. It might be a review of a film, play, book or a concert. It could be a biography about someone within a community (a social worker or elderly citizen, for instance), or even an interesting family member or friend.

Importantly, in writing an informative piece, the writer must constantly address its purpose and for whom the work is intended, adjusting the language to suit the target reader. It should be clear and concise, aided by economical sentences and a sequential approach to the topic. If in an essay format, depending on the topic, you may need to do research, and of course, reference your sources. Check with your teacher.

Remember, you only have one shot at an introduction. Make the most of it! Your conclusion, however, is just as important. If you can leave your reader satisfied, thoughtful, moved, motivated, dare we hope, excited—or any other positive response—be assured, you have done a very good job. In other words, always aim to take your writing beyond being *just interesting.* Make it compelling! The more widely read you are on your topic, the better equipped you will be to formulate a convincing, sequential, informative piece that will keep your reader absorbed from beginning to end.

Here are some informative essay topics; most will require research. The titles are:

- My favourite uncle. An interview (humour an option)
- A report on the current status of aged care in our community and the Government's responsibilities
- The impact of post-European settlement on aboriginal culture
- The phenomenon of reality television
- A film review of (a film of your choice)
- The effects of gambling on today's society
- Biography of an unsung hero
- Multiculturalism in our country today
- A history of the Internet
- South Africa today. A weekend news portrait

Here is an example of an opening paragraph of one of the above titles. At first glance, it may seem a timeworn theme: post-European aboriginal culture. Not so! Dig deeper, and beneath the layers of stories told, are as many or more, yet to be revealed. Against a background of rich cultural history, one can draw human tales of struggle, conflict and disillusionment, and sometimes, of inspiration and triumph. Research uncovers a wealth of material and provides the opportunity for a colourful and moving retrospective to introduce an informative essay.

Introduction

Essay title: 'The impact of post European settlement on aboriginal culture'
Essay type: Informative news article

Statement of Intention:

The following article will seek to convey, using examples, how post-European settlement has had a largely negative impact on aboriginal culture. It will do this by relating the present day circumstances of two aboriginal family members, and recounting the circumstances of the brutal death of a third family member. It will seek to illustrate the negative impact of European culture on this family (and thus a large sector of aboriginal people in Australia), and the mechanisms involved.

This piece, written as a feature article in a weekend news magazine, is aimed at a typical adult reader of such features. It seeks to appeal to the egalitarian instinct in thinking people, to arouse fresh public debate on the unsatisfactory conditions, both physical and psychological, that many aborigines today, (by virtue, largely, of Anglo Saxon culture, policy and influence) are forced to bear.

His name is Wally. His skin gleams like burnished leather. His deep-set eyes are troubled. He has nine kids, is loved by two women and hasn't a brass razoo to call his own. Wally is also an inveterate drinker and has several mates just like him.

His younger brother, Maxwell, died in a police lock-up at seventeen. Wally's mother, Belle, has diabetes. In this modern-day, materialistic world of post-European settlement, such stories illustrate too often, the desperate plight of the Australian aborigine. Who are Wally and Belle, and what of Maxwell? Has their culture been sabotaged by the burden of change? If so, who or what is to blame?

Firstly, you will note that the Statement of Intention is longer than others we have presented. This illustrates a more diverse statement where the following key questions are answered:

- What is the purpose of the piece?
- Who is the target reader?
- In what format or context is the piece written?
- What strategies will be employed to elicit a response?

This is a handy way, also, to plot the course of your essay and ensure, on revision, that you have not strayed from your intentions. Apart from the first and second above points, your teacher will advise you what other aspects should be covered in the Statement of Intention.

You will note that although the article may be about to dip into the history books from 200 years ago to the present day, an informative essay by virtue of its function need not always be formal and without its personalities. Subject matter usually involves people one way or another. If you have the opportunity to weave a human story through an informative piece, (that is, aboriginal culture and the impact of European settlement, for example), it can make for a very compelling read.

See also, how the Main Ideas have been set up nicely in the opening paragraph, inviting the Supporting Details to be provided in the paragraphs to come. Of course, there is the story of a troubled Wally and his drinking mates, and the factors that influence their lack of economic and social well-being. And what of the story that lies behind Maxwell's death in custody—and how is that linked to post-European settlement? Belle is a diabetic. This allows the history of diabetes in aborigines to be traced back to a cultural change from a traditional hunter-gatherer diet to the alien high-fat Western diet—a change totally influenced by post-European settlement and highly unsuited to aboriginal digestive systems. In fact, research will show that this cultural change has impacted heavily on aboriginal health.

The Main Ideas are:

1. Wally, his drinking habits, his family responsibilities, and his mates; the forces that have created their situations.
2. Maxwell's story; the forces and their impact.

3. Belle's story; the forces and their impact.
4. Is aboriginal culture flourishing or is it in shreds? Is post-European settlement a target of blame? The answer lies in the above stories to be developed in the main body of the article.

Instructional essay writing

Imagine you are a journalist working for a popular women's magazine like 'Cosmopolitan' or 'Glamour'. You have been assigned the task of writing a 'how to' article entitled 'How to catch your man, hook line and sinker!' Voilà! You are looking right down the nose of an instructional essay.

The title could just as easily be 'How to drop him without denting his ego!' or 'How to throw a party without breaking the budget!'—but it all boils down to a similar quest: the delivery of some pretty snappy advice on how to rise to a challenge and sail through with flying colours.

Your target reader, of course, will have already been defined for you by virtue of the magazine's readership. Language and tone therefore need to be set accordingly—this article title suggesting a humorous slant and a good bit of tongue-in-cheek for a more light-hearted approach.

Your choice of humour or otherwise is something to keep in mind when considering different instructional topics. Something as dry as 'How to change a bicycle tube', for example, would be a true test of ability—not in terms of your subject knowledge—but your skill in taking the inexperienced reader through the steps without boring the bike pants off them. In this case, the use of humour would provide an attractive fillip to your 'how to' monograph. In fact, many instructional topics seem to invite a comic angle or nimble wit (if you can manage it; don't try it otherwise) to raise it from the doldrums. Look at these examples and you will perhaps see the possibilities:

- How to survive a day-out with your parents and their friends
- How to raise funds for charity
- How to draw attention to yourself without looking like a geek
- How to choose a birthday present for your grandmother
- How to become famous
- How to win a person over—on the telephone
- How to become a billionaire
- The art of repartee at lunch with a crown prince/princess
- The art of eating globe artichokes, escargots and Spaghetti Bolognese like a true professional

The key to writing a good instructional essay or article is research. As with any such writing, the more you know of your topic, the more examples you will have for making your point and thus, the chance of a good mark will be.

What *is* the 'true professional's' modus operandi when it comes to eating Spaghetti Bolognese, anyway? Does one suck it off the plate with pursed lips, doing one's best not to flick the sauce over the person opposite? Or does one bite it off mid-slurp, allowing the remainder to splash back onto one's plate—and *then* over the person opposite? Does one twirl it around a fork until it's the size of a walnut or a tennis ball?

Does one use a rounded spoon for twirling, or the bottom of the plate? Indeed, does one *twirl* at all? Unless you have studied the etiquette of this issue you will be unable to present it in a credible, convincing style with the expert tone of a connoisseur!

Whatever you do, make your instructional piece as clear as possible. Use short sentences. Think your instructions through carefully, mapping them out as you go. In defining your target readers, you should ascertain how well informed on the subject they are likely to be. Are they complete novices or can you assume some level of expertise?

Don't ever talk down to your reader; adopt a friendly didactic (teaching) tone and impart your knowledge and information sequentially to maintain clarity. A concise, step-by-step format will help you to achieve this. You don't necessarily have to *write* it this way (that is, Step 1, Step 2, etc.)—but it will definitely aid the planning process.

The use of smart, eye-catching sub-headings, particularly for a magazine article, will help you to define the stepped process without numbering, per se. A flip through any popular magazine of the genre will soon have you dreaming up your own sub-headings. Puns and alliteration work well: study the article titles under 'Instructional essay writing', (page 156, second paragraph) for a play-on-words. Incidentally, ask someone who represents your target reader to look your piece over to ensure it is coherent, crystal clear and *hitting the bull's eye.*

Following is an introductory paragraph example, using the topic suggested earlier, to give you an idea how such a piece might be introduced:

Introduction
Essay title: 'How to catch your man, hook line and sinker!'
Essay type: Instructional

Statement of Intention:
Written for a popular, young women's magazine, the following article is aimed at 18-22 year old female readers. Although the text follows an instructional style, its primary design is to entertain by offering frivolous, rather than serious advice.

He's gorgeous and you're smitten! Your mother adores him. Your father wants to take him off to the club, and your sister is green with envy. You've just landed yourself the biggest, the best catch you're ever likely to see on the end of your line. And he's fallen for you—hook, line and sinker! Trouble is, will that alluring package you offered as bait be enough to sustain his fascination? Will your sexy chat, designer pants and strawberry lip gloss keep him permanently breathless—or will you need a deeper net to draw him up the aisle? Hooking your man is one thing. Keeping him interested is altogether another story! Here are five tried and true, ultra feminine techniques that will help you snare your man and keep him happy—forever! The first is as old and mysterious as the Mona Lisa herself.

This concludes our descriptions of the nine different essay types.

Brainstorming comes next. Whether you are about to write a creative, issue-based or informative style essay, once you have a topic—even before the planning begins—the first thing you'll need is to stimulate some fresh and innovative ideas.

Let's do it!

33

Skill 5: Brainstorming

Whatever you do, don't overlook brainstorming.

When presented with an essay topic, ask yourself: 'Are the criteria already established?' That is, are the guidelines already in place (as with various analytical essays, for example); or do I need to stimulate ideas? If it's the latter, and a successful essay is what you want, brainstorming will be as integral to the process as having lunch.

Hungry for more? Let's say you establish the essay needs brainstorming. You've identified your *target reader* (see, 'Reading the essay question', page 108). Right. Now you need a bit of quiet to do some thinking, so seek solitude in your study or bedroom or somewhere else nice and peaceful.

Brainstorming can be tackled several ways, depending on the essay type. Issue-based are seen differently to creative or informative style essays.

Issue-based style of essay

A common criticism of student writers is their superficiality when discussing issues. I have therefore devised a brainstorming checklist to ensure virtually all perspectives are covered when issue-based essays are being addressed during the brainstorming phase. This means that whether a perspective applies or not, you can address it and assess its relevance.

Twelve perspectives

Our checklist for brainstorming issue-based essays contains six criteria that offer different perspectives: the 'political' perspective, the 'economic', 'psychological', 'social', 'moral' and 'environmental' perspectives. Potentially, each criterion may be seen from two viewpoints, the 'micro' view and the 'macro'. This offers a total of 12 perspectives that need to be considered and evaluated relative to the topic discussion. Each perspective can then be prioritised for inclusion in your essay writing Plan (see next chapter).

With micro and macro views, the micro view considers the impact the issue has on individuals in the immediate surroundings. The macro view, which pupils often neglect, is the far-reaching impact of an issue. That is, the influence upon wider society. For example, if you were asked to write an essay on the pros and cons of gambling, you would need to ensure that as well as discussing its impact on individual victims and their families, you address the broader repercussions gambling has upon society as a whole:

The billions of dollars spent on gambling each year suck vital money out of the economy contributing to the downturn or failure of local businesses; social disharmony can be caused by broken marriages from gambling; people out of jobs through failed businesses or the direct results of gambling may rely heavily on social services funded by the tax payer—and so on.

This is how the brainstorming checklist looks. A full-page version can be found at edworksglobal.com, and in the Appendix, page 248, for printing.

BRAINSTORMING ISSUE-BASED ESSAYS
CHECKLIST FOR SECONDARY STUDENTS

Essay title:

Essay type: Argumentative or Persuasive

Essay's aim/s:		
PERSPECTIVES	**MICRO VIEW (Impact on Individuals**	**MACRO VIEW (Impact on Society)**
POLITICAL		
ECONOMIC		
PSYCHOLOGICAL		
SOCIAL		
MORAL		
ENVIRONMENTAL		
OTHER		

Our pupils find this checklist invaluable for preparing issue-based essays; Try it for your next issue-based essay and you'll see what we mean by 'working smart'. Incidentally, for a more detailed explanation of how to use such a checklist, read Chapter 23, page 83, and specifically, the point-by-point discussion that follows the checklist.

A checklist for printing is on page 248 and also on Edworks' website, edworksglobal.com. Click on 'Checklists and Templates'.

Creative and informative style essays

Generating ideas for a creative style of essay ('creative', 'descriptive' and 'personal') can be a lot of fun, using non-critical, free idea association exercises. Test the following two methods, for your preference: 'Triad' and 'Clustering'. The format for the Triad Method is also suitable for plotting the course of your informative style essays ('informative' and 'instructional').

The Triad Method

In the example given, following, your essay topic is, 'A day at the beach'.

Firstly, on a blank page, you draw three circles and brainstorm what the plot of your story might be: (i) about *a rescue?* (ii) finding *treasure?* (iii) perhaps *an event centred around people* and their reactions? Write your suggested plot in each circle. (Be warned here. Every second person thinks of *shark attack* the minute 'a day at the beach' is suggested. It's a big yawn for most teachers, so unless you want to be predictable, give this topic a miss and fossick around for something different.)

Secondly, draw three arrows or lines, radiating from each circle. Brainstorm again as to the possible subject matter for each scenario you have proposed. For example, will your 'rescue' be of a child, a dolphin or a boat, perhaps?

Check the following diagram for the remaining examples:

BRAINSTORMING: TRIAD METHOD

Essay title: 'A day at the beach'
Essay type: Creative

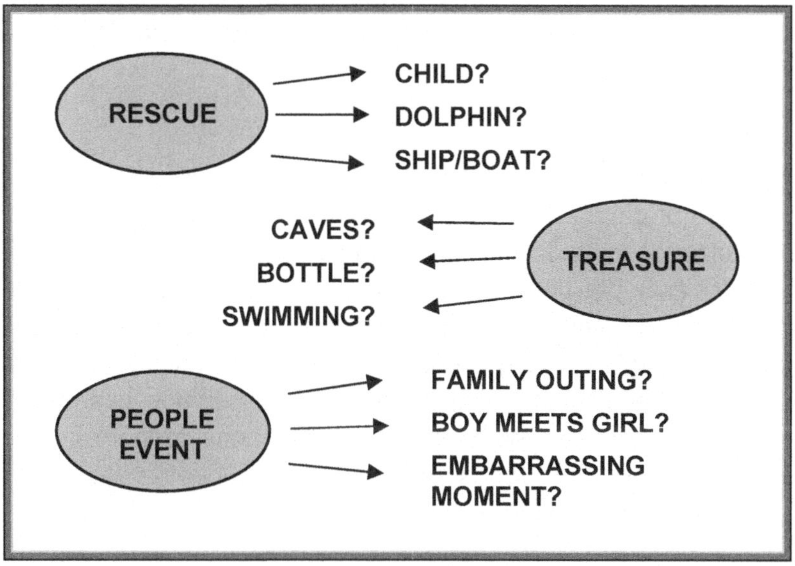

Spend one minute only, completing your triad and deciding the theme you want to develop. Then draw another circle to fill in additional details. For example, you may have decided on the last scenario shown in the diagram: 'An embarrassing moment', perhaps drawn from a personal experience.

This might mean your main character loses a swimsuit in a giant wave and has to face the embarrassment of getting back to a highly populated beach. In the circle, therefore, you may write: 'lose swimsuit'. Then your three radiating notes might ask: (a) 'join mermaids?' (b) 'dodge behind pylons?' and (c) 'steal child's bucket/protection?'

The possibilities are only restricted by your own imagination. Brainstorming here, is an opportunity to give your thinking a non-critical free rein. So, dream, be inventive, fanciful, original—and stretch that grey matter to its outer limits! Let it run riot! It could be very funny when you think about it.

Be aware however that comedy or humour, if you do choose it, can sometimes be difficult to write convincingly. What may be hilarious to you, may not strike a chord with others. If you are working smart and have planned ahead, leave your completed essay for a day or so. Then read it back as if for the first time. If it still works for you, ask a reliable friend or family member to read it, too. Honest feedback can be a great help in assessing your own work before handing it in.

This advice, of course, stands for any essay type. Learn to view valid criticism as an opportunity to grow, to improve your essay technique or content. Receive it with a gracious, open mind and a willingness to see that someone else's point of view may have more to offer than your own.

Be willing to modify or change your ideas in your quest for self-improvement. Remember, there may not be a wrong or right side to an issue. The aim is to present your ideas with originality, clarity, validity, and with a good pinch of imagination.

The Cluster Method

The Cluster Method is also a non-critical, free idea association exercise. You choose a word or phrase and encircle it in the middle of a blank page. From this, brainstorm associated ideas that spring spontaneously into your mind.

The essay example title, opposite, is 'I couldn't believe my eyes'. You might instantly write 'fear' in the centre of your blank page. Associated words might be 'screaming', 'flapping wings', 'escape', 'stranger', 'dark woods', and so on. Once you have exhausted the immediate possibilities, use a highlighter to mark the words that you feel have the most obvious connections: perhaps 'screaming', 'escape', 'dark woods', 'stranger', and so on. We've left one circle empty. What are you thinking? Go on, write it in!

BRAINSTORMING: CLUSTER METHOD

Essay title: 'I couldn't believe my eyes ...'
Essay type: Creative

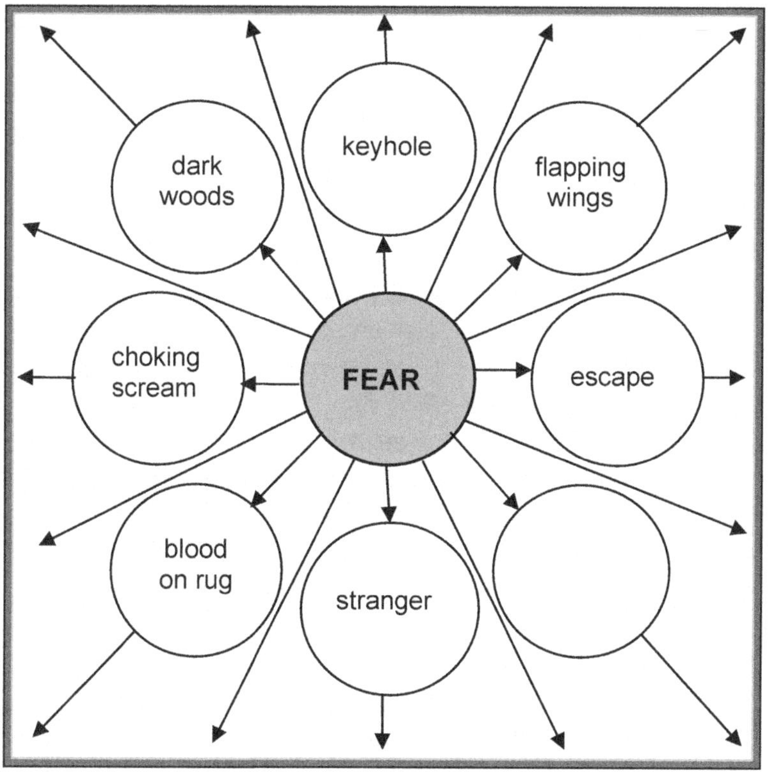

Brainstorming in this manner can suggest a possible story line and set your mind racing.

Great! Jot down the ideas that flow from this. This is what brainstorming is all about: generating one idea from another. Try your own ideas, using the Triad or Cluster Methods on scrap paper. Practise whichever method you prefer. The more you do it, the easier it will be at exam time.

A word of caution

Make sure you don't labour over brainstorming. See it for the device it is meant to be: a spontaneous ideas generator. Like sparks! In an examination setting you don't have time to loll around for half an hour dreaming up the perfect scenario.

So let the brain sparks fly for just *one minute,* grab your ideas, juggle them around a bit and quickly select the ones that give you the basis for a storyline—*and then run with it.*

Remember, it's *the skill* of your essay writing and your ability to entertain your reader that are at stake. It's the story *telling,* not the clever idea for a story that you'll be mostly marked on. Imagine, for example, James Cameron waking up one night after brainstorming for two months, thinking, 'What a great idea! I'll do a blockbuster movie about the sinking of the Titanic.' Now that was a great idea. But the success of the movie didn't pivot on the idea alone. Apart from its popular young stars and the visual effects, it was Cameron's script, his editing and brilliant direction that spearheaded the movie's mammoth success.

On the other hand let's say after this great idea the fans flocked to the cinema. As the opening titles dissolved from the screen, up came the words: 'In 1912, the RMS Titanic hit an iceberg and sank! The End.' Oh, dear! Not much of a story. Would crowds have swamped the cinemas on hearing of the movie's abysmally inept script? Of course not! This 200 million-dollar epic would have been a gigantic box-office flop. Cameron would probably have scratched his head and said, 'Mmm. Seemed like a good idea at the time.'

The moral of this tale is that good ideas will count for nothing unless you can breathe life into them by learning the key skills of competent writing. More to the point, even a simple or ordinary idea can be, and often is, transformed into an acclaimed work. It is *what you do* with your idea, how you present it, how you craft your storyline, and whether you can capture your reader's imagination that counts for everything.

Look at it this way: If you had two choices: (i) write a great essay on an ordinary topic or (ii) write an ordinary essay on a great topic—which would win the day? This all means, ultimately, in the exam, do not spend more than *ten per cent* of your time reading the question, brainstorming and planning (to be discussed). That is, devote three minutes for a 30-minute essay—about 1½ pages—and 27 minutes to the actual writing and reviewing.

Practice = proficiency

This may sound difficult at first. However, the purpose of this book is to have you working smart. That includes alerting you to the preparation that is required *before* you reach the exam room door. So grab some essay topics and practise brainstorming plus other essay phases discussed. Incorporate the exercises into your regular study routine. Even when you think you have it covered, as with tennis or music, practise your essay writing exercises on a regular basis. This means slotting practice times into your timetable. It will keep you well primed for big essay writing events, allowing ideas and formats to be generated quickly in your mind when you need them most.

You could also check out our 'Time out 15' skills practice program in the last chapter on page 211.

Here are a few creative style topics to play around with. They can be creative fantasy—or factual personal or factual descriptive essays. Others can be found in the ensuing chapters. For more inspiration, ask your teacher for some good essay topics or scan the news media for ideas and create your own titles. The idea is to practise what you are learning now as a matter of routine. Use any spare time from working smart in other areas to sharpen and refine your writing skills. Moving the time saved in one exercise to an area of need makes sense, doesn't it? The outcome will mean less time and effort spent in *all* areas for a greatly improved result.

Essay title:

1. **'He walked deliberately towards me'**

   Possible scenarios:

   - He was up to no good.
   - You have just won a major prize.
   - He was the bearer of bad news.
   - You have run out of petrol on a lonely, country road.

Essay title:

2. **'The morning began like almost any other. By dusk, my day had been thrown into turmoil and my life was changed forever. I would never be the same again.'**

   Possible scenarios:

   - The trigger event that leads to life changes may be subtle or ordinary; the chain of events that follow may be surprising.
   - A cataclysmic event.
   - Ask yourself from which viewpoint the essay will be: reality or fiction? If you are a brain surgeon, a life-changing event may be different to that if you are, say, a sporting hero, a pop star, or a prime minister.

Essay title:

3. **'At last, s/he had achieved her/his goal!'**

   Possible scenarios:

   - Published a magazine.
   - Passed the Bar Exam to practise law.
   - Flown in a hot air balloon.
   - Invented the world's first ...

By now you should be versed on brainstorming. Next, we dip into some research advice with a few clues on how to narrow searches on the Web. Using the novel as a model, there's also a 'Text Analysis Checklist' for researching/reading and analysing texts. It's a great support tool.

34

Skill 6: Doing your research

As a senior student, you will already know how to carry out research. However, you may be looking for some extra pointers. Or you may be a younger student looking to prepare for later years. Knowing how to access research data takes only a little tuition, but will pay huge dividends.

Make sure you use as wide a research base as possible. Using the Internet alone may not be enough. In fact, the Internet is not the 'be all and end all' when it comes to research information. There is a good deal to be had from books and journals in libraries. Remember, your teachers and examiners know their subjects intimately. This means they are pretty much aware of the available research material. If your essay shows a broader and deeper understanding that goes beyond the nominated texts, there's a good chance your initiative and zeal will be recognised and rewarded.

Research sources are, of course, the Internet, school, public and university libraries, news articles, seminars, and parliamentary documents (proposed bills). Treat your school or local librarian as a valuable information resource: if you don't know how to do anything, or where to look, your school (or public) librarians will help you. And if they don't know the answer, they will find out for you.

Librarians will certainly help you to use the Internet. Importantly, if you can't find what you're after, vary your search terms. For example, if 'global warming' doesn't yield what you need, try 'climate change'. Failing that, source another search engine. You'll find a good many at your fingertips simply by Googling 'top search engines'. Tap into the first few to learn how the search engines are rating to make your choice.

Google itself (http://www.google.com) is currently, one of the biggest and most popular databases and rated as the fastest and most comprehensive. As you are probably aware, it features tabs such as Images, News and Videos, allowing you to target things like photos, illustrations, news articles and video clips.

Bing (www.bing.com) is ranked right up there with Google in terms of popularity and is fast gaining a reputation for providing the most relevant results. Others prefer Yahoo! Search (search.yahoo.com) as their first stop search engine. Incidentally, check the dates that information is published. Some are well out-of-date.

You can also use *directories* on the Web to source information. Directories are collated and compiled by people rather than automated programs. Results are categorised based on website content as a whole, as opposed to web searches which focus on particular keywords. Some of the better all-purpose directories include Yahoo! Directory (dir.yahoo.com), Open Directory Project (ODP)/Dmoz Directory (www.dmoz.org) and Best of the Web (http://botw.org), to name a few.

The key in searching for information is not to waste time! Knowing a few basic short cuts to locating what you want on the Web will help. At university level, some courses require that students do a two-hour compulsory presentation on how to access data bases, or students are expected to take the initiative and do a brief seminar for some instruction. This teaches them how to access electronic journals and periodicals using author names or key words to source data. But, that's for later.

What we want is to avoid the junk while our search terms need to be broad enough not to miss anything of interest. In dealing with one of the main search engines, you should firstly read its instructions for getting the best, most efficient result from your search. This will teach you:

- how to create a phrase that will bring the best results
- how to exclude words to narrow your search
- how to search using more than one phrase

Some of the search conventions are different, which is the reason you should read their blurb. Google, Bing and Yahoo! Search have similar basic search conventions, but the number of results may vary.

Let's say you are studying honey and beekeeping. You know, at least, that a Winston Lamb is an expert on the subject. Entering *winston lamb* by itself, for any search engine, would be a mistake. For the search engines discussed, this will mean that the results will have both names on the same page, but not together. If you asked Bing, for example, you'd receive more than eight million results!

So to find this chap, Winston Lamb, you'll have to treat it like any exact phrase you might want to find and enclose his name in double quotes as "winston lamb". The Bing results are dramatically reduced to about 400 and contain both words, together, on the same page. Thus it becomes easier to find our beekeeper.

Now if we type in "winston lamb beekeeper" our Bing search fails with no results. This simply means that no pages contain the three words as a single phrase. However, when we submit—"winston lamb" beekeeper—bingo, we find who we are looking for with five results mentioning Winston Lamb, and the word 'beekeeper' elsewhere on the same page.

To exclude things you don't want, Google's convention requires the insertion of a minus (–) sign before the word to remove it from the search. Sometimes, for example, a word will have two meanings: 'bass' could refer to music or mean the fish. Thus, you would type *bass –fish* to target your music theme. To include a common word like 'how' that Google would normally leave out to speed up the search, simply type a plus (+) sign before the word. (Leave a space *before* the plus or minus signs discussed.) Play it smart by spending a little time checking the various search engines' conventions; it will pay dividends and make your research more pleasurable.

For other research, your national Bureau of Statistics has statistical information available both from libraries and the Internet. Some may require payment by credit card—so seek assistance from your school or parents if necessary. Governments also have websites from which research material may be sourced.

Researching for text analysis

Essay questions require that your answers demonstrate your understanding of the text. Your research for the novel (or plays, film and television) needs to be conducted therefore from an analytical point of view.

To assist our senior students, I created a checklist for analysing text which they find immensely useful (see the reduced format, next page). It will prompt you all the way through the reading exercise. It may even surprise you to learn, once you have identified the issues, how easy analysing the text really is. When you're ready, take up your class novel/play and we'll get down to some research and analysis that will see you working smart.

Motivators revisited

If you have not already done so, I urge you to read or re-read pages 139-140 from the 'text analysis' chapter. The emotions or states which humans experience and which lie behind the issues you will find in your texts—such as love, envy, betrayal, and so on—I call 'Motivators'. Motivators 'motivate' us to respond or take action to restore homeostasis.

'Belief Systems' influence the Motivators. That is, the way we respond to our environments is largely determined by our Belief Systems. Personal beliefs, in turn, are inspired by personal histories, including childhood experiences. In analysing text, I divide the Belief Systems into two distinct categories: 'Fatalists' and 'Non-fatalists'.

Fatalists

Fatalists are reluctant to accept responsibility for their actions or to control situations, viewing everything as inevitable, or *fate*. They often have irrational beliefs and engage in self-defeating behaviour.

Non-fatalists

These people take responsibility for their actions and control of situations. They accept that, while they can't change circumstances, they can change *how they choose* to respond to situations.

First reading

Prepare a working copy of the 'Text Analysis Checklist' seen below, from the Appendix, page 249, or print a big one from our website, edworksglobal.com at the 'Checklists and Templates' tab. Keep it in front of you at all times as you read. Also equip yourself with coloured stick-on paper tags that you can number in accordance with the numbered Motivators on the checklist. Several different colours may assist in easier retrieval, later. Set up your own ID system.

TEXT ANALYSIS CHECKLIST

MOTIVATOR	PAGE: QUOTES/ PASSAGES	IMPACT	AUTHOR'S INTENTION
1. Love: passionate			
2. Love: companionate			
3. Hate			
4. Conformity			
5. Rebellion			
6. Greed			
7. Selfishness			
8. Envy			
9. Power			
10. Courage			
11. Fear			
12. Loyalty			
13. Betrayal			
14. Loss			
15. Jealousy			
BELIEF SYSTEM	**PGE: QUOTES /PASSAGES**	**IMPACT**	**AUTHOR'S INTENTION**
16. Fatalist			
17. Non-fatalist			

Think! Then read

Remember, you are not reading for entertainment!

The purpose is analysis. Therefore, it is important to begin from a position of awareness to avoid wasting valuable time. You will recall the scavenger hunt analogy: you need to know what you are looking for, *before you start*.

Firstly, become acquainted with the Motivators and Belief Systems in the 'Text Analysis Checklist'. As you read your text, when you think something significant is occurring, use your tags and/or highlight the text with an identifying number: for example, 'greed' is '6'.

Don't worry if you are not sure exactly what it is. Mark it with a question mark if needs be and analyse it later.

Second reading—addressing the essay question

Having read your text and identified the Motivators and Belief Systems, you should now study the essay question.

Look at the question within the context of the Motivators that cause the characters to behave the way they do. This means you need to record the issues you have highlighted, using your 'Text Analysis Checklist' and jotting down brief details. Don't forget to make good use of the note-taking tips we discussed on pages 54-65.

In other words, don your cap and cape and borrow the skills of a regular Sherlock Holmes.

When reading any text, (novel, play, research data, news article and so on), should you come across a word and are unsure of its meaning, stop for a moment and grab a dictionary to look it up.

Dictionaries that offer phonetic pronunciations and context examples are the best to have on your bookshelf. You'll find one at your bookshop. Note the word's meaning in your pocket book and memorise it over time. Use the word whenever appropriate until it becomes a part of your vocabulary. If you are unsure as to the word's context, consult Answers.com online or ask a parent or teacher. *That's the fast track to building word skills!*

Look closely and identify *the impact* of these Motivators and Beliefs, and interpret the *author's intention* in creating a situation. Make your notes brief and to the point. For example, let's say you are reading the novel, 'Animal Farm', by George Orwell, discussed on page 141. On page 12 of the book, the farm animal rebellion against the intemperate and cruel Mr. Jones is described. Later, the same pigs that fought for equality and justice begin to copy the departed Mr. Jones by living in his house.

The author illustrates here how power corrupts. The pigs eat the farmer's food (keeping the best for themselves) and ultimately walk on two legs. Orwell's intended message is that when leadership is corrupted by power, its impact upon successful revolution is rendered ineffective as it prevents the process of democracy from occurring.

Therefore, at point 9, 'Power', in the Text Analysis Checklist you might say:

TEXT ANALYSIS CHECKLIST

MOTIVATOR	PAGE: QUOTES/ PASSAGES	IMPACT	AUTHOR'S INTENTION
9. Power	P 22. After rebellion. Chant, '4 legs good 2 legs bad' rally cry (contempt). In spite of animal creed, pigs later imitate Jones (eat his food, live in house, walk on 2 legs).	Power corrupts.	Shows leadership in rev. process becomes ineffective when corruption prevents democracy.

Having recorded all significant and relevant observations, the research phase of your text analysis will now be complete. The planning and first draft chapters will take you through the next steps to editing, before the submission of your final copy.

Excellent! With research done, we now need to get on with an often-neglected aspect of writing a good essay: the all-important, planning stage. In fact, if you take our advice for working smart—including employing an effective essay writing Plan, you might surprise yourself.

Your next essay could be brilliant!

35

Skill 7: Planning your essay

Winning is intrinsic to the human spirit!

Since the mists of time, it has meant the scooping of spoils, the reaping of rewards, the hailing of heroes. Winning elates the ego and opens the doors of opportunity. Winning, in fact, is all about success and feeling good!

The glory and prizes that big win's earn are also why sports coaches earn top salaries: Experience, Success and Wisdom are the coaches' tools of trade. These they use to impart their skills to the athletes who seek to follow their winning example. Motivation aside, an important part of a coach's skill, is having a game plan—or a coaching strategy—that will lead to winning.

Imagine the opposite for a moment: a soccer or football team is ready for a big game. A theme tune blares, the cheer squad cheers, the crowd roars like Romans in the Coliseum. And the players stream valiantly onto the field—*without a game plan!* What a debacle! They all try to hog the ball. They run the wrong way. They despatch goals right through the middle of . . . the opposition goal posts! What an unruly bunch. What a perfect recipe for failure!

This is all a bit of fun of course. No worthy coach would send a team out unprepared like that, let alone expect it to win.

You don't have to be a rocket scientist to see planning is important. It's as vital for success as being physically fit enough to take on the challenge. Yet, when it comes to essay writing, time after time our staff members encounter blank looks on the faces of new pupils who have never considered such a thing. 'An essay *plan*?' they say sceptically. 'What's that?' On a scale of importance from one to ten, it's probably worth a good nine, that's what!

This may come to you as big a surprise as it did recently to a mature-aged Bachelor of Arts, Literature Major.

At 34, Glenn was keen to take up study again to do his Masters in Literature. He knew he had good ideas (after all, he had achieved his degree using many of them). Even so, he felt there was something missing.

Glenn knew it concerned his writing skills, but couldn't identify the problem. I showed him some worksheets, including how to plan an essay.

It was as if a light switch had suddenly been flicked. Glenn's face lit up. 'That's what's missing!' he said emphatically. 'It's the structure. I've never known how to put my concepts together really coherently or to link the paragraphs through main ideas and supporting data.'

Glenn needed no more convincing to become one of our growing number of university students who are brushing up their essay writing skills with our help. It's never too late to learn how to work smart, and if ever those skills are needed, it's during the tertiary years. Be glad you're looking at them now.

Linking note-taking to essay writing

It may pay you to look back on page 55, Step 1 of 'Smart note-taking' dealing with understanding text structure. The structure that helped you understand the writing of others, will also guide you in the planning of your own writing. It will also greatly enhance a key requirement of your writing style: clarity.

Any essay you write will be improved by ensuring it contains the following four criteria: clear structure, personal style, emotional accord and imagery.

While the different types of essays require varying measures of each component, a good essay will seek to use all four to the best effect. Even for an informal issue-based piece such as an editorial or speech, the use of imagery through vignettes or anecdotes may enhance its presentation as discussed on page 130.

1. Clear essay structure

CRITERIA FOR ESSAYS

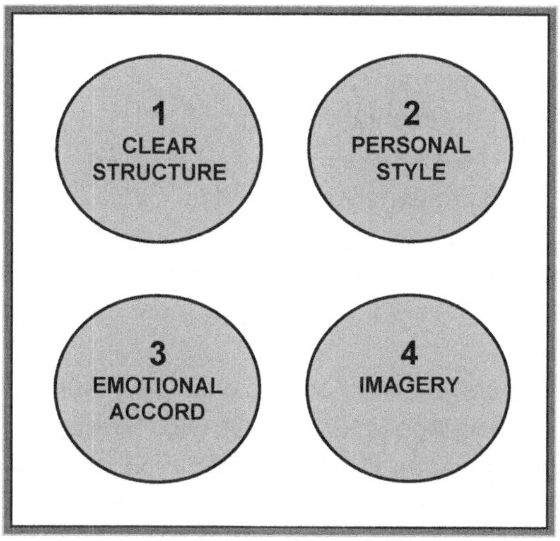

Remember the adage, 'The purpose of the written word is communication'?

When you are planning your essay, make sure it is clear and makes sense. This means your essay should follow a Plan and address the essay topic. Your essay should be well structured so that one point builds upon another. If you aim to please both teachers and examiners, your Main Ideas should be linked back always to the essay topic. This aids clarity and allows the development of a sequence of ideas.

2. Personal style

We might call this, 'personality'. It is your personal stamp on your writing. Read two or three books by the same author and you will get a good idea of what personal style means. Reading a diversity of others' works offers a melting pot of styles and will put you well on the road to developing your own. Importantly, it will also improve your vocabulary and grammar.

Don't commit the sin of writing essays like a list of events. Aim for dimension in your writing style through language, wit or insightful comment. Allow descriptions or imagery to express your thoughts or feelings.

Best advice? Read, read, read!

Take home a library book. Download an e-book. Tap into media magazines and read articles. They are all written by people; people who incorporate their personal styles in what they write.

3. Emotional accord

This was discussed in Chapter 27, page 115. Check it again if you need to.

4. Imagery

The use of imagery has been well covered, particularly in Chapter 27, 'Creative essays', beginning on page 111.

Planning

We are now on a new starting block.

We are about to put our brainstormed ideas into an essay Plan. But first, we identify four different planning approaches for the different essay types. These come under the headings of:

1. General Plan
2. Argumentative Plan
3. Text Analysis Plan
4. Language Analysis Plan

Our essay writing G-Plan (General Plan) discussion is back at 'Smart note-taking,' page 56. As a guide, most essay types can be planned using the G-Plan.

However, the conventions are different for argumentative, text analysis and language analysis essays. To avoid possible confusion, we therefore have separate Plans for each type of essay: the A-Plan (Argumentative), T-Plan (Text analysis), and L-Plan (Language analysis). These Plans will assist you to think with greater clarity and depth about your topic and will assist the quality of your essay structure. As you gain experience and develop your skills, you may wish to devise your own.

The G-Plan (General): This essay plan example is comprised of six paragraphs. When writing your essays within the essay guidelines, naturally you will include as many paragraphs as you need. Here is a reminder:

**SKELETON G-PLAN (GENERAL)
PARAGRAPHS FOR AN ESSAY**

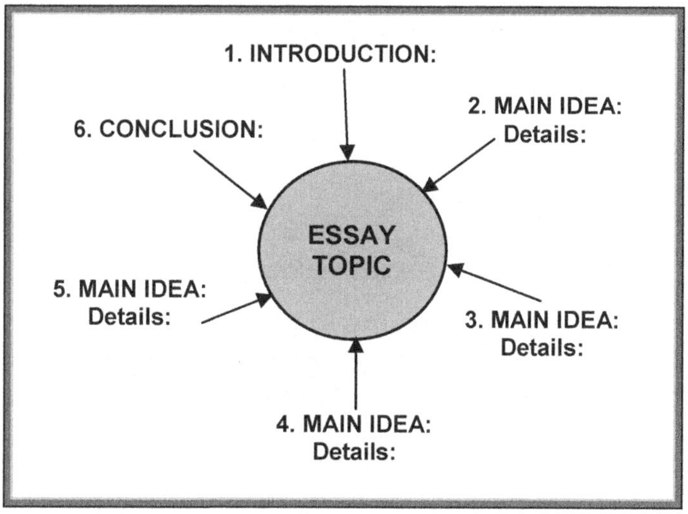

The A-Plan (Argumentative): This essay writing plan is essentially different due to the arguments 'for' and 'against' (the *positive* and *negative* stances) which characterise this type of essay. Again, the six paragraphs shown in the example can be reduced or increased, depending on your essay.

**SKELETON A-PLAN (ARGUMENTATIVE):
PARAGRAPHS FOR AN ESSAY TOPIC**

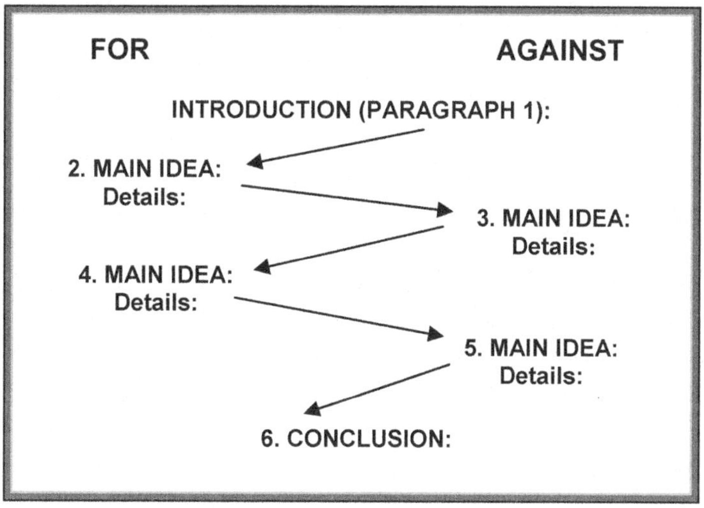

These are the bare bones of course. Let's see how the Plans look adding the flesh of our ideas. Here are two examples: the first is the creative essay, 'Visions', from page 116. All seven paragraphs cannot be fully addressed on these pages; however, this does not prevent you from using A4 sized paper during study or in an exam, to plan all the paragraphs your essays require.

As you plan, focus on:

- keeping to the essay topic (very, very important)
- good time management
- clarity and,
- sequential flow

G-Plan for essay writing—example:

As 'Visions' comprises seven paragraphs, we have bonded the fifth and sixth into one, as paragraph 5, for convenience. Paragraph 7 becomes 6.

G-PLAN (GENERAL): EXAMPLE
CREATIVE ESSAY: 'VISIONS' BY YOLANDE

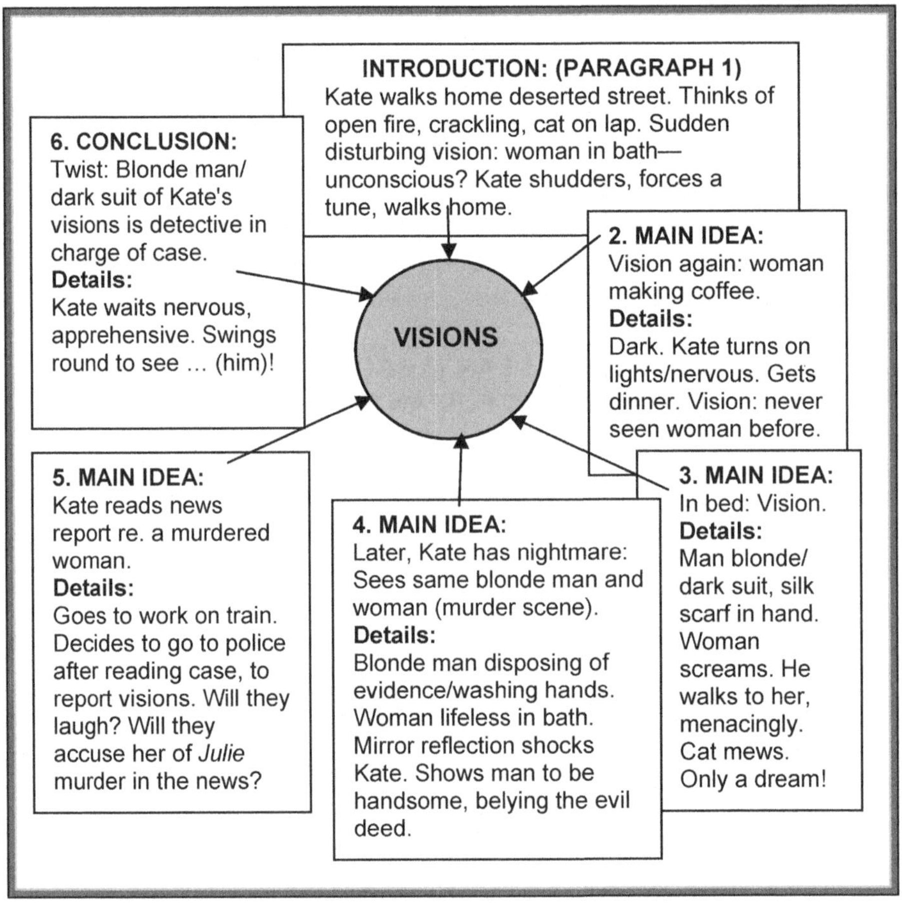

Our notes are mostly written in full for understanding. However, a quickly written Plan using shorthand notes will serve you best in exams. Regular practice is again the key to working smart and achieving a good result.

A-Plan for essay writing—example:

Next is the Plan for our formal, argumentative essay, 'Does the Internet serve democracy?' Although the essay has not been shown in full, the introduction is on page 128 and the conclusion, page 201. Note that in the discussion (pages 128-9), points 6 and 7 form the basis of the conclusion in our following A-Plan.

A-PLAN (ARGUMENTATIVE): EXAMPLE 'DOES THE INTERNET SERVE DEMOCRACY?'

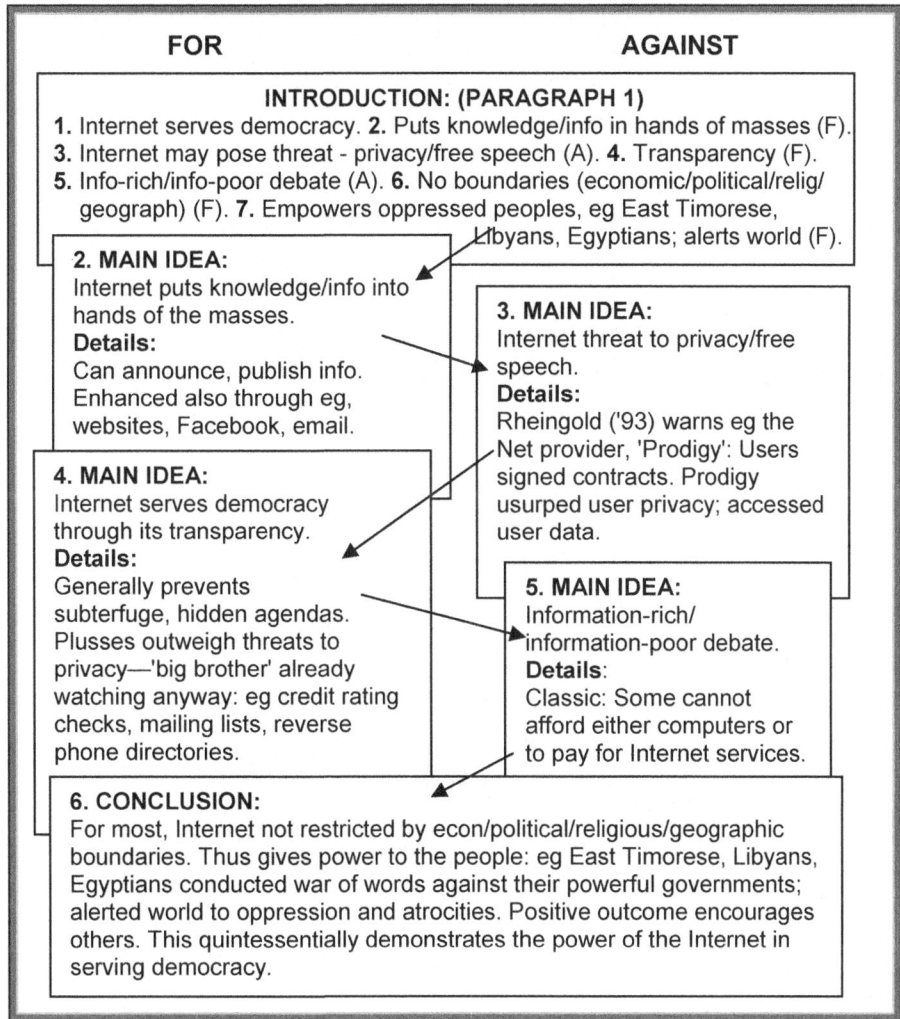

FOR | **AGAINST**

INTRODUCTION: (PARAGRAPH 1)
1. Internet serves democracy. **2.** Puts knowledge/info in hands of masses (F). **3.** Internet may pose threat - privacy/free speech (A). **4.** Transparency (F). **5.** Info-rich/info-poor debate (A). **6.** No boundaries (economic/political/relig/geograph) (F). **7.** Empowers oppressed peoples, eg East Timorese, Libyans, Egyptians; alerts world (F).

2. MAIN IDEA:
Internet puts knowledge/info into hands of the masses.
Details:
Can announce, publish info. Enhanced also through eg, websites, Facebook, email.

3. MAIN IDEA:
Internet threat to privacy/free speech.
Details:
Rheingold ('93) warns eg the Net provider, 'Prodigy': Users signed contracts. Prodigy usurped user privacy; accessed user data.

4. MAIN IDEA:
Internet serves democracy through its transparency.
Details:
Generally prevents subterfuge, hidden agendas. Plusses outweigh threats to privacy—'big brother' already watching anyway: eg credit rating checks, mailing lists, reverse phone directories.

5. MAIN IDEA:
Information-rich/information-poor debate.
Details:
Classic: Some cannot afford either computers or to pay for Internet services.

6. CONCLUSION:
For most, Internet not restricted by econ/political/religious/geographic boundaries. Thus gives power to the people: eg East Timorese, Libyans, Egyptians conducted war of words against their powerful governments; alerted world to oppression and atrocities. Positive outcome encourages others. This quintessentially demonstrates the power of the Internet in serving democracy.

To stimulate your thinking about issues, why not become a current affairs buff? Watch news and quality current affairs programs and scan news articles for topical stories. To view it positively, plan reading and watching times as part of your timetable. You will vastly improve your knowledge this way while gathering a wealth of material for some great essays.

Here are some guidelines for planning an argumentative piece:

- Check each point 'for' and 'against' for its sense of logic and reason.
- Plan your notes with clarity (even if quickly written) using rational arguments to refute opposing views.
- Use your most powerful arguments to support your case. For example, in arguing for a total ban on smoking, citing the number of trees that had to be cut down to manufacture the cigarette packets would not serve you well. Rationally, your biggest argument should be: smoking can cause cancer and death!

The T-Plan (Text Analysis): The T-Plan structure is similar to the G-Plan, featuring Main Ideas and Supporting/Substantiating details. However, a separate Plan for text analysis allows us to highlight additional key points: the need for adopting a personal viewpoint on issues or instead posing a stance by the author, plus the importance of substantiating *all* the points used for your Main Ideas. This provides insight to an examiner as to your understanding of the text. (See opposite.)

SKELETON T-PLAN (TEXT ANALYSIS)
PARAGRAPHS FOR AN ESSAY

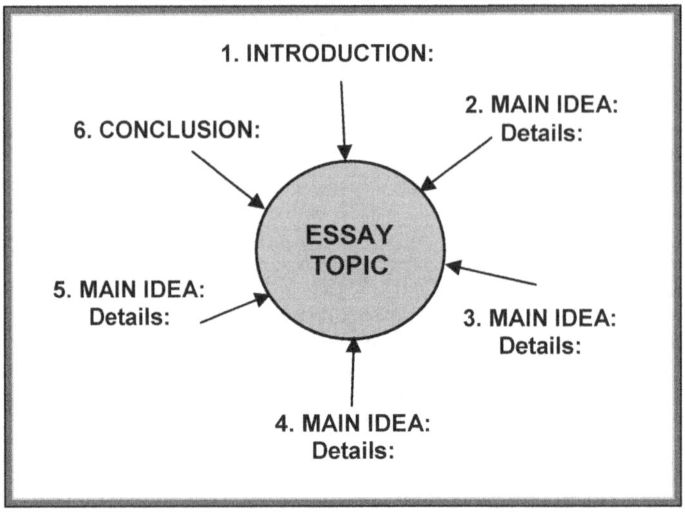

T-Plan for essay writing—guidelines
For clarity, our 'fleshed out' version contains general text analysis guidelines rather than notes on an essay example. Keep this T-Plan open on your desk and follow its guidelines as you plan your next text analysis essay.

Incidentally, as mentioned previously, this is *not* the only way you could plan such an essay. With experience, you may well improve on our idea.

T-PLAN (TEXT ANALYSIS)
ESSAY PLAN GUIDELINES

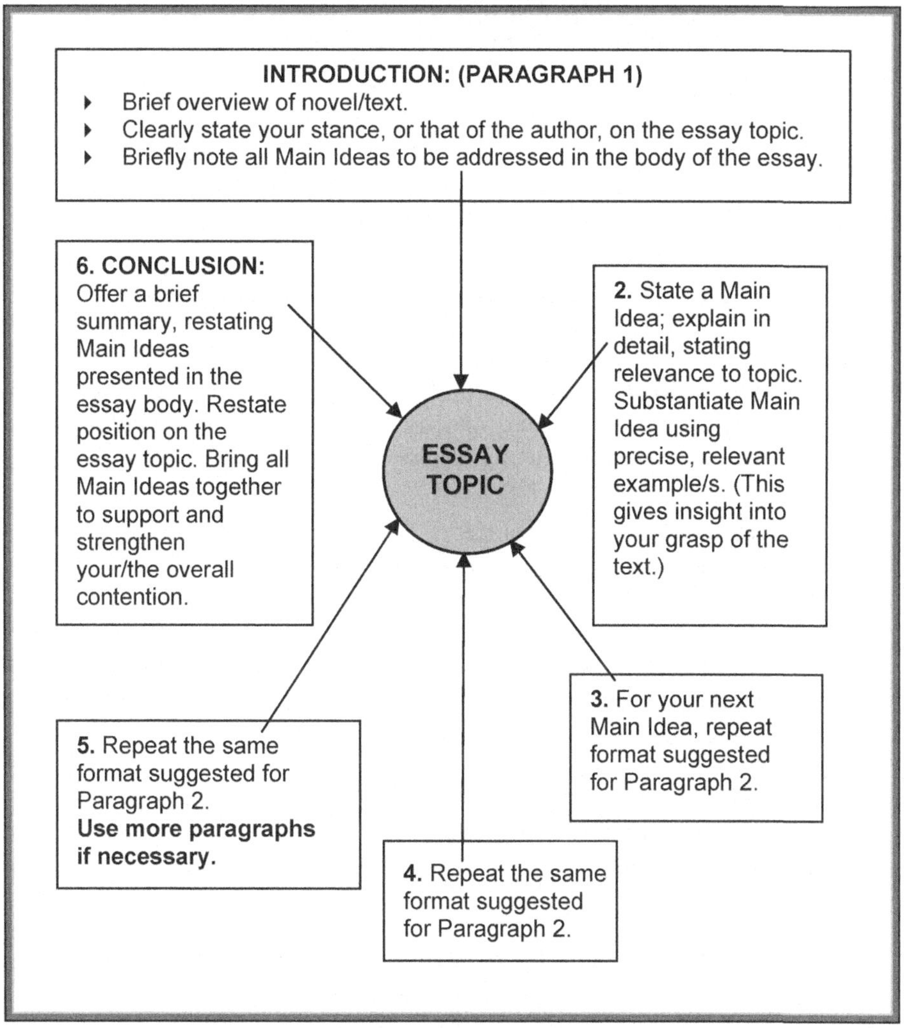

The L-Plan (Language Analysis): This Plan, overleaf, is different again. Instead of identifying Main Ideas or arguments, we identify and analyse the use of language. Keep in mind that more paragraphs may be needed than the six that are shown. The bare bones L-Plan looks like this:

SKELETON L-PLAN (LANGUAGE ANALYSIS) PARAGRAPHS FOR AN ESSAY

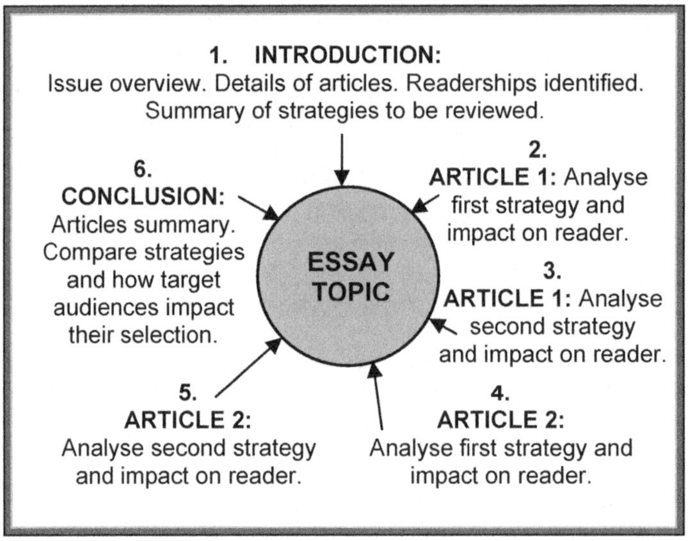

Our detailed L-Plan, over the page, also offers general guidelines rather than specific notes on an essay example. This is to achieve greater clarity. Your teacher will undoubtedly have offered sound advice for selecting issues and articles for language analysis. However, keep these pointers in mind:

- Select topics that are controversial. Controversial issues guarantee broad media coverage and diversity of opinion.
- Collect articles that cover a wide range of formats: editorials, cartoons, Letters to the Editor and so on. Be aware, informative news articles will provide background knowledge of an issue, but are not suitable for language analysis.
- Issues that provide extremes of opinion (ie either 'for' or 'against') provide good language analysis material. They are more likely to provoke controversy and provide colourful discussion—for example, 'euthanasia', 'illegal immigrants' and 'sending troops to war'.
- Avoid selecting an issue for its personal appeal; choose something that offers substance and broad-ranging material.
- Try to find articles that express strong opinions, have distinct viewpoints and that use language clearly intended to influence the reader. Our 'Clauses and Phrases for Plaudits and Praise' checklist, page 246, will help you to fluently express strategies employed in a polemic.
- Ensure your articles cover *a variety* of publications.

Language analysis essays: preparation phase

This requires a little application.

Make copies of our 'Language Analysis Checklist' from the Appendix, page 242, and 'Identifying Tone', page 247, or print them from Edworks' website, edworksglobal.com. You may recall we discussed these checklists on page 132. For more on analysing language and the checklist, see Chapter 31, page 145, 'Language analysis essays'. Become well acquainted with its contents.

You should also organise two enlarged copies of each of your chosen articles. (Use one; keep one handy as a spare.)

1. Read the articles carefully one at a time. Using the 'Language Analysis Checklist', highlight passages where you are able to identify language strategies and intentions to influence the reader. Also tap into your 'Identifying Tone' checklist to help you with tone.

2. Number each highlighted segment in accordance with your 'Language Analysis Checklist'. For example, you may identify where a writer is using emotional blackmail. As that's number 7 strategy on your checklist, mark your highlighted text accordingly. The numbers will then clearly indicate to you the strategies being used by the commentators in each of your chosen pieces, as you write your essay.

3. When choosing article quotes for your essay to illustrate language strategies, keep them short and precise.

4. Get acquainted with our 'Clauses and Phrases' checklist, page 246.

L-Plan for essay writing—guidelines

Now, to your Plan. Following the L-Plan guidelines below, quickly map out your own Plan on paper, using the data highlighted in your articles. *Express no self-opinions.* Language analysis is the nub; check Emily's essay, page 148. If required, state more strategies and/or use more articles and paragraphs.

L-PLAN (LANGUAGE ANALYSIS): ESSAY PLAN GUIDELINES

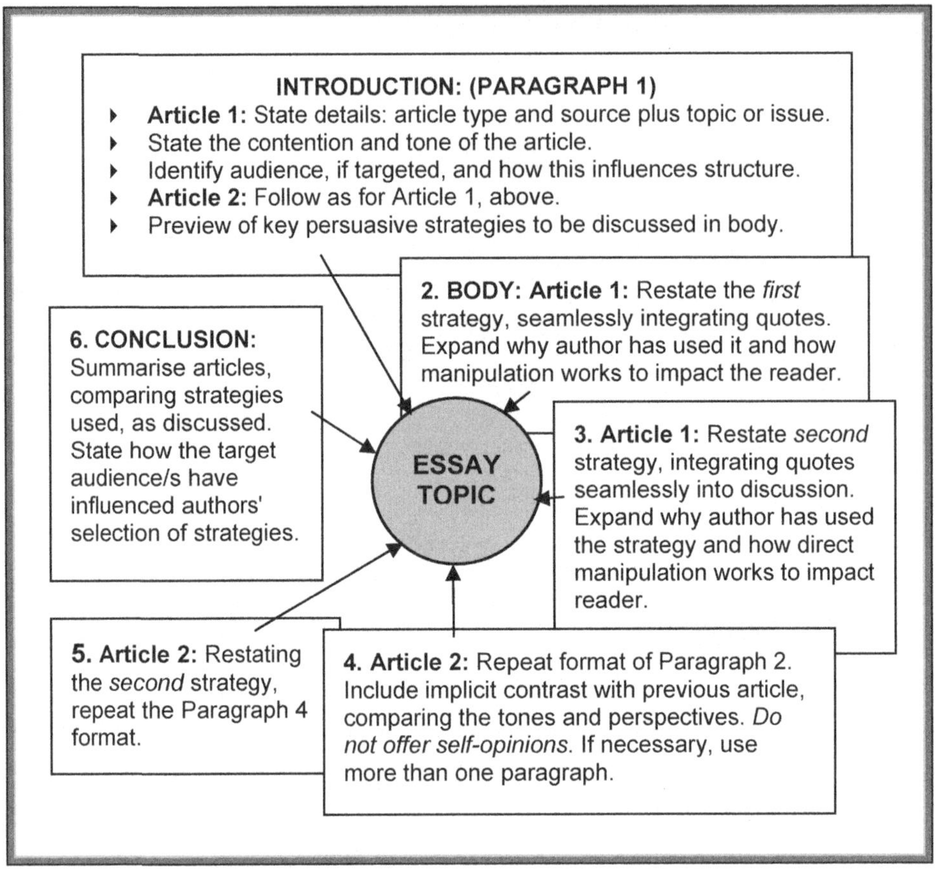

Key guidelines for writing your essays can be found in Chapter 36, page 186 and Chapter 37, page 193.

Planning practice

Unless you practise, you can forget the whole thing. During exams, the ability to plan essays *in a limited time frame* plays a key role in success. Recently, a final year student, Kee-Lin, and her father rushed in to us three weeks before final exams for emergency assistance. While Kee-Lin had performed well in class written assignments, a practice exam had just sent her into a tailspin.

In a one-hour exam, she had only produced one page of an essay!

Although quantity isn't everything, Kee-Lin had been unable to address all the issues in the exam. Why? Firstly, she had no idea that *planning* was a vital part of essay writing; secondly, that *practising* the planning phase would have brought its rewards. I cited a typical analogy of a sports star practising a special aspect of a game in preparing for a tournament. Having shown her how to plan, I suggested to Kee-Lin that she not only put in plenty of practice planning some essay topics, but also into writing quickly and legibly.

Despite her initial scepticism, after just two sessions, for a half-hour essay, Kee-Lin was preparing a clear but brief essay Plan in three minutes, and writing her essay at an average rate of five minutes a paragraph. It's a very simple strategy. But it works! Experience shows that when planning is a well-practiced exercise, it pays high dividends.

You could test this yourself, from the topics, below. Pick a subject or one from the media, a great source of popular issues. Create a question as your essay title and using current knowledge, the Internet or what you learn from a news article, practise your planning only. If you're new to it, once you have your information, aim to complete a six-paragraph Plan in ten minutes. [It would be expected, if you later write the essay, you'd be finished within half an hour, at the end of which, (as exam conditions testify) *your hand should hurt!*] So do a Plan, then grab another topic and do another one. Then select another. You'll become faster each time—and improve on your personal best with each topic. Do just ten minutes practice each night for two weeks. You'll find it a stunning confidence-booster for your next exam!

Following 'Choose a topic: Practise your planning', below, is a very valuable tool: your 12-Point Planning Checklist. This will ensure that your planning stays on track. In other words, before, during and after completing your essay Plan, it will give your brain a nudge to ensure you've addressed all the requirements. You will find another copy in the Appendix, pages 250-251, in case you want to photocopy it and put it in a prominent position.

CHOOSE A TOPIC: PRACTISE YOUR PLANNING

▪ Fast foods	▪ Gambling
▪ Drugs	▪ Equal opportunity
▪ Religious intolerance	▪ Advertising industry
▪ Political corruption	▪ Cosmetic surgery
▪ Violence in society	▪ Fashion
▪ Pollution	▪ Censorship
▪ Invasion of privacy	▪ The manipulated male
▪ The diet industry	▪ Teenage alienation
▪ Unemployment	▪ Political prisoners
▪ Animal liberation	▪ Multiculturalism
▪ Genetically modified foods	▪ Conservation and the environment

12-POINT PLANNING CHECKLIST

Point	Planning Phase 1: COMMENCEMENT—I have:	☑
1.	Read the essay question thoroughly, several times, and understand its requirements. (See pages 57-8 and 108-9.)	
2.	Identified essay type and style: eg **'argumentative' type, 'creative' type, analytical style,** etc. (See pages 108-9.)	
	Planning Phase 2: BRAINSTORMING—I have:	
3.	Reviewed 'brainstorming' guidelines (page 159); also ensured that, where appropriate, the following have been completed: **Issue-based essays:** brainstormed the perspectives, eg Political, Environmental, Social, etc, to be addressed; also Micro and Macro Views. (See pages 83-93 and 159-60.) **Creative type essays:** brainstormed action/direct speech/thoughts and plotted story line. (See pages 111-114.)	
	Planning Phase 3: RESEARCH—I have:	
4.	**Where appropriate:** if essay is an assignment, not an exam, researched data from a broad cross-section of resources (page 166). **Text analysis essays:** having thoroughly read the text (novel or play, etc), identified and highlighted human Motivators and Belief Systems in text. (See pages 139-44 and 168-71.)	
	Planning Phase 4: MAKING MY PLAN—I have:	
5.	From my notes (see 'note-taking' chapters, pages 54-65), or otherwise: **made a G-Plan, A-Plan, T-Plan or L-Plan** according to suggestions on pages 175-182, 'essay planning' chapter.	
6.	**In the 'first draft' chapter (see page 193):** reviewed the relevant section of the essay type I am planning, to confirm that my Plan has followed its guidelines. **For all essays, I have thought: 'press buttons'.**	
7.	Ensured that the Plan consists of key words or phrases, *not* lengthy sentences. (See note-taking examples, Page 60.)	
8.	**Where Main Ideas feature:** ensured they **can be linked to the essay topic.**	

12-POINT PLANNING CHECKLIST (Continued)

Point	Planning Phase 4: MAKING MY PLAN—I have:	☑
9.	**Where Main Ideas feature:** clearly noted Main Idea for each paragraph. Ensured Main Ideas have Supporting Details. **For issue-based and text analysis essays:** ensured any points to be used to elaborate Main Ideas can be supported/substantiated with precise, relevant details. **Paragraph by paragraph:** planned that each Main Idea will build upon the previous Main Idea, to give my essay sequential flow (page 191). Considered **conscious** and **subconscious** writing levels (page 192).	
10.	**For creative type essays:** planned to bring the threads of the story together to a *button-pressing* finish (page 105), ensuring resolution of any plot or sub-plots (if used). (See pages 111-2.)	
11.	**For any essays where Main Ideas feature:** planned that the conclusion (one or two paragraphs) will have a summary, with the key Main Ideas *clearly restated.* (Check chapter that deals with relevant essay type and 'Skill 8: First draft', page 193.) **For issue-based and text analysis:** planned that the summary will support and strengthen my/the main contention (see relevant essay chapter and also the 'first draft' chapter, page 196). **For language analysis:** planned summary of the issue's current situation. See Emily's essay, page 148, and also next point, below.	
12.	**For issue-based essays:** planned conclusion offering possible future directions or alternative solutions to issue (see page 195). **For language analysis essays:** compared strategies used in articles and how audience type influenced their selection (see 'first draft' chapter, page 198, also L-Plan guidelines, pages 180/182, and Emily's essay, page 148). ⌘	

Once the preparation and planning phase of your essay has been completed, you will almost be ready for your first draft. What a great feeling! Your Plan will be set out in front of you, your ideas or arguments already in place. You can be confident about what you are going to write. No more procrastination. No uncertainty. No panic attacks. But wait! What about grammar, fluency, tone and personal style? Check the next chapter to see whether these areas can be brushed up a little. Then we can go to our first draft.

Are you due for a five-minute break? I know I am!

36

Habit is second nature

Grammar, punctuation, fluency, tone, rhythm, sequential flow, plus all the other components we have discussed at greater length already, make up the package that is to become your completed essay.

Before you faint, consider this point: Do you play tennis? If so, think of all the components that make up the entire tennis package. You need to know: court etiquette, dress, equipment, line rules, net rules, how to score, fitness needs, co-ordination, foot work, how to serve, play backhand strokes, forehands, lob shots and volleys. That's 14 different features of the game. But do you have to think of all of these things as you enter a court to play? Of course not! You would certainly be a very distracted player if you did.

The reason you don't mentally contemplate all of these issues at once is the very reason that writing a good essay will become second nature to you: preparation. You have studied the tennis rules and learned how to play the game. You have taken lessons, perhaps watched videos of the tennis Opens or Wimbledon. You have practised religiously. You've honed your skills and gleaned what finer points will help you win your game. Before long you consider yourself a tennis player. The components of the game have been stamped on your memory and stored in your subconscious ready for calling upon whenever you play. And guess what? You don't even have to think about them. Why? *Consuetudo est altera natura:* 'Habit is second nature'. It is the same for any activity that is learned and practised.

So let's revisit the essay components of our opening paragraph. Then, in the next chapter, we can go through the first draft step-by-step.

Grammar and punctuation

When writing an essay, keep a good eye on your personal style; it should be lucid, individual and above all, credible. This means having a competent command of language, spelling and knowing where to put a comma or full stop.

Otherwise, be warned: no matter how insightful, lyrical or witty your personal style, your credibility as a writer will immediately fly out the window if your grammar and punctuation skills are poor. If you are writing a creative piece, for example, your *story* can be as *in*credible as you like. However, if you make a mess of it with long ungainly sentences, little punctuation and grubby work to boot, it is *you* who will be without credibility—and there's the rub! It reflects on you, personally, rather than your creativity. More to the point, you will have no buttons to press. It's the same for any essay. Your work will be considered unworthy and given a mark to match.

If you think your credibility may be at risk for the reasons mentioned, we offer a few tips. Our essay writing guidelines are presented on the assumption that you possess reasonable skills in this area. However, if you are feeling a little rusty, you should consider sourcing a text that will teach you the areas you need to know, *before it's too late*.

Your local educational bookshop is a good start. Nonetheless, to brush up on some fundamentals, turn to the Appendix on page 238 for a table of random tips on grammar and punctuation. You will also find some grammar and punctuation exercises on page 250 in the Appendix.

Fluency and tone

Both components of fluency and tone should be an integral part of your writing style and these come with practice.

Fluency

When you think of fluency, think clarity. Think of a written piece that flows gracefully through an association and connection of ideas; think of a smooth liquid. (A liquid with lumps is a text that jars.) 'Fluency Links' were introduced on page 76. They are easy to learn and will assist your fluency when crafting an essay. You'll find a list over the page.

To recap, a Fluency Link is a word or words linking ideas contained in a sentence or clause to the ideas contained in the following sentence/clause. For example: 'however,' 'nonetheless,' 'furthermore', etc. Used to commence a sentence, they may also precede clauses within a sentence, often with conjunctions such as 'or', 'and' and 'but'. (For example: 'She had not only planned her trip for this year, but furthermore, the following year as well.')

Note also that the old idea of commas separating conjunctions and conjunctive adverbs (our Fluency Links) is becoming less common (eg 'but, furthermore,') and may be written 'but furthermore,'. Also, the comma is sometimes dropped after a conjunction, even when it's not followed by a Fluency Link. It depends on the flow of the sentence the writer wants to create. Check with your teachers; they may prefer the old way.

Fluency Links allow sentences and paragraphs to hang nicely together. They alert the reader to the relationship of one idea just made, to one about to be proposed. Keep your Fluency Links close by when drafting your essays. You may think of more to add to the list.

FLUENCY LINKS

AIM	FLUENCY LINKS
To list ideas in order of priority or sequence	firstly; secondly; etc; first; second (also an option); first of all; for one; then; next; initially; finally.
To add another idea	furthermore; what is more; by the way; in addition; additionally; also; moreover; not only that; and; as well as that; besides; incidentally.
To add or introduce an opposite idea	however; nevertheless; on the other hand; but, even though; while; whilst; notwithstanding that/this; nonetheless; although; still.
To add a similar idea	similarly; likewise; also; and; into the bargain; certainly; sure; by all means.
To offer an example, to illustrate	for example; for instance; for one thing; for another thing; that is; namely.
To give a cause or reason	since; as; for; anyway; at any rate.
To give results or effects	consequently; so; yet; therefore; hence; thus; as a result; accordingly; in this respect; in this regard.
To sum up	in brief; briefly; to sum up; in summary; to summarise; in short; ideally.
To add a conclusion	in conclusion; above all; on balance; finally; as a final point; when all is said and done; in the end.
To show emphasis	of course; obviously; certainly; clearly; indeed; naturally; in fact.
To signal the nature of a comment you are about to make	interestingly; sadly; happily; unfortunately; fittingly; fortunately; funnily enough; coincidentally; strangely; regrettably (feeling sorry); regretfully (full of regret); stupidly, disturbingly; unthinkingly; on reflection; surprisingly; not surprisingly; in comparison; aptly; comparatively speaking; understandably; admittedly.

Tone

There are two aspects of 'tone' here to note: the tone of *your* writing as it pertains to a persuasive essay, for example, or a Letter to the Editor, or an instructional essay or any other type—and the tone used by others—commentators, that is, who contribute to public debate and whose tones you may be expected to identify and interpret in a language analysis essay.

When it comes to tones that *you* express, think of your *voice* coming from within your writing. Is it sharp, comforting, angry, weak, light-hearted, confronting, overbearing? Naturally, in *pressing buttons* we want only positive tones, not the negatives—so we can side-step 'weak' and 'overbearing' for starters. (You can be angry, by the way, as long as it's controlled. Listen to your *voice:* don't shout! Remain rational, allowing carefully chosen words to achieve your goal. As Emily highlighted in her essay on the climate change polemic, in the media scientist, Tim Flannery, used 'tones of reason' in responding to a columnist's blistering attack on his scientific credentials and beliefs (although he also returned a good serve of derision in defending his professional reputation). The scientist was clearly incensed by his opponent's criticisms, yet chose to interweave language restraint into a reasoned response, which heightened his convincing, educated tone and, no doubt, respect for his views. In our writing, too, we should seek acceptance and agreement or support from our readers, not alienation.

Remember, some readers may have opposing views. Your role is to sway them therefore through intelligent persuasion, not lose them through offensive or inflamed verbal posturing. Check your tone by reading your work aloud after putting it aside for at least 24 hours. That means, work smart and plan ahead! (For your language analysis essays, to assist you to identify and report the tones adopted in a public debate, check out page 247, or 'Checklists and Templates/The Tone Zone/Identifying Tone' at edworksglobal.com.)

Rhythm

Did you realise that rhythm is essential for good writing? As in music, rhythm of course is a pattern of weak and strong beats, and yes, believe it or not, it exists in the writing of words. The following exercises will help you to find it. *Re-write* the texts inserting the missing elements as explained over the page. Some words need small changes in grammar to make sense. For example, in Exercise 1, paragraph 3, the first line should read: 'Salt was treated like gold!'

Each exercise comprises a paragraph. *Be sure to punctuate and use appropriate grammar as you go.* When finished to your satisfaction, check the completed exercises on page 258. (Be aware in some cases, there may be more than one acceptable answer.) Amend your work if necessary, then read it aloud several times. It is important to pause in your speech where punctuation indicates. This will help you to feel the rhythm.

The inserted slashes indicate missing punctuation, missing or wrong letters or a missing word/words (eg 'refine / ' = 'refined'); '/ / roman' = 'the Roman'.

Exercise 1:

1. Evidence indicate / that refine / breads of / / roman era / contain / small amount / / sugar and salt as / / modern breads.
2. However / salt / / roman times play / / far less humble role outside / nobleman's kitchen.
3. / salt / treat like gold! In fact / as part of / wage / / soldiers / / Imperial / roman / army / pay / *salt money* for / sole purchase / salt—thus the derivation / / word *salary.*
4. Indeed / early as 2200 BCE / salt / value / such that / tax / impose / upon / by / Chinese / emperor.

Exercise 2:

1. Erase from / mind image / / industrial settings: / smoke stacks / / noxious effluent gushing / once pristine waterways / / cacophony / whirring / thumping / metal machinery / / smell / oil / scorching steel.
2. / expunge visions / cogs / wheels / conveyor belt /. Instead / consider / for / moment / somewhere in / microcosm / may seem obscure / separate from your own but which / nonetheless inextricably linked / a wondrous biological phenomena / / occurring.
3. Amidst / complex mixture / fragrant earth / nitrogen / fixing microbes / leguminous plants / playing out / symbiotic roles / Each gains mutual benefit / / other:
4. the microbes live in / root nodules / fixing nitrogen / use by / plant which cannot absorb / from / air; in turn / / microbe / drew / on nourishment / / roots of / host.

Exercise 3:

1. As you wander / stall / stall / relax / enjoy / experience. Visualise / dish you / prepare / home with / wealth / ingredients on offer /
2. / fresh red peppers / garlic / tomatoes / pungent fresh herbs / have you thinking / / thick sauce nestled / spaghetti.
3. A fragrant pineapple / crisp / brightly / coloured vegetable / will / you off looking / buy / new wok. Barrel / / red apple / perfumed peach / / have you headed / / park for / feast.
4. And / overlook the fact / as / pause / smell / mango / gently prod / avocado / that these / Nature's perfect foods; / culmination of / vibrant forces / life that emanate / / element / of / earth: / sun / / air, / water and / soil. Make / a part / you. / that / Nature's design.

Sequential flow

'Fluency' describes sequential flow pretty well: a text that flows, through an association and connection of ideas. However, the word 'sequential' is an important reminder of the need to ensure that paragraph-by-paragraph, each Main Idea builds upon the previous Main Idea in an ordered, sequential manner to expand the topic. But don't worry! This will be assured when you employ your essay Plan.

Creating a symphony

Regard rhythm, fluency and tone as elements in a symphony you are creating. As you read your essay to yourself aloud, listen critically and modify your work if you detect any *off* notes. Unfortunately, it's the jarring elements that people will remember. Sure, it may only represent one per cent of your entire essay, but it can have a 110 per cent negative impact!

The good news is that when you fix that one per cent, the reverse is true: it will instantly have a 110 per cent impact on enhancing your writing style.

Sometimes you don't have to do much to achieve a quantum leap in terms of improvement!

Conscious and subconscious writing

You may not have thought about it, but writing involves two levels: the conscious and the subconscious. Test it, next time you read a book or article.

Say, for example, you are writing an issue-based essay or editorial piece. The conscious level is the line of discussion that conveys your message. But messages alone can be ordinary and uninspiring. Your reader may tire and fall asleep. So you need to do something. The use of carefully chosen words, emotive language and rich or restrained imagery (depending on the mood), empowers your writing and nourishes the reader at a subconscious level. This gives an otherwise prosaic piece an emotional or persuasive edge, and offers a firm connection between the reader and writer.

For example, return for a moment to our informal persuasive piece (written as an editorial or a speech) about homelessness, beginning on page 130. Towards the end of the introduction's third paragraph, the following *message* is conveyed about John Doe, a homeless man found dead at first light of day: *He'd had his last meal at the soup kitchen. Usually he walked around all day to nowhere in particular.*

However, instead of delivering only the bare bones of the message or thought, we have embellished it with imagery and a more emotive turn of phrase: 'A watery stew had been his last meal from the soup kitchen—but hopelessness had been his daily bread, the road to nowhere his daily path.'

When read within the context of the two opening paragraphs, do you think this language brings John Doe more to life, allowing you to feel a little sorry for him? You may even feel angry with the Government for allowing it to happen. Good. This means we have delivered a message with a subconscious *hook* to elicit a reader's supportive response.

Note also that the language in the sentence is both restrained while conveying life's stark reality—('A watery stew had been his last meal from the soup kitchen')—and emotive and richly symbolic—('but hopelessness had been his daily bread, the road to nowhere his daily path.'). One technique acts as a foil to offset the other.

We see the strategy of the powerful delivery of words and emotive language all the time on television. Watching a barrister in action underlines the importance of these tactics in winning over the jury. It all boils down to the use of language. The defence uses words to play down the severity and intent of a crime. The prosecution wields its skill to heighten the emotion surrounding it. Speaking of wielding skill, with your essay Plan on the ready, let's see how good you are at transforming it into a first draft.

Don't worry! We'll guide your every step.

37

Skill 8: First draft

With all we have now learned from other chapters, let us consider the steps for putting your first draft onto paper.

Naturally, you will have your prepared essay Plan and our 12-Point Planning Checklist, from the Appendix, pages 250-251, in front of you as you work. Remember, aim for clarity! Don't get caught up with the notion of using long words. See words essentially as vehicles for your self-expression. Keep them relatively simple and your sentences concise. This will allow you to impart any complex ideas, concepts and images with clarity.

Creative and informative *style* essays:

▪ creative ▪ descriptive ▪ personal ▪ informative ▪ instructional

Introduction:

If writing a creative *type* essay, write a Statement of Intention according to your teacher's directions. Next, write your introduction following your prepared G-Plan and the advice contained in Chapter 27, 'Creative essays', page 111. (Our G-Plan example is on pages 175-6.)

Use the G-Plan example as a guide for an essay such as those mentioned above. Where no specific format has been provided by your teacher, the Funnel Approach described over the page, may suit the opening paragraph of your G-Plan essay. This can be used when a more general approach to an essay topic is called for. That is, one that doesn't begin in the style of a creative essay with speech, thoughts or action, or one that doesn't contain a vignette (a short graceful literary description).

The following example features a reflective personal essay. As you will see, the Funnel Approach encourages the writer to begin by giving a general overview of the topic before becoming more specific and setting up the Main Ideas for later discussion in the main body of the essay.

FUNNEL APPROACH
TO INTRODUCTIONS

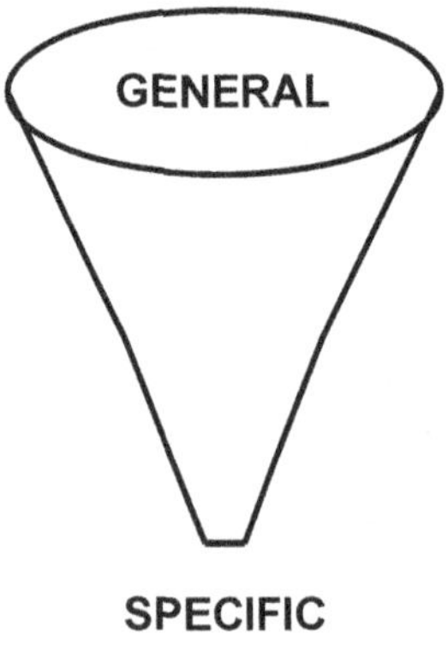

The Funnel Approach

The funnel graphic reminds our students to avoid a common mistake: using the essay title as the first sentence. This is excusable for nine-year-olds but not senior students.

For the introduction to this reflective personal essay, 'What concerns me most about growing old', an average Grade 5 student might begin: 'What concerns me most about growing old is . . .' A senior student is expected to write something along the lines of the following:

With improvements in medicine, sanitation and better living conditions, people now find that they are living longer than ever before. However, an important consideration is the degree of real pleasure and satisfaction people may experience by living longer. I would hate to think of living to 100 or more, if I couldn't enjoy life to the maximum. I remember that as a 12-year-old, I felt invincible. However, through my widowed grandmother, I've seen things of late that have begun to make me think. The atmosphere in government nursing homes makes me shudder. My grandmother is fine because she has us. But the others: I see their isolation and loneliness. I see an old man with vacant eyes and gnarled hands in a wheelchair. The nurses call him 'Doctor Watts'. A former heart specialist, he spends his day aimlessly patrolling the nursing home passages. Sometimes he charges uninvited into people's rooms. That's what I find unnerving about old age and is perhaps what concerns me most: the loss of one's mental faculties and dignity, particularly after a fruitful and meaningful career.

As the foregoing opening paragraph shows, the Funnel Approach is so named as it encourages students to view essay introductions like a funnel: broad at the top and narrow at the bottom. This means beginning your essay by generally discussing broader issues, perhaps using topical researched news events where possible. Following a general overview, you can then become more specific, introducing your Main Ideas and perhaps the essay topic in, or near, the final sentence of the first paragraph (see underlined sentence in the above example). Check pages 72-75 for further information.

Main body of essay:

Using your prepared G-Plan and the 12-Point Planning Checklist, pages 250-251, continue to develop your essay in the manner discussed, ensuring to incorporate the four criteria of *clear structure, personal style, emotional accord* and, where appropriate, *imagery.* Refer also to the G-Plan example, page 176, to help you in the early stages of your writing practice.

Conclusion:

An essay's conclusion is as important as its introduction. So think it through and make sure you *press buttons* when concluding your essay according to your Plan. Look back on the chapters dedicated to the essay type you are writing for more assistance.

Issue-based essays: ▪ argumentative ▪ persuasive

Introduction:

For an argumentative or a persuasive essay, write a Statement of Intention according to your teacher's directions. Keeping your prepared A-Plan (for argumentative essays) or G-Plan (for persuasive essays) and the 12-Point Planning Checklist handy, offer a brief overview of the issue. Clearly state whether you agree or disagree with the topic. Briefly note all the Main Ideas you intend addressing in the body of the essay. Check page 125 which deals with these essay types, as a reminder of guidelines. The introductory paragraphs there will assist you in getting underway with your own topic.

If your essay is argumentative, keep the A-Plan example on page 177 open; it may be helpful for checking points you need to review. For a persuasive essay, guidelines are on pages 129-34. A discussion on persuasive essay writing for younger students is in Chapter 24, pages 95-9, and a G-Plan example on page 96. It may prove very useful to you.

Main body of essay:

In conjunction with your prepared essay Plan and the 12-Point Planning Checklist, pages 250-251, continue to develop your essay in the manner we have discussed, ensuring you incorporate the four criteria of *clear structure, personal style, emotional accord* and, where appropriate, *imagery.* Refer also to the A-Plan example and the persuasive essay guidelines, to help you in the early stages of your writing practice.

As with any essay, the ideas in the last sentence or two of your general introduction should link up to the ideas in the first sentence or two of the essay's main body to impart sequential flow from one paragraph to the next (page 191). Check the following excerpt from our informal persuasive piece on homelessness, page 130-1. Here, we repeat the latter sentences of the general introduction in paragraph 4 and reveal the first two sentences of the main body—not previously shown—to make this point. Note also the use of two Fluency Links (underlined for your benefit) which aid the flow of ideas.

'Homelessness is not a self-inflicted condition. It is a disadvantaged human state conferred by circumstances some call "fate" and sustained by a grossly inadequate, government fiscal policy. <u>Yes, the Government can spend a lot more to fight this growing problem.</u>

``````````````````````````````````````````````````````````
``````````````````````````````````````````````````````````

Disturbingly, however, the Government is spending less! Funding for public housing was slashed by almost half, last financial year—a sum of $247 million—attributable largely to federal funding cuts, and rendering our most vulnerable citizens worse off than those in any other state or territory. (Cook; 2014)'

The body of your essay should contain some three or so more paragraphs developing each Main Idea one by one (in the case above, perhaps beginning with: 'John Doe returned from Vietnam a heroic but damaged man.') For argumentative and persuasive essays, develop *each paragraph* as follows:

1. Clearly state the Main Idea (wherever appropriate in the paragraph, usually, but not necessarily, at the beginning).
2. Develop the point, explaining in detail and stating its relevance to the topic. Remember, your aim is to expand the topic.
3. Substantiate each point with precise, relevant examples. Executed properly, this will provide an insight into your grasp of the topic.

Conclusion:

As mentioned, an essay's conclusion is as important as its introduction. You are seeking to maintain a positive impact on your readers. Keep this in mind as you consider your strategy for sustaining their attention.

For issue-based essays remember to restate your position on the essay topic. Bring all your ideas together to support and strengthen your overall contention. One strategy in the Pressing Buttons Department is to propose future directions of research or suggest alternative issues that you believe should have been incorporated in the essay topic. This should please your examiners: it will show you can think for yourself. For example, you might say: 'Future governments might consider (this strategy) . . .' or 'A United Nations policy where all nations are brought to understand the problem may be a solution.' Avoid 'I' statements, however, such as 'I believe that . . .' And remember, the conclusion is not the place to introduce a new idea!

Text analysis essays:

Introduction:

Complete your Statement of Intention. With your completed 'Text Analysis Checklist' and 'T-Plan Guidelines' in front of you, offer a brief overview of the novel or work, stating your position relative to the topic question/s. That is, the essay question may infer blame upon a character or situation and ask you to discuss it. You should therefore establish in your introduction, a point of view as to whether blame is justified or otherwise. The Main Ideas to be addressed in the body of the essay should be clearly and briefly stated, linking them to the position statement, and thus the topic.

When adopting a stance, or observing that of an author, remember convention. Do not write in the first person such as, 'I believe that . . .' Consider the texts you read in the media. Journalists generally remove themselves from the personal view and write in the third person. Note an example of writing style taken from our essay on Orwell's 'Animal Farm':

'Set in the English countryside, George Orwell's timeless novel, "Animal Farm", is a political satire on Stalinism and the Russian Revolution. The satirical nature of the novel, with pigs depicted as the ruling caste, clearly reflects Orwell's contempt for the revolutionary and leadership processes. Importantly, it also offers a critical insight into the inherent weaknesses of the revolutionary process.' (See page 141 for more.)

For your text analysis essay, keep the T-Plan example on page 179 bookmarked; it may be helpful for checking any points you need to review, especially in the early stages of your writing practice.

Main body of essay:
In conjunction with your prepared essay T-Plan and the 12-Point Planning Checklist, pages 250-251, continue to develop your essay in the manner discussed, ensuring to incorporate the four criteria of 'clear structure', 'personal style', 'emotional accord' and, where appropriate, 'imagery'. When addressing the second and remaining paragraphs in your essay, ensure there is a link to the essay topic or a common idea pertinent to the topic that leads from one paragraph to the other. See a reminder illustrating this point, beginning the penultimate paragraph on page 195.

The body of your essay should involve some four or more paragraphs developing each Main Idea one by one in the following manner:

1. Clearly state the Main Idea (wherever appropriate in the paragraph, usually, but not necessarily, at the beginning).

2. All the points made to develop the Main Idea should be fully supported or substantiated with the use of specific relevant examples from the text: quoted dialogue or descriptive passages. Without this substantiation, you may as well pack up and take a holiday. The whole point of the essay exercise is to illustrate to the teacher/examiner that you have read the novel or work properly, dissecting it chapter by chapter and putting it under a microscope. In turn, this has enabled you to not only study the human Motivators and Belief Systems integrated into the story line, but to acquire insight into, and form opinions about, the authors strategies and intentions. *It shows you can think for yourself!* Remember, there are two questions examiners ask as they pick up your essay:

(i) Does this student understand the text?
(ii) How well is the understanding demonstrated?

Imagine a searchlight beaming from their foreheads. Will your effort stand up to the scrutiny? Better still, will it stand *out?*

As you develop your work, always step back from it and judge it from the reader's angle. When quoting from texts to support a point, be short and precise and don't overdo their use. Avoid quoting merely for the sake of quoting. Use your own words to express your ideas and personal style, thereby removing any tendency to plagiarise. Constantly refer back to the essay question/s to ensure your writing is on target and relating to the topic. In other words, don't wander off on your own little pilgrimage. Stay within the parameters of the topic and respond only to *what the task is demanding.*

Conclusion:

There is little point in crafting a strong essay if the conclusion lets you and your readers down. So think it over carefully, jot down a few notes and deliver a great finish that reflects the attention you have given it.

Over one or two paragraphs, your conclusion should be imaginatively and thoughtfully presented, restating the Main Ideas covered in the essay and also restating your position on the essay topic. Your Main Ideas should culminate in such a way as to both support and strengthen your contention.

Your conclusion should aim not only to achieve this end, but to also provide a quality that raises your work above that of your peers. Classroom discussions are common to everyone, so present your work in a manner that reflects further ideas or introspection. Follow the philosophy of working smart and use your time effectively so that you can plan ahead and *think your ideas through.* Look beyond being ordinary. Aim for excellence!

Language analysis essays:

You'll need a kitbag of support tools for this essay. As well as enlarged copies of your highlighted articles and your completed L-Plan, you might source:

1. The 'Language Analysis Checklist', page 242 (for reviewing any point).
2. The L-Plan Essay Guidelines, page 182, (as backup during the early stages of your writing practice).
3. The 'Clauses and Phrases for Plaudits and Praise' checklist, page 246, will aid your expression of commentator strategies. An expanded version is on the Edworks website, edworksglobal.com; click Checklists and Templates.
4. 'Identifying tone', page 247, will help you to distinguish writer tone of voice.

Introduction:

Begin your essay with a Statement of Intention, guided by your teacher. You are expected to adopt formal language, so be clear and precise in your choice of words. Emily's essay, page 148, may prove a useful reference. Your introduction should contain an overview of your selected articles and include:

- the details of each article, including the format, source and dates
- the contentions, writer tone and readerships stated
- a preview of the key persuasive strategies about to be discussed

Main body of essay:

In conjunction with your prepared L-Plan, your selected articles and the tools in your kitbag, just mentioned, continue to develop your essay in the manner we've discussed, ensuring you incorporate the four criteria of *clear structure, personal style, emotional accord* and, where appropriate, *imagery.* (Remember Emily's use of metaphor, for example, in her introductory paragraph, page 148: 'Tim Flannery stoked the fire of debate').

In the main body of your essay, follow a simple format, systematically identifying the key strategies in each article and detailing why and how they have been used to manipulate and influence the readers. When reintroducing each article, give the title and writer's name, noting the general tone. Where relevant, expand on the writers' contentions, and describe their target readers. Be aware, your article quotes should be seamlessly integrated into your discussion. Again I stress, your role is to analyse the *language,* not the issue: the language strategies used, and what intentions to influence the reader—in order to achieve certain outcomes—lie behind them.

As a rule of thumb, dedicate one paragraph to each strategy, although shorter essays may demand more than one strategy to a paragraph. This is conceivable where, a writer perhaps uses an inclusive pronoun (strategy 27) while appealing to pride (strategy 6) by saying: 'We, as thinking people . . .'

After discussing the strategies in article one, proceed to article two. Remember to compare and/or contrast the strategies, intentions, tones and stances of your cited articles. Tones and stances may change at times as writers develop their arguments. For example, for effect, a writer may support aspects of an opposing view to offer a balanced perspective. Such changes in tone and/or stance should be identified and defined in your essay.

Conclusion:

For the desired impact, your conclusion is as important as your introduction! So wield a little strategy of your own and press a final button or two. Re-read your essay and think it through. Keep your eye on the ball then give it your best shot.

Having crafted your essay, a conclusion should draw the threads of your paragraphs into a confident summation which compares/contrasts the articles' strategies. Note that when the minds of writer and reader meet over controversial issues, the power of language and strategy pose an interesting dynamic. To demonstrate the depth of your analysis, your summary might therefore explore the question, does symbiosis exist between writer and reader and, if so, wherein lies (if any) the greater influence: reader upon the writer (whose strategies are tailored to fit the reader) or the strategy, itself, upon the reader.

On completion of any essay

Before turning off the desk light, check off your 12-Point Planning Checklist, pages 250-251, or make any necessary amendments. Then put your essay aside for a day or so before editing. This allows a more objective review of your work plus you may have a flash of inspiration that you'll later wish to add.

Checking for the four essay writing criteria

You've now finished your edit, so how does your essay stand up as a whole? Remember in our 'planning' chapter, page 173, we discussed the four criteria: *clear structure, personal style, emotional accord* and *imagery*. Although you should aim for all four, the weight assigned to each will depend on the essay type. Even so, a good essay will display all four elements to best effect.

To assist you in addressing this question, having given your essay an honest appraisal, assign a mark out of five for each of the essential essay writing criterion in the following table. For example, if you have written an economics or history-based, argumentative essay, the presence of *clear structure* and *personal style* should be in high evidence, while *imagery* and *emotional accord* might be less so. If you have given appropriate weight to each criterion you might therefore score 5 for *clear structure* and *personal style,* and perhaps 1 or 2 for *imagery* and 1 for *emotional accord.* Naturally, were you submitting a persuasive piece (for example, a 'Letter to the Editor' where emotive language techniques are used), you might expect that *emotional accord* would feature more prominently and perhaps score 3 to 5. A creative piece would probably see all four components receiving equal consideration.

CRITERIA TO INCLUDE IN ESSAYS

How did you do? Give each essential essay writing component a score out of five, according to the weight of its presence.

Clear structure	**/5**	**Personal style**	**/5**
Emotional accord	**/5**	**Imagery**	**/5**

This exercise will help you to address, recognise and move away from the 'list of events' approach to your writing, discussed on page 174.

Remember, your aim should always be to transcend the mere *reporting* of ordinary, dry and unpalatable information. As a writer, your obligation is to present appealing and appetising work; to impart style and, where appropriate, to write with *insight*, imagination and wit. Above all, you must engage and *entertain* your reader!

Ignorance is not bliss!

Do you wish your writing or debating skills could set you apart? Well, there is no magic. You don't even have to have a brilliant mind—your brain just needs *stimulation* and *exercise*.

So, number one, *become aware* of what is needed. Then take action to achieve that wish!

Here's the nub: Become a listener, become an observer, and become a reader of literature and media issues. Unless you have a sound background knowledge of community and current affairs, how else are you to evaluate issues and their relevant research with any depth of understanding? Test it for a week and *feel* the power of awareness; feel your confidence soar!

Concluding paragraph—example:

To finish, we present the concluding paragraph of our argumentative essay, 'Does the Internet serve democracy?' Although not shown in full, this essay's introduction was used as an issue-based example (see page 128). The essay was also used to demonstrate the A-Plan format on page 177.

Here, we use the essay again to illustrate a conclusion that exhibits sound and clear structure and a convincing personal style that is given further weight through a well-chosen, age-old quotation in the last line.

The concluding penultimate paragraph has not been given here. However, you need only be aware that it briefly summarises the essay's Main Ideas found in the introduction, (page 128) of 'transparency, the information-rich/information-poor debate', and 'the absence of political, geographic and other boundaries'. The essay then concludes:

The Internet may be young, but it has already served democracy well in regions such as Bosnia and East Timor, and against powerful military governments which met their end during the Arab Spring. Through a war of words the East Timorese, the Libyans and the Egyptians, for example, were able to awaken the world to the oppression and often, atrocities, occurring behind their closed borders. The subsequent withdrawal of the Indonesian military in East Timor and the overthrow of the decades-long, dictatorial regimes in North Africa have consequently inspired other oppressed peoples to take up the fight and not to give in. This demonstrates, quintessentially, the power of the Internet in serving democracy and above all, that the pen once more has proven mightier than the sword.

38

Skill 9: Editing your essay

A perfect first draft is quite uncommon. Practically unheard of, in fact!

Even the world's top writers put their drafts aside for a spell. They then return to them afresh to prune and strengthen them. This allows objectivity and the assurance that the writers are producing their very best work. They often also show their manuscripts to others for reviewing. With these thoughts in mind, this is how you might now proceed.

Once your draft is completed, you need to do about five things:

1. Check it against the 12-Point Planning Checklist (pages 250-251) and amend any text, if needed.
2. Set it aside for *at least* a day. (Two or three days are better.)
3. Read the draft aloud.
4. Correct the flaws (neatly, if written by hand).
5. If appropriate, ask your teacher to review it for you.

You will gauge from this that you need to plan ahead as discussed. Time management is crucial when undertaking an essay assignment. If you are required to produce your essay assignments entirely in class, a teacher review of your draft/s is unlikely to be possible. However, if you are not governed by this, producing your draft as far ahead as possible will improve your chances of your teacher agreeing to look it over before you proceed to final copy. Therefore, you should ideally allow three weeks from the time you complete your first draft to the due date. No teacher wants a bunch of pupils clambering for attention a week before final submissions are due.

Having ensconced yourself in the privacy of a room, armed with your draft and a coloured pen, read the essay aloud. Our pupils are taught to do this as a vital part of the editing process. This enables them to use two senses at the same time: sight *and* sound. When reading silently, we tend to focus on the meaning of the passage and may overlook repetitious words or poor grammar. Reading aloud provides a double-checking mechanism.

As you edit, check the draft again against the 12-Point Planning Checklist for omissions: have you followed your Plan point-by-point? Have you made a conscious effort towards self-expression, grammar and punctuation; towards the fluency, rhythm and tone of your work? Listen for that symphony. Do you detect any off notes? As you check your work, if you are writing by hand, make your corrections neatly. This aids clarity if your teacher reads it prior, and when you address your final copy.

If possible, asking your teacher to review your work is a great shortcut to identifying the flaws in your presentation of ideas or writing style. It's like doing a trial run. I didn't discover the value of this until university, and wish I had employed it more during my last years at school. With a teacher's help, your essay writing will improve in leaps and bounds.

But be warned! Teachers definitely appreciate initiative and are usually pretty obliging. However, don't go rushing in waving drafts under their noses at the last minute. (You see why you need leeway of about three weeks?) Teachers are busy people. If you ask them to review your work, you should at least extend the courtesy of giving them adequate time to fulfil your request.

Once your draft is returned, make the appropriate amendments, produce your final copy and submit your essay on or before the due date.

Well done! If you have diligently used our guidelines, you should be on your way to achieving a mark to be proud of. Not only that, with continued practice your knowledge will become second nature and your skills—skills for life!

Before we leave this subject however, we need to review some helpful key points for sitting for exams. Our closing chapter will then provide you with plenty of material for staying focussed and on track, and for developing and fine-tuning those all-important skills for working smart.

39

Preparing for exams

There is no escaping it! The responsibility for exam preparation rests firmly on your shoulders alone.

In a sense, you have to be your own coach. To use our tennis analogy, if you were about to enter a tennis tournament for the first time, there is no way a good coach would allow you *not* to be ready. All your preparation, your practice and refining of skills would be completed well before the eve of the tournament. In fact, to be in the winning stakes, a week away from a tennis tournament—and an exam as well—your skills should be as sharp and keen as it's been humanly possible to make them. In fact, the last week should be dedicated only to quiet practice and a little fine-tuning, and *not* with an expectation to achieve great strides in performance.

It is a time to say to yourself, 'I have achieved my skills through constant practice. Therefore I *know* I can do well.'

Big pay-off for a small investment

If you have incorporated exam preparation time as part of your weekly study routine, there is no reason this should not be so. The maths look like this: setting aside just 45 minutes a *week* for 30 weeks of a school year means you will have assigned more than 22 hours to examination preparation time even *before* the exam looms. Whether you spend the time on a weekend or as part of your weekly study timetable is up to you. Importantly, your reward system should also be a part of your study routine.

How can we rationalise such preparation if exams are months away?

We all know that the capacity of the human brain is greatly under-utilised—so there's plenty of room! Look upon exam study as systematically acquiring skills and knowledge (the purpose of learning, after all; of equipping yourself for adult life and your future career) and storing it in your brain cells week-by-week. The pay-off will far outweigh your small investment.

For optimum impact, I strongly encourage you to commence your 30-week exam study program no later than five weeks into the new school year.

Spend the time you allocate, making exam study notes. Don't forget the note-taking advice on pages 54-65. Then, add to and review your notes regularly. Ensure you completely understand topics; if you don't, ask your teacher! Use your time to memorise quotes and formulae. If you adopt this working smart strategy, you can count on it: you will be up there with the best of students at exam time, less stressed, and primed for the last few weeks of steady preparation. No matter what objectors may say, cramming is stressful and nowhere near as productive as establishing a weekly exam-study routine.

The prima donna syndrome

Do you become a bit of a prima donna at exam time? If so, shame on you! There are higher ways to achievement. Occasionally, I speak to parents who are wringing their hands and bearing the scars of battle with their teenage children as a result of exam time stress. It is unnecessary, and usually occurs when students adopt an exaggerated sense of self-importance. They believe their final year gives them carte blanche to strut about the house on a short fuse, ready to snap the head off anyone who dares challenge them. They operate on the principle that 'if I have to suffer, you can all suffer with me'!

Some well-intentioned parents believe that to avoid rocking the boat, it is a cross they must bear. This can lead to a power switch, where the obnoxious student takes unfair advantage of parents who have adopted accommodating behaviour. Clearly this is a *lose-lose* situation for everyone and above all, for the student. Throwing your weight around will earn you no points for integrity, respecting others, exercising dignity and maintaining a pleasant disposition. Not only that, it bodes poorly for your skills as an adult and suggests a continuum of selfish and unsatisfactory future behaviour.

Study and the stress associated with it should really be seen as a long-term advantage. It is a time for personal growth. It should be viewed positively by students and parents alike as the student's rehearsal for adulthood; as a time for displaying strength of character by showing common sense and goodwill to others, when under stress.

And that is the test. Anyone can be pleasant when things are going well. So if you tend to get a little steamed up and crotchety around exam time, take a minute to look back over the chapters on stress beginning on page 43. Sound time management and positive thinking are the basic answers to keeping a lid on stressful outbursts. This means no procrastination and getting down to study in plenty of time in a peaceful environment. Once the source of the stress is removed, you may surprise yourself what a thoroughly nice person you really are.

Concentration fuel

When studying for your exams, here's another no-no to consider: for keeping your brain cells jumping and to extract the most from your study time, treat junk foods like a virus. High sugar energy drinks and caffeine will give you a lift, sure. But they will just as quickly dump you without mercy, just when you need your concentration most. Fatty foods can make you sleepy; salty foods, thirsty. So do your poor body a favour and look after it: snack on an apple or a banana or munch on a carrot! Prepare them on a plate before you start or during your FMB.

Prep

Let's assume you have followed our guidelines and put in plenty of practice. Here are some final points to consider as you prepare for exams:

- In the months leading up to your exams, you should have written up your exam study notes on each topic, using the note-taking skills you have practised from pages 54-65.

- You should also have practised doing speedy essay writing Plans (see 'essay planning' chapter, pages 176-82). Do your Plans quickly and time yourself. Apart from homework assignments, you should practise Plans when preparing your study notes for exams, when you are doing a practice exam or even by getting together with friends and making up exam questions together.

- Just prior to the exams, don't panic and don't over dramatise! You're not going to war, you're not making a maiden speech in parliament, your head is not about to come off. It is merely an exam.

- As a study aid, you might use mental images of animals and so on to link them to different aspects of your topics. Acronyms can be useful, too. For example: 'PEACSI' might help you recall the four key criteria for your essays: **P**ersonality (Personal style), **E**motional **A**ccord, **C**lear **S**tructure and **I**magery. Understanding their meanings, by association you will introduce other significant features such as Main Ideas and Supporting Details. The perspectives required for issue-based essays might be remembered as PEPSMEMM (**P**olitical, **E**conomic, **P**sycho-logical, **S**ocial, **M**oral and **E**nvironmental, plus **M**icro/**M**acro).

- On exam day, make sure you're physically comfortable. Check your writing aids (at least three good pens, sharpened pencil and rubber) and don't allow others' trivial chatter to undermine your confidence.

- Once seated, breathe evenly and remember, you are well prepared. For some, the fear of the unknown means this is the most stressful time of all. But *you* are ready and have the skills to do well. A reminder: you are not about to face a firing squad! It's only an exam.

- During the reading phase before you are allowed to write, read *all* instructions carefully, including if appropriate, the script book covers. When the supervisor gives the word to write, clearly fill in your candidate number *immediately.* If you leave this until the end, you may forget it or run out of time and the whole exercise will be wasted.

- During the reading phase also, if you are reading a multiple-choice question, a thumbnail indentation will help to indicate your choice when you come to write. Don't assume you will always remember.

- Once writing, you will be operating at conscious and subconscious levels. If an answer won't come to you, don't panic; it's there, just waiting for you to calm down a bit. Leave it alone and go on with another paragraph or something else. It will come to you later.

- Once you are writing, if you have been asked not to mark the exam question paper and an idea comes to you that might be, say, three questions away, write a key trigger word very lightly in pencil beside the question and carefully rub it out later. Don't assume you will remember when you come to the question. Chances are, you won't.

- Time management is critical. You have several phases to consider: your planning phase, answering each question and reviewing.

- When faced with a choice of written responses, 'feeling comfortable' about a topic may be misleading. So ask yourself, 'Can I think of, say, four Main Ideas (that relate specifically to the topic)?' This helps you to choose the one that suits your knowledge the best. Be aware also that longer questions usually contain more guidelines than generic questions that simply say, 'discuss'. Longer questions often have the Main Ideas built-in for you and may be easier to follow than generic questions involving your interpretation of the question (a hazardous path if you wander off the topic). This is a common problem even at tertiary level. Recently, I gave a guest lecture at a local university and in discussion afterwards with the lecturer, she commented that 60 per cent of her students were going to fail their most recent written assignment due to *their inability to stick to the topic.*

- If writing an essay, naturally we wish to avoid shadow behaviour or old faulty habits due to panic. So write systematically, using time as your guide to ensure control: for a half-hour essay, allocate about five minutes per paragraph. With ten minutes to go, if you've misjudged time and are left short, immediately start modifying your conclusion. You should be operating at two levels: be involved in your writing but at the same time look over your own shoulder to objectively check what you're doing. Once, a pupil told me he achieved this by asking himself, 'What would Edworks tell me to do?' This kept him on track in the exam.
- Edit as you go.
- Do *exactly* what questions ask; not just parts of them. Lightly pencil-highlight key words in the question and make sure you respond to them. Do a quick Plan before you begin your answer. Then tick off the points in your Plan as you check the points of the essay question. Physically checking in this way will keep you on the ball.
- It's important to remember to *only answer what is asked.* Do not invent your own questions.
- Fine-tune your exam paper if you have time after completing it. If you amend areas, use correction tape or cleanly cross out what you don't want. Correction fluid wastes precious time and can make a mess if you are rushed. Worse, you may forget to write in vital information.
- Once you've left the exam, put it behind you. Move on to the next one. Don't be influenced by others' behaviour and remember, too, how you feel as you leave won't necessarily reflect the outcome.

With all your exams over, it will be a time for celebration and claiming the well deserved rewards you promised yourself. Unfortunately, I need to remind you that these pleasures await you in the future. Right now, I assume you are reading these pages to give yourself the optimum opportunity for a strong performance and successful study year/s ahead.

There is still much to do. Our following practice chapter will assist you in bringing our essay writing guidelines together and give you an easy weekly program to follow.

A wise person once said:

'There's no time like the present to begin.'

40

Reach for the sky

Click! . . . Click! . . . Click! Who is the solitary lad in Shepherd Street, scuffing his feet under a clear Australian sky, and what is he doing? It is a young Don Bradman practising his cricket, striking a golf ball with a cricket stump against a brick tank stand in the yard.

Thwack! . . . Thwack! Who is the boy on the beach, laughing with friends under a bright West Indian sun, and what is he doing? It is a young Garfield Sobers, practising his cricket with a makeshift ball and bat.

With the passing of the supreme, Australian batsman, Sir Donald Bradman, at age 91, a book he had authorised revealed he had regarded West Indian cricket legend, Sir Garfield Sobers, as 'the best of the best'.

Consider for a moment: what gave these men of might their greatness? Inherent skill? Genius? Gritty determination? Of Bradman, English batsman, Lord Cowdrey, once wrote, 'He had astonishing fleetness of foot, sharpness of eye and timing, but it was his mind that powered his success.' Of Sobers, Professor Henry Fraser of the University of the West Indies has said, his desire to do well combined with 'a rare ability to concentrate on the task in hand, to apply himself to the task, and to enjoy every minute of it.'

Is greatness really inherent?

With the brilliance of Bradman and Sobers in mind, you might ask, what makes some people more successful than others? Are they, as the saying goes, 'born great'? Truth to tell, success rarely springs from natural skill alone—innate ability needs a helping hand! On pages 27-28, we discussed that the path to success begins with 'awareness'. Remember, the equation went like this:

Awareness + Motivation + Skills = Working Smart

Awareness, we found, is our starting block: there, we learn *what* to do! But our actual success lies in knowing the *how* of things, where we develop the skills to achieve our goals. And like the young Sobers swinging his home-made bat in the salty Caribbean air or the young Bradman swatting a golf ball with a narrow cricket stump hour after hour—to achieve personal success you can count on it: *practice* plays a major role!

Hold that thought! Putting our working smart guidelines to use, let's look at ways of converting *what* we know, into the *how* of achieving our goals. Every student is encouraged to learn from this chapter. The answer lies in regular practice—exercises readily slotted into a weekly timetable that won't intrude greatly on your study commitments. This means gaining the skills for success can become part of your routine. Seniors, these exercises will prove useful for your exam preparation, discussed in the last chapter. Once you're in the swing, the more practice you put in, the easier it will be.

Above all, don't throw in the towel before you give yourself a chance. Sure, it will be irksome at first. New activities often are! Overcoming procrastination and getting started is the key. So, give yourself the challenge and if you want it *enough,* motivation will follow. Focus on your goals and the sweet rewards riding on their fulfilment. Then—become your own coach. Aim a little higher each time you improve. Who knows, by applying yourself to the task in hand, like the great Garry Sobers, you might even enjoy every minute of it!

Time Out 15

Okay, here's the drill: find and boldly mark the cover of a standard exercise book: 'Time Out 15'.

You've guessed it! All you need to do is take time out, 15 minutes a day, five days a week to practise and hone your new skills. Remarkably, if you dedicated this small amount of time to the final two years of your senior schooling (for an average 40 weeks a year), you would notch up a gigantic *one hundred* extra hours towards skill development. How bad can that be?

Your Time Out 15 exercises are already written into a timetabling format for easy use. Don't cheat! Remember, each day requires at least 15 minutes, but longer *if you choose.* However, don't allow extra time spent to compromise your study assignments. Note your Time Out 15 commitments on your regular study timetable so as not to forget them. Refer to this section of the book for your daily suggested exercises. Why not tag it now for later?

The first thing is to ensure that you know the basics of grammar and punctuation. Once that's done, we'll systematically go through some tuning up exercises covering everything from brainstorming to editing. If your G. and P. don't need brushing up, get hold of a news article, book or magazine instead, and for 15 minutes try identifying text fluency, personal style, tone and rhythm. Find material you can mark if possible, highlighting noteworthy sections or jot notes in the margins. Reference any such areas in your Time Out 15 exercise book and keep the text handy or filed away clearly labelled; you may need it later. Stationers sell filing boxes with lids if you don't have a special drawer.

Before commencing a Time Out 15 exercise, identify and tag this book's chapter dealing with the essay type to be tackled. Next, check the chart below and tag the principal Guideline Chapters for reference as you plan and write your essays.

Don't forget rewards; they'll fire up your motivation to begin.

TIME OUT 15

GUIDELINE CHAPTERS	PAGE	GUIDELINE CHAPTERS	PAGE
SKILL 5: Brainstorming	159	Habit is second nature	186
SKILL 6: Doing your research	166	SKILL 8: First draft	193
SKILL 7: Planning your essay	172	SKILL 9: Editing your essay	202

To keep track of the exercises you've done, in the correct 'day' column of the following pages, fill in the date you complete the exercise. You may later repeat the exercise using a different topic, so start at the top to leave room.

WEEK 1 **Time Out 15**

DAY	EXERCISES FOR WORKING SMART
MONDAY	**1.** Refer to our 'Grammar and Punctuation Tips' in the Appendix, on page 238. Revise your understanding of the first section headed, 'What is?'. Begin using newly learned tips in all writing, including your essay writing. Otherwise, read as suggested. **2.** Refer to the creative titles, page 118, in our chapter on 'Creative essays'. During the week, give conscious thought to ideas that you could use for three different creative type essays. Younger pupils: think of nursery rhymes and fairy stories. Take any two stories, for example, 'The Three Little Pigs' and 'Little Red Riding Hood'. Plot a new story using all their characters. Consider others. Think, 'clever twists'. You'll be asked to record your topics later in the week.
TUESDAY	Refer to our 'Grammar and Punctuation Tips' on page 238. Revise your understanding of the latter section headed, 'When do I use?' Incorporate newly learned tips in your essay writing. Otherwise read as suggested on the previous page, paragraph 3.
WEDNESDAY	Exercises for rhythm, and grammar and punctuation improvement are in Chapter 36, page 189-90. Do one program a week until competent. Once happy with your skills, read a preferred text for 15 minutes in coming weeks, identifying writing criteria, fluency, personal style, tone, rhythm, etc. as suggested on page 211. Highlight and reference selected texts for later.
THURSDAY	Referring to Exercise 2 on Monday, revisit, think about storylines and plots, and record the titles of three different creative *type* essays.
FRIDAY	Using the Triad or Cluster Methods, (pages 161 and 163), brainstorm ideas for the three creative type essay titles from yesterday. (This has been an easy week. Consider it a warm-up!)

Time Out 15 **WEEK 2**

EXERCISES FOR WORKING SMART	DAY
1. If necessary, continue your revision of 'Grammar and Punctuation Tips', page 238, (the same as last Monday)—or read as suggested. **2.** Select a creative essay writing topic from Friday. Using the G-Plan format, pages 175-6, plan the paragraphs in your exercise book within the Time Out 15 timeframe. (You will be expected to become faster with familiarity and practice.)	**MONDAY**
1. If necessary, continue your revision of 'Grammar and Punctuation Tips', page 238, (the same as last Tuesday) or read as suggested. **2.** Writing clearly and quickly, complete the first two paragraphs of your creative type essay, using your planned G-Plan as a guide. Use the Fluency Links, page 188, the Verb-Speak list, page 241 in the Appendix, and the 12-Point Planning Checklist, page 250. Remember the Time Out 15 timeframe.	**TUESDAY**
As for last Wednesday, complete exercises for rhythm and grammar and punctuation improvement, pages 189-90. Do a program a week until competent. Once happy with your skills, read a preferred book or magazine for 15 minutes in the ensuing weeks, identifying writing criteria as suggested on page 211. Remember to use your exercise book for referencing.	**WEDNESDAY**
Having put your creative essay paragraphs aside for a day, edit your text, referring to our editing chapter on page 202 for guidance. Practise clean corrections, using a line to cross out mistakes if hand writing your text. Any insertions should be neat and legible.	**THURSDAY**
Select a descriptive type essay topic from the list on page 122. Using your preferred method (Triad or Cluster, pages 161 or 163), brainstorm ideas for the essay.	**FRIDAY**

WEEK 3 **Time Out 15**

DAY	EXERCISES FOR WORKING SMART
MONDAY	**1.** Continue, if needed, revision of 'Grammar and Punctuation Tips' (as last Monday). **2.** If on the Internet, research an aspect or two of the descriptive essay topic you brainstormed on Friday. Otherwise, attempt to locate background information from the news media or other sources on hand, eg a place on a map; old family photographs, information from an encyclopaedia, etc.
TUESDAY	**1.** Continue, if needed, revision of 'Grammar and Punctuation Tips', (as last Tuesday). **2.** Using the G-Plan, page 175-6, plan the paragraphs for your descriptive essay, with the 12-Point Planning Checklist, pages 250-251, as a guide. Refer to the appropriate descriptive essay writing chapter, page 120. If choosing to describe the topic details through your or another's eyes, consider a vignette (see page 130), or the Funnel Approach (pages 72 and 194).
WEDNESDAY	Write the first two paragraphs of your descriptive essay using your planned G-Plan as a guide. Refer to Fluency Links, page 188, the Verb-Speak list, page 241, (Appendix) and the 12-Point Planning Checklist, pages 250-251. Note the points made on Tuesday regarding the Funnel Approach. *Write clearly and quickly.* Remember the Time Out 15 timeframe.
THURSDAY	G. and P. Or if successfully revised, read a preferred book or text for 15 minutes identifying writing criteria (page 211) as already discussed. Remember, record references you may need later in your exercise book.
FRIDAY	Edit the text of your descriptive essay paragraphs, checking the editing chapter, page 202. A reminder: practise clean corrections, using a line to cross out mistakes. If using the computer, print out and edit *by hand,* for practice. Keep any insertions neat/legible.

Time Out 15 **WEEK 4**

EXERCISES FOR WORKING SMART	DAY
Today, revisit our personal essays chapter, pages 122-4. Select a personal essay topic from page 123. Using your preferred method (Triad or Cluster), pages 161-3, brainstorm ideas for the essay.	**MONDAY**
Research the personal topic, if necessary. You may need to make research phone calls (family or other relatives) or check dates, geographical features or photographs as background material. (Discussing grandpa's pigeons for 15 minutes doesn't count, unless its part of your essay.) Otherwise, use your time productively by reading, as discussed.	**TUESDAY**
Using the G-Plan, page 175-6, plan the paragraphs for your personal essay, using the 12-Point Planning Checklist, pages 250-1, as a guide. Refer, to the appropriate chapter, pages 122-4, for further guidance, and others you have earmarked, as required.	**WEDNESDAY**
Write the first two paragraphs of your personal essay using your planned G-Plan as a guide. Refer to Fluency Links, page 188 and the 12-Point Planning Checklist, pages 250-251. Remember the Time Out 15 timeframe. *Write clearly and quickly.*	**THURSDAY**
Edit what you have written so far of your personal essay referring to our editing chapter on page 202 for guidance and adhering to the usual suggestions regarding clean corrections. Then continue writing and complete paragraphs 3 and 4. Write speedily and neatly. Edit these paragraphs on Monday.	**FRIDAY**

NOTES:

WEEK 5 **Time Out 15**

DAY	EXERCISES FOR WORKING SMART
MONDAY	Edit Friday's paragraphs. Select an argumentative issue-based essay topic from page 126 and brainstorm your ideas using an enlarged photocopy of the Brainstorming Issue-based Essays Checklist (Appendix pages 237 and 248), or draw up your own in your exercise book or print from edworksglobal.com.
TUESDAY	Research the topic as per our 'research chapter' suggestions, page 166. If not on the Internet, make a note to briefly research your topic *within the next two days.* Or source material from books or the news media in your home environment. Otherwise, use your time productively by reading, as discussed.
WEDNESDAY	If research has been undertaken, using the A-Plan (pages 175 and 177), plan the paragraphs for your argumentative essay, referring to the 12-Point Planning Checklist, pages 250-1. Refer to the chapter on 'issue-based essays', page 125, for further guidance. If not yet researched, read productively instead.
THURSDAY	If you're A-Plan is completed, write the first two paragraphs of your argumentative essay using your Plan as a guide. Refer to Fluency Links, page 188, and the 12-Point Planning Checklist, pages 250-1. Remember the Time Out 15, timeframe. *Write clearly and quickly.* Put your paragraphs aside till Monday. If not researched, read instead.
FRIDAY	If you have only just completed your research for your argumentative essay, complete the drill for Wednesday and Thursday, today. If your paragraphs are written, do G. and P. or read, as discussed, keeping references and filing your texts for later. ***Note:*** *Your argumentative essay writing skills are also assisting your text analysis skills. See top of page 222.*

Time Out 15 **WEEK 6**

EXERCISES FOR WORKING SMART	DAY
1. Having put your argumentative essay paragraphs aside for the weekend, edit your text, guided by our editing chapter, page 202. Practise clean corrections. **2.** Select a persuasive issue-based essay topic from page 129, and brainstorm your ideas using an enlarged photocopy of the Brainstorming Issue-based Essays Checklist (Appendix pages 237 and 248), or draw up your own in your exercise book or print one from edworksglobal.com.	**MONDAY**
Research the persuasive topic in accordance with our suggestions in Chapter 34, page 166. If not on the Internet, make a note to briefly research your topic *within the next two days.* Or source material from books or the news media in your home environment. Otherwise, use your time productively by reading.	**TUESDAY**
If researched, using the G-Plan, page 175-6, plan your persuasive essay paragraphs, guided by the 12-Point Planning Checklist, pages 250-251, Refer to the appropriate persuasive essay section, page 129, for further help. If not yet researched, read instead.	**WEDNESDAY**
If your G-Plan is done, write the first two paragraphs of your persuasive essay guided by your Plan. Refer to Fluency Links, page 188, and the 12-Point Planning Checklist, pages 250-251. Keep to the timeframe; Write clearly and quickly! If not yet researched, read.	**THURSDAY**
If you have only just completed your research for your persuasive essay, complete the drill for Wednesday and Thursday, today. Edit text on Monday; or do G. and P. Or read, filing texts and references for later. ***Note:*** *Over the weekend, source at least two different weekend news articles that both cover the same one or two controversial issues of which you are aware. You will need these on Monday for language analysis.*	**FRIDAY**

WEEK 7 **Time Out 15**

DAY	EXERCISES FOR WORKING SMART
MONDAY	**1.** Edit your persuasive essay paragraphs, guided by our editing chapter, page 202. **2.** Scan the weekend news for a lively discussion and choose a topic for language analysis. Select the articles for analysis. Revisit our chapters 'Language analysis essays', page 145, the 'planning' chapter, pages 180-2, and 'first draft' chapter, page 193. Bookmark them for tomorrow. Take your selected articles to school for photocopying and enlarging, tomorrow, and if desired, photocopy our 'Language Analysis Checklist', page 242, to keep with your work.
TUESDAY	Organise your photocopies at school. During Time Out 15, return to your marked pages and, using the L-Plan, plan your language analysis essay. Don't forget the 12-Point Planning Checklist on pages 250-251.
WEDNESDAY	Write the first two paragraphs of your language analysis essay using your planned L-Plan. Check your 'Language Analysis Checklist', page 242, Fluency Links, page 188, the 12-Point Planning Checklist, pages 250-251, and the 'first draft' chapter, page 193. Stick to the timeframe. Write *clearly* and quickly.
THURSDAY	Review the first two paragraphs of your language analysis essay. The detail in your L-Plan and your highlighted texts should allow you to continue paragraphs 3 and 4 today, without too much trouble. Plan to conclude your essay tomorrow.
FRIDAY	Review your language analysis essay so far. With clarity and speed, write your conclusion, paragraphs 5 and 6. Continue to refer to guideline chapters already indicated. *Don't assume you know it all already!* You may miss vital points. Avoid establishing faulty new behaviour: check back to the guidelines. Check the 12-Point Planning Checklist, pages 250-251.

Time Out 15 **WEEK 8**

EXERCISES FOR WORKING SMART	DAY
1. Edit your language analysis essay, referring to our editing chapter on page 202 for guidance. **2.** Today, find three interesting pictures from a magazine or news article; nothing too detailed, say, two people drinking coffee, or a policeman with an elderly person; a bushfire or political scene, etc. Choose one picture and brainstorm story ideas. Decide on an essay: 'creative', 'issue-based', 'personal' or 'descriptive'. Go beyond your comfort zone here. Practise essays needing more skill development. Select the appropriate Plan (G-Plan or A-Plan) and do your plan.	**MONDAY**
Write the introductory and second paragraph of your chosen essay. *Write clearly and quickly.* Edit the text; check the 12-Point Planning Checklist, pages 250-1.	**TUESDAY**
Select another picture from Monday's picture cuttings or print-outs. Brainstorm ideas for a new story and choose an essay *type.* Select the appropriate Plan (G-Plan or A-Plan) and plan your essay.	**WEDNESDAY**
Write the introductory and second paragraph of your chosen essay. Write clearly *and quickly.* Edit the text; check the 12-Point Planning Checklist, pages 250-1.	**THURSDAY**
Repeat the exercise practised during this week, using your final picture for inspiration. Today, you must brainstorm ideas, plan *and* write the first two paragraphs of your essay. In 15 minutes, brainstorm and plan in the first five minutes and allow ten minutes for writing (ie, five minutes a paragraph). <u>Note for tomorrow</u>: Source two issue-based weekend news items, for Monday's activities. *Note that with experience you are building speed and an ability to 'think on your feet'. Keep sourcing and using your support systems: chapter information, checklists, Plans, appendix templates and other guidelines.*	**FRIDAY**

WEEK 9 **Time Out 15**

DAY	EXERCISES FOR WORKING SMART
MONDAY	**1.** Edit last Friday's paragraphs. **2.** Today, select an informative type essay topic from page 154, or a topic which can be written in an informative style from 'Choose a topic: practise your planning', page 183. Scan the news for articles to support your topic. Scan and mark research for Main Ideas, storing it for tomorrow.
TUESDAY	Using the G-Plan, pages 175-6, plan the paragraphs for your informative essay. Be guided by the 12-Point Planning Checklist, pages 250-1, and the informative essays chapter, page 153. Incorporate references from your researched data.
WEDNESDAY	Refer to the literary sections of weekend news articles and learn from their informative styles. Then write the first two paragraphs of your informative essay using your planned G-Plan as a guide. Refer to Fluency Links, page 188, and the 12-Point Planning Checklist, pages 250-1. Consider the Funnel Approach, see pages 72 and 194, or a vignette (see page 130). Remember the Time Out 15, timeframe. *Write clearly and quickly.*
THURSDAY	Continue your news article reading today for Time Out 15. Highlight and file any texts you think may be useful to cite in the future, or any writers from whose styles you can learn.
FRIDAY	Having put your informative essay paragraphs aside for a day, edit your text, referring to our editing chapter on page 202 for guidance. Practise clean corrections, as usual. Review the section on instructional essay writing, page 156, and choose a topic for next week from the suggested texts or invent your own topic for a 'how to' type essay. Put it aside for Monday. *Have a good weekend!*

Time Out 15 **WEEK 10**

EXERCISES FOR WORKING SMART	DAY
Today, having selected your instructional type essay topic from the list on page 156, or invented your own, brainstorm your ideas using the 'Triad or Cluster Methods' (pages 161-3). Do any necessary research, consulting magazines, the Internet, or any instructional books that you may have in your home library.	**MONDAY**
Using the G-Plan, page 175-6, plan the paragraphs for your instructional essay, using the 12-Point Planning Checklist, pages 250-1, as a guide. Refer back to the relevant text, page 156, and revisit Chapter 37, 'Skill 8: First draft', page 193, for further guidance.	**TUESDAY**
Referring to the Guideline Chapters and texts mentioned on page 211, write the first two paragraphs of your instructional essay guided by your planned G-Plan. Refer to Fluency Links, page 188, and the 12-Point Planning Checklist, pages 250-1. Consider the Funnel Approach; see pages 72 and 194. Remember the Time Out 15 timeframe. *Write quickly and clearly!* On completion, put your essay aside for a day.	**WEDNESDAY**
Read any short article from a popular magazine that exemplifies the 'instructional' genre. Make notes and keep references in your exercise book. Highlight and file any texts you think may be useful to cite in the future, or any writers from whose styles you can learn.	**THURSDAY**
Having put your instructional essay paragraphs aside for a day, edit your text, referring to our editing chapter on page 202 for guidance. Practise clean corrections, as usual. *Congratulations and very well done! You have now notched up a solid, 12½ bonus hours of skill development towards your future success! It's time to collect that reward you promised yourself!*	**FRIDAY**

Text analysis essays

Since text analysis requires the study of a novel or other literary works, it has not been included in the ten-week program. However, to improve your skills in this area, revise 'Text analysis essays', page 135, so that you are well aware of the requirements when responding to the subject in class. The issue-based and language analysis essay exercises will have aided you in presenting the required formal essay structure. Always remember to plan, (see T-Plan, pages 178-9), and that within the context of the topic question you must develop a coherent contention, substantiated by quoting the text, to clearly *demonstrate* your understanding.

Once is not enough!

By now, you should have developed a regular routine for your Time Out 15 study. We have now brushed up on grammar and punctuation, and covered all the essay types previously discussed. If you have fully utilised the guideline supports, as suggested, even if not yet fully learned, these should be at your fingertips or easily accessed from the index.

But we can't stop here of course! Using the established regular format, I urge you to continue undertaking your self-improvement exercises. Choose different topics from here or school, mixing your essay types. Concentrate more on your areas of greatest need. You will note that throughout these exercises, we have made 'writing clearly and quickly' a constant theme. If you take this advice, you will be well prepared when your exams arrive to achieve the clarity and speed necessary to acquit yourself under stress.

Although many exercises only involved an essay's first two paragraphs, in regularly completing your school assignments, you will have plenty of solid practice in crafting main bodies and conclusions in your essay writing. Always keep your working smart guidelines handy.

Once read, some people find it difficult to re-read and revisit old ground. Revision of a text, such as this book, not a compulsory part of the curriculum, may be readily overlooked as a result. However, I cannot stress strongly enough, the importance of regularly returning to the guidelines in these pages as you continue your studies. Not to do so would be a bit like spending time and money on a one-day seminar or workshop. You walk away, fired up with enthusiasm to conquer the world. Then, bingo! A week later the event is almost forgotten, the burning principles that fanned your excitement, no more than a speck at the edges of your mind.

Once is not enough! To grasp the important principles of working smart takes practice. But as you have seen, your commitment need only be a few minutes a day—such a small investment for a return with the potential to change your school life, and the events that are to shape your future years.

The power of working smart revisited

In 1823, a Scot, Charles Macintosh, invented a cotton coat treated with waterproof rubber. In Britain, of course, it was called a mackintosh or mac, elsewhere, simply a raincoat. Thanks, Charlie! Nice work. Where would we be today without the dependable comfort and fail-safe protection of a raincoat in a storm?

Like a raincoat in a storm, this book has been about how you—with the help of your family and teachers—can *future-proof* yourself against the uncertainties and challenges you will meet in your lifetime. By applying its principles, working smart can become your safeguard, your fail-safe protector against the great unknowns that lie ahead.

But—it can also be so much more.

Working smart can inspire you to find your passion and help you shape your goals. It can open the door to unexpected and exciting opportunities; to a productive, innovative and happy future—and because it widens choices—to a job you'd love to do and relationships you'd love to have. Your future begins today and stretches before you. But before you set your stride to begin your journey, let us revisit the intrinsic parts of working smart one last time:

Awareness, Motivation and Skills

Awareness, and how we might effectively harness and use it, has formed the essence of this chapter. Accordingly, our Time Out 15 practice routine helps us to transform our 'awareness' into 'skill'. In getting the job done, however, we also need motivation as the driver behind our goals. Thus, as seen in Chapter 7, we create a reward system for ourselves, to provide that motivator: the force that propels us towards the greater purpose beyond the task.

As you take on and use the guidelines in this book, and as your skills grow day by day, you may sense something curious emerging. Care to guess what that might be? Developing the skills, alone, begins to generate your motivation. Indeed, it is 'having the skills' which propels you towards the greater purpose—the fulfilment of your dreams. Here then is our last pearl of wisdom:

**'When I gain the skills for working smart,
my motivation will have no bounds!'**

Having the skills feels pretty powerful—especially as it means less time and effort for better results. Certainly, it's rewarding. In fact, when you think about it, the rewards are far from ordinary. Applying newly learned skills is greatly rewarding; accomplishing sound results is mightily so.

But the reward that takes the gold?

Achieving the skills for life—*and the power to be extraordinary*—when you reach for the sky!

PART 4

GO!

APPENDIX

Dear Student,

In Part 1, I congratulated you for having opened this book in a bid it was hoped, to improve your academic performance and therefore the course of your entire future.

If you have studied 'Reach for the Sky' from *ready* through to *go*, I commend you highly. You are clearly a person of spirit, vision and commitment who has all the earmarks of success and perhaps leadership in your chosen field.

Remember, the power of the written word and the intermediate steps you take to achieve it will stand you in good stead throughout your whole life. So think before you write; think after you write; then fine-tune what you have written *before you present your work.*

Now for some action! The Appendix will provide you with the 14 tools you need to bring all the advice contained in this book to fruition.

Very well done! I wish you every success and happiness for your future!

Greg Nicholson

Contact: www.enquiry@OldTreesPress.com

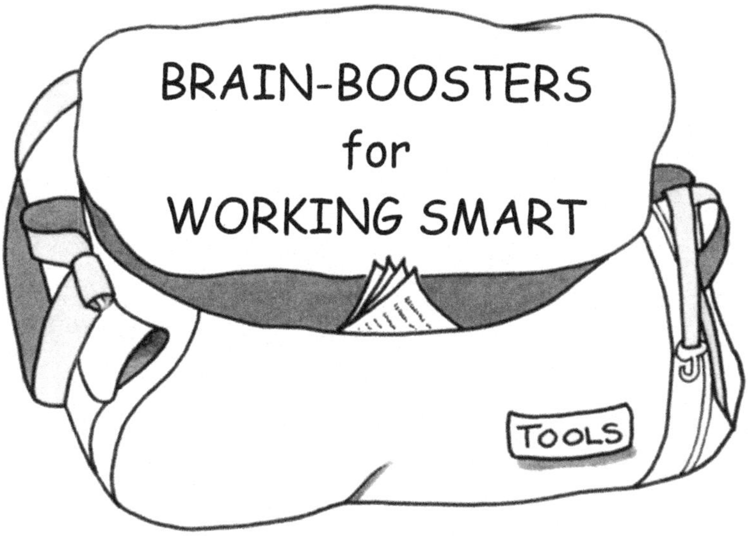

*** Note:**
Shaded areas are removed from templates for photocopying clarity.

▸ From page 38:

Our suggested priority of Tasks, below, has been transferred to the time-tables, next page, where shaded boxes denote expected times for Tasks.

THE TWO-FACTOR MODEL (Example)

LEVEL OF IMPORTANCE (High – Medium – Low)		
High	**BOX 3** **ENGLISH due 16th Aug.** ① Brainstorm and plan: ½ hour. **(Task 3)** ② First draft: 2 hours. **(Task 9)** ③ Edit and final copy: ½ hour. **(Task 10)**	**BOX 1** **MATHS due 9th Aug.** ① Researching and collecting data: ½ hour. **(Task 1)** ② Interpret and write report: 2 hours. **(Task 4)** ③ Edit and final copy: ½ hour. **(Task 5)**
Low	**BOX 4** **FRENCH due 11th Aug.** ① Translation: 1 hour. **(Task 6)** **GEOGRAPHY due 13th Aug.** ① Research: 1½ hours. **(Task 7)** ② Note-taking: 1 hour. **(Task 8)** ③ First draft: 1½ hours. **(Task 11)** ④ Edit and final copy: 1 hour. **(Task 12)**	**BOX 2** **ART due 6th Aug.** ① Answer questionnaire: 2 hours. **(Task 2)**
	LEVEL OF URGENCY: Low – Medium	High

Note:

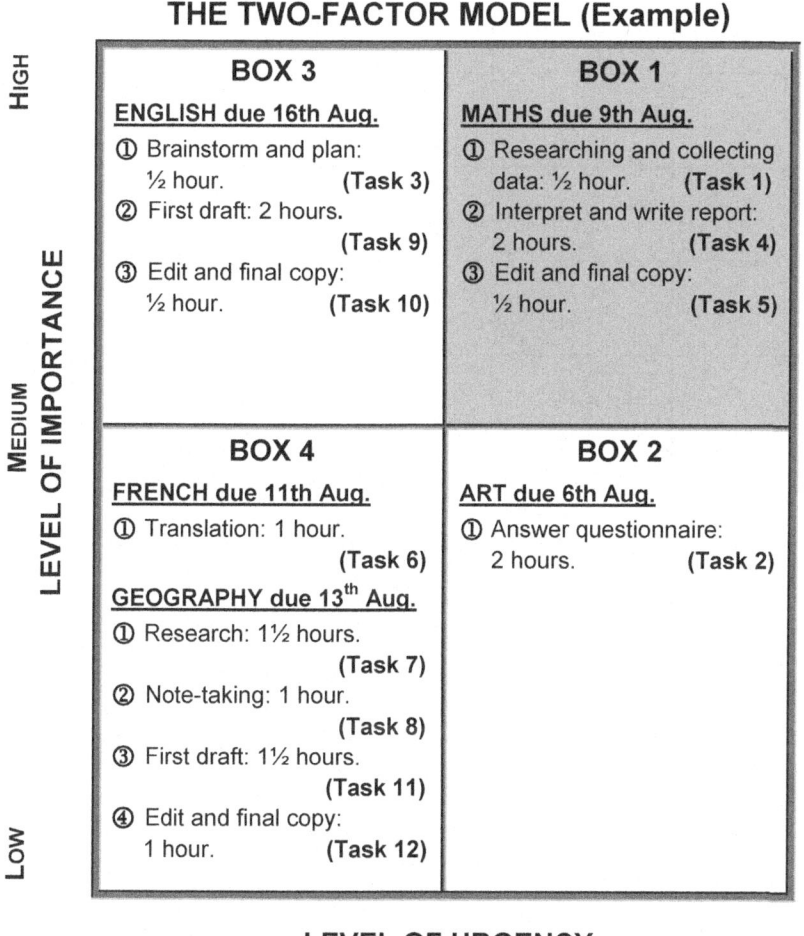

As discussed in 'Breaking down tasks', page 37, at the end of each homework assignment (pages 35-6), the suggested times depicted are considered appropriate for pupils learning to pace themselves in the completion of quality assignment-based work. In an exam setting where time limits are shorter, sharper response rates are naturally required. (See pages 29-30.)

TOOL 2

WEEKLY TIMETABLE BEGINNING MONDAY, 2ND AUGUST

🕐	MON 2	TUE 3	WED 4	THU 5	FRI 6	SAT 7	SUN 8
9 AM					ART DUE		
10 AM							
11 AM							
NOON							
1 PM							
2 PM		E①T3					
3 PM						E②T9	
4 PM							
5 PM			M③T5		G②T8		
6 PM			F①T6				
7 PM	M①T1	M②T4					
8 PM	A①T2			G①T7			
9 PM							E③T10

Next week has to make way for more new assignments, of course. Our English assignment has been completed in the first week, above, with a week to spare. However, you may have decided to take the weekend off to go away camping, for example. That's fine. However, the impact of new assignments the following week

WEEKLY TIMETABLE BEGINNING MONDAY, 9TH AUGUST

	MON 9	TUE 10	WED 11	THU 12	FRI 13	SAT 14	SUN 15
9 AM	MATHS DUE		FRNCH DUE		GEOG DUE		ENG DUE MON
10 AM							
11 AM							
NOON							
1 PM							
2 PM		G④T12					
3 PM							
4 PM							
5 PM	G③T11						
6 PM							
7 PM							
8 PM							
9 PM							

is something you should consider. Some may be urgent! And that means a heavy workload that perhaps you haven't anticipated. If nothing special has cropped up, it might therefore be wise to heed the 'be prepared' motto: think smart, put in a couple of hours' study on the weekend and give yourself plenty of time to spare.

TOOL 2 (Continued)

Naturally, as individuals at different year levels and stages of study, you should structure your timetable to suit yourself. Older students during the final years of school will have heavier workloads than younger pupils. For seniors, workloads will also vary during certain times of the year with weekend timetables being fuller than at other times.

Senior students should of course allocate blocks of time for study in their weekly timetables in the months leading up to examinations. Study can be approached in the same way as homework, using The Two-Factor Model. For example, if you are studying for a science exam worth 50 per cent of your final marks, and a geography exam worth 25 per cent, all things being equal, it would make sense to allocate twice the study time to science.

Your template for The Two-Factor Model and the Weekly Timetable follow. If you wish, photocopy and enlarge them for everyday use or print them, as suggested, from the Edworks website at edworksglobal.com. ⌘

TOOL 3

THE TWO-FACTOR MODEL (Template)

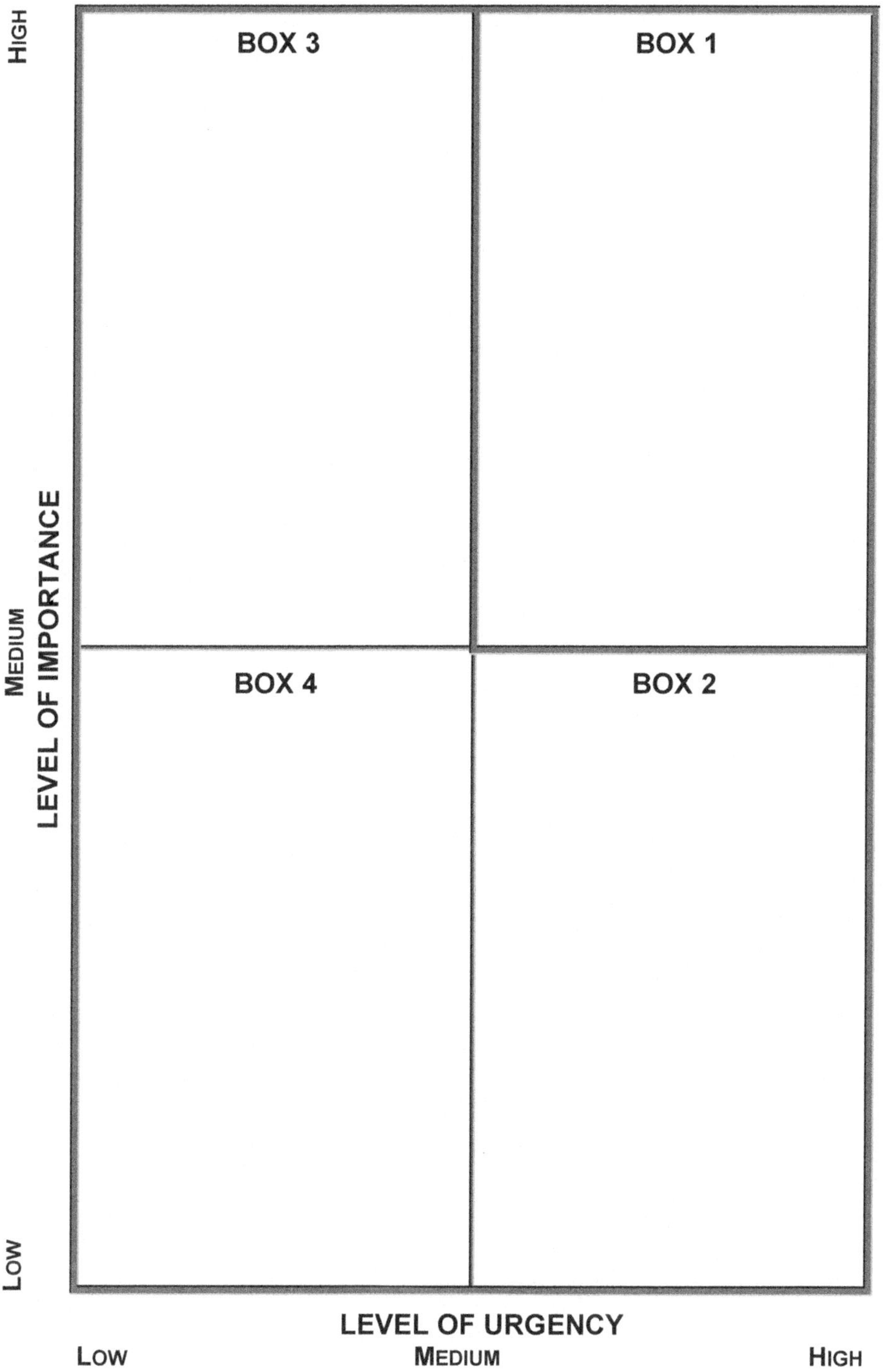

TOOL 4

WEEKLY TIMETABLE (Template)

⏱	MON	TUE	WED	THU	FRI	SAT	SUN
9 AM							
10 AM							
11 AM							
NOON							
1 PM							
2 PM							
3 PM							
4 PM							
5 PM							
6 PM							
7 PM							
8 PM							
9 PM							

TOOL 5

BRAINSTORMING ISSUE-BASED ESSAYS CHECKLIST FOR UPPER PRIMARY STUDENTS

Essay title:

Essay type: Argumentative or Persuasive

Essay's aim/s:		
A. ANGLE (Perspective) **Ask: Can the issue or outcome be seen from this angle?**	**B. SMALL PICTURE** (Micro View) **Would/does the issue affect individuals? How?**	**C. BIG PICTURE** (Macro View) **Does the issue affect the community or society? How?**
1. MONEY (ECONOMIC)		
2. GROUP (SOCIAL) (Family, school, club, society, etc.)		
3. RIGHT OR WRONG (MORAL) (According to law)		
4. STATE OF MIND (PSYCHOLOGICAL) (Happy, sad, angry, worried, etc.)		
5. ENVIRONMENTAL		
6. OTHER		

TOOL 6

GRAMMAR AND PUNCTUATION TIPS

WHAT IS?	ANSWER
A SENTENCE	A group of words that expresses a complete thought or meaning. It contains a subject and a predicate. eg 1. *The black cat, her pride and joy, purred softly, twitching his whiskers.* 2. *He purred.* NB A sentence should always begin with a word, never a number. eg Incorrect: *1991 marked the end of the war.* Correct: *Nineteen ninety-one marked the end of the war.* In this case it is better to reword the sentence: *The war ended in 1991.*
THE SUBJECT (Using sentence examples 1 and 2, above.)	The entity about what or whom we are speaking. ie 1. *The black cat, her pride and joy* (The long group of words here simply enlarges the subject, *'The black cat'*.) 2. *He*
THE PREDICATE (Using sentence examples 1 and 2, above.)	A word or group of words within a sentence, telling something about the subject. ie 1. *purred softly, twitching his whiskers.* 2. *purred.* (If Example 2 were, 'He purred softly.', then *'purred softly'* would be the predicate.)
A NOUN	Any word which names something. Distinctions follow below:
A COMMON NOUN	Expresses the general name of things. eg *cat, boat, man, cathedral*.
A PROPER NOUN	Expresses the individual name of a person/thing or place and usually carries a capital letter. eg Kermit, *River Queen, Robert, St. Paul's Cathedral*.
A COLLECTIVE NOUN	A singular noun that expresses the name of certain things when in a group. eg *flock (of birds/sheep), gaggle (of geese), herd (of cattle), class (of students), crowd (of people), murder (of crows), crash (of rhinoceros/es), pride (of lions/peacocks), school (of fish) or shoal [(i) of fish, or (ii) any large group of people or things], etc.* Continued ...

GRAMMAR AND PUNCTUATION TIPS (Continued)

WHAT IS?	ANSWER
A COLLECTIVE NOUN (continued)	NB The verb following a collective noun may be singular or plural, depending on the meaning inferred. eg (i) The group was unanimous. (ii) The group were divided
AN ABSTRACT NOUN	Defines non-physical things; a quality, state or emotion, eg *fear, beauty, anarchy*.
A PRONOUN	A word used in place of a noun (a person, place, animal or thing). It must agree with the word for which it stands, in number, person and gender. A singular pronoun must agree with a singular noun: eg *Every dog* will have *its* day; *Each man* removed *his* hat; A plural pronoun must agree with a plural noun; eg The *men* removed *their* hats. Technically speaking, you may run into a spot of bother when a noun represents either gender, eg student. *Incorrect: Each student* must study *their* work. *Correct: Each student* must study *his or her* work. Overcome the awkwardness of using *his or her*, if possible, by changing the sentence to read: *Students* must study *their* work.
A VERB	A word/s expressing action or state of being. eg She *sat*, and *was* glad to *be* there; He *is* brave and always *will be*.
AN ADJECTIVE	A word that describes or gives more meaning to a noun. eg The *pale thin* boy wore a *tattered, mud-smeared* cap. Commas were once used after every adjective except the one before the noun. Today, this generally holds only where greater clarity/readability is required. Follow your teacher.
AN ADVERB (SIMPLE)	Any word that adds to the meaning of a verb, adjective or other adverb, by telling how, when, where, why, or 'how much' an action or state of being occurs. eg She played the piano *beautifully*; She is due *tomorrow*; They have searched *everywhere*; *Why* does he sit there all day? Although *very* wealthy, they lived *quite* simply.
THE DEFINITE ARTICLE	The word *'the'*. *The* indicates a particular person or thing. eg *The* girl was dancing.
AN INDEFINITE ARTICLE	The words *'a'* and *'an'*. *A/an* do not specify which particular thing. eg He asked for *a* kitten for his birthday. Continued ...

GRAMMAR AND PUNCTUATION TIPS (Continued)

WHEN DO I USE?	ANSWER
A CAPITAL LETTER	To mark: ▪ the first word of a sentence, full quotation or line of a poem. ▪ a proper noun, ie a person, place or thing. eg *William Shakespeare, Australia, United States of America*, the *Tower of London*, the *Taj Mahal*. ▪ a proper adjective, eg an *English* village, a *Chinese* city, an *African* country, the *Victorian* era. ▪ a race, eg *Caucasian, Jewish, West Indian*, or religion, eg *Judaism, Christianity, Islam, Hinduism*. ▪ deities, eg God, Allah, Brahman, *Zeus, Venus, Apollo*. ▪ things personified, eg The *Chair* closed the meeting. ▪ geographical divisions, eg the *West*, the South Pole, *Fleet Street*. ▪ other: days and months, companies, clubs, organisations, academic courses, titles of distinction; also for official bodies such as *the Government* but note lower case when used as an adjective: *government policy*.
A COLON (:)	Before a list, quotation, statement or explanation, etc. It signals reader to anticipate more information. eg ▪ *There are two kinds of pupils: the aware, who work smart and the unaware, who work hard.* ▪ *He wrote: 'Habit is second nature.'* ▪ *I made a list: pens, dictionary, box-file, markers.* ▪ *All you need is one thing: the will to succeed!* Note: Lower case letters usually follow colons in British/Australian English (except to begin quotations). Capital letters may be used if colons precede several related sentences. (In American English, colons are usually followed by capital letters.) Do *not* use the colon like this: eg *He admired: the bold and the brave.* This should be simply: *He admired the bold and the brave.*
A SEMI COLON (;)	To separate clauses or introduce a pause longer than a comma. It is closer to a full stop than a comma. Can be like another comment or thought of equal rank. eg ▪ *He had talent enough to learn the skills; he simply lacked motivation.* ▪ *Some students believe there is no choice; that hard work is the only road to success.* ⌘

TOOL 7

▸ **From page 114: For creative style writing,** most of the listed verbs describe the tone or manner in which a character may speak, lending atmosphere to your text. Be careful not to spice the pot too much. If in doubt, 'said' is always a reliable word to use. Some authors use little else.

S/he: *said,* etc.

VERB-SPEAK

acknowledged	croaked	intimated	screamed
acquiesced	declared	intoned	shouted
affirmed	demanded	joked	shivered
agreed	droned	lamented	shrieked
announced	disclosed	laughed	shuddered
answered	exclaimed	maintained	sighed
apologised	explained	mentioned	snapped
argued	fumed	murmured	snarled
asked	fussed	panted	sobbed
asserted	granted	proffered	squeaked
barked	grimaced	purred	squealed
bawled	grinned	quipped	stammered
bayed	growled	quivered	stated
begged	grumbled	remarked	stuttered
bellowed	grunted	replied	suggested
breathed	guessed	reported	threatened
cackled	gulped	responded	twittered
chirped	gurgled	retaliated	uttered
chortled	heckled	retorted	wailed
commanded	hedged	returned	warbled
commented	hinted	revealed	wept
conceded	hooted	roared	whispered
continued	howled	said	winced
countered	inferred	sang	yawned
cried	interrupted	scoffed	yelled ⌘

TOOL 8

LANGUAGE ANALYSIS CHECKLIST

STRATEGY	DEFINITION	INTENTION
1. Euphemism	A mild or indirect expression in lieu of one which may upset or offend. eg *passed away = died.*	Shields reader from reality. Aims to assuage impact.
2. False analogy	Comparison of two totally different things. eg *Environmentalists are just like hippies as they don't see the value of progress.*	To benefit the contention by imposing a false relationship, often to instil fear.
3. Rationalism	Where politicians, for example, 'rationalise' a salary increase on the premise such salaries are key for political parties to attract top people. Reality is they want more money.	To justify an action in the eyes of readers/audience when it is not accurate or correct.
4. Appeals to tradition	The past is cited to excuse future or current behaviour. eg *When I was young, we learnt by rote and it didn't do us any harm.*	Aim is to offer an excuse to prevent change or protect own interests.
5. Misuse of statistics	Beware! Statistics are often used to stretch/misrepresent truth. eg *Half the children are below average in maths!* Used to alarm reader when in fact that's how averages are obtained: 'average' is the mid-point, so half must be above and half below the average.	Attempting to validate an argument or point of view by representing statistics in the most positive light.
6. Appeals to pride	Use of phrases that appeal to vanity or pride. eg *Any intelligent person can see that . . .*	Ego is used to deflect reader from taking a more critical standpoint against argument.
7. Emotional blackmail	Statements often involve projecting guilt feelings to influence the reader. eg *Every child deserves the best education money can buy.*	Plays on the insecurity of the reader/listener to influence them to more readily accept the contention.
8. Appeals through use of 'authority' figures	Uses authorities/personalities to gain credibility for views. eg *Often seen in U.S. politics where movie stars endorse candidates.* Used to influence public perception as to quality of argument.	Attempting to validate arguments or position and gain credibility by association.

LANGUAGE ANALYSIS CHECKLIST (Continued)

STRATEGY	DEFINITION	INTENTION
9. Appeals to fear	Threatens a negative consequence if author's argument is not adhered to. eg *If we don't adopt this Bill the economy will become a basket case.*	This strategy is used to elicit an irrational response by instilling fear in the reader or listener. Also often used to avoid analysis of an argument's validity and exploration of reasonable options.
10. Invalid causal relationships	Attempts to link unrelated causes and effects. eg *Since we have had the new neighbours, our hens have refused to lay.*	To impose or assign a negative or positive cause-and-effect link to strengthen an argument, where no link exists.
11. Labelling	Seeks to undermine the opposition by using terms or remarks which are disparaging or which have socially negative connotations. eg *extremist, radical, communist, un-Australian, un-British.*	Used to instil fear in the reader or listener to undermine the credibility of the opposition with sweeping and unsubstantiated terms or names on the basis that 'mud sticks'.
12. Personalise the issue	Refers to a personal aspect of the opposition or to something personal in their past, irrelevant to the issue. eg *He's got shifty eyes. What do you expect, he got caught drink-driving (fifteen years ago!).*	Often utilised to divert attention from the real issue and undermine the integrity of the argument by attempting to denigrate the authority of those who disagree.
13. Comments not substantiated or provable	Here, assertions are often boldly presented as the truth, but are not supported by evidence or substantiated. eg *Many letters received from consumers complained about . . .* (How many letters were actually received? Three or four!)	Relies on the readiness of readers to accept generalised statements without question because it sounds authoritative.
14. Attributing blame to minority groups	Where a small sector of society is blamed for a situation arising. eg *Unemployment is due to all those migrants.*	Used to deflect blame onto a group unable to defend itself. Strategy takes advantage of inherent bigotry where the reader accepts such assertions without question.

LANGUAGE ANALYSIS CHECKLIST (Continued)

STRATEGY	DEFINITION	INTENTION
15. Conspiracy theory	Where disagreement with a line of argument is seen as admission of association with the perceived traitor. eg *Anyone who disagreed with the war in Iraq, must be a terrorist sympathiser.* This strategy is often used by politicians.	Often presented by those who see the world as 'black and white'. It is used to deflect attention from alternative views. Also used to subdue possible critics who may fear being dubbed as conspirators.
16. Inferred association (A)	Over-generalising: from the specific to the general. eg *I couldn't trust your father; men can't be trusted!*	Used when an argument cannot be readily substantiated. Relies on the reader who does not question the over-generalisation of the association.
17. Inferred association (B)	In our need for homeostasis (ie a sense of order), this sees us trying to group/classify people while failing to acknowledge the individual. eg *Teenagers are reckless. She's a teenager, so she, too, is reckless.*	Takes advantage of the human tendency—in desiring a sense of order—to want to group things together.
18. Jargon	Language that is normally associated with a restricted audience or profession. eg The use of terms or phrases, the meaning of which are often only understood within a profession.	Used to establish a degree of authority and to illustrate intellect. Also used to confuse and distract the reader or listener from the real issue.
19. Persuasive language	Alliteration may be employed to add a sense of colour to language. Also, word repetition is often used to elicit an emotional response. This was used to good effect by Western world leaders, John F. Kennedy and Sir Winston Churchill.	Used to encourage the reader or listener to be swayed by the subjective/emotional elements of language.
20. Selective evidence	Selects only evidence that will support the line of argument. Interest groups such as the cigarette industry have used restricted data to support their line of argument.	To present an argument in a favourable light that may otherwise lack strong support.

LANGUAGE ANALYSIS CHECKLIST (Continued)

STRATEGY	DEFINITION	INTENTION
21. Misquoting or selective editing of material	Selects material that will support argument. Misrepresent the truth by omitting a quote's key parts. Current affair programs are full of examples!	To misrepresent or distort the truth to advance the author's argument.
22. Rhetorical question	A question where answer is obvious and does not need expression as it can never be known, or because the answer is assumed clear to both writer and reader. eg *Who wouldn't want to win a million dollars?*	Asked for effect only, as a persuasive device to reinforce the obvious or a lack of reasonable options to a particular line of argument.
23. Loaded language	Words used to create images that manipulate the way people think. eg The *unemployed* may be called *dole bludgers.*	Connotations associated with such words are used to manipulate reader in a positive or negative sense.
24. Conformity	Such arguments elicit a need to conform; not to draw attention to one by being unusual or holding unfavourable ideas. eg *If other people do it, then it is a good and desirable thing to do.*	Aims to stir fear of ridicule based on being seen as different. Manipulates person to justify his or her response through the supposed actions or attitudes of the majority.
25. Self-interest	Presents issue from perspective of self-interest. eg *Maintaining gambling and casinos means we pay less tax.*	Attempts to focus the reader or listener on what they can personally gain from a line of argument.
26. Tone	Author's attitude shown through the strength/quality of his/her writing. Tone adopted may be empathic, emotive, authoritative, objective, conciliatory or humorous. Tone may alter as passage progresses.	To convey author's attitude and facilitate adoption of the contention. Also used to convey personality and manipulate reader's response beyond the facts.
27. Inclusive and/or authoritative use of pronouns	Often pronouns, 'we', 'us' and so on are used to offer a sense of inclusiveness, eg We*, as responsible senior students, should . . .* In contrast, 'I' is used to offer a sense of authority and credibility to the issue, eg *I believe . . .*	Used to present a softer line to the argument or to add a sense of inclusiveness and credibility to the issue presented. ⌘

TOOL 9

For Language Analysis, you have researched your articles. You've done a clear plan. You know your material. You're ready to start your essay, then—suddenly your brain is scrambled eggs! Welcome to the writer's block solution and strings of words to lend credibility, fluency and colour to your assignment. (Underlined words define the use of your objective view. Such use prevents you making the error of presenting the assumption that a polemicist's strategy was successful.)

CLAUSES AND PHRASES FOR PLAUDITS AND PRAISE

Opposing the contention, he argues that . . .	Using wit as her currency, . . .
The use of . . . signals the writer's belief in . . .	He deftly argues that . . .
A series of rhetorical questions highlights . . .	Readers are <u>urged to</u> . . .
The writer employs such emotive phrases as . . .	The belief that . . .
In a carefully constructed manner . . .	A contentious issue . . .
<u>In order to</u> instil in readers a sense of . . .	This editorial contends . . .
The author insinuates/suggests/implies . . .	These phrases are coupled with . . .
Drawing a new arrow from his quiver, . . .	Having sewn the seeds of doubt, . . .
<u>Seeks to</u> add grist to his mill by offering . . .	The constant theme of . . .
Tailoring her comments to suit her readers, . . .	Pursuing his point further, . . .
Appealing to our <u>assumed</u> anger over the . . .	Conflicting views raise . . .
<u>Attempts to</u> influence his readers by . . .	The writer embarks upon . . .
<u>Seeks to</u> grab readers attention by . . .	He launches an attack on . . .
<u>Attempts to</u> give wings to her theory by . . .	The purpose being to . . .
His selective use of words evoke images of . . .	<u>In attempting</u> to undermine . . .
The writer <u>seeks to</u> maintain his authority . . .	Adds more fuel to the fire by . . .
His questions <u>are designed to</u> coerce/coax . . .	Seeking to deflect concern, she . . .
She rekindled/fuelled the fires of debate, . . .	In response to . . . ; In contrast, . . .
Throws cold water on the line of argument . . .	He addresses the need to . . .
The writer has been successful in . . .	Targets an audience . . .
She elucidates her concern with examples of . . .	To draw his readers towards . . .
Adds legs to his line of reasoning by . . .	The image depicts . . .
This initial use of rhetorical questions . . .	This visual <u>is intended to</u> . . .
Embroidering her point further by adding, '. . .'	The article opens with . . .
The graphic depicts/illustrates/<u>aims to</u> . . .	This ploy <u>acts to</u> elevate/evoke . . .

Note that longer lists can be found at edworksglobal.com. The verbs below may assist you to describe persuasive techniques in essays. Example: The verb, 'to accentuate', might be used to demonstrate your grasp of a writer's strategy: 'Use of the inclusive pronoun *accentuates* the idea of nationhood in the reader's mind.'

accentuate	deflect	encourage	inform	provoke	strengthen
acknowledge	diminish	evoke	inspire	rebut	suggest
allude to	dismiss	expose	intensify	recognise	summarise
appeal to	elicit	expound	label	reflect	underscore

TOOL 10

Be aware, when comparing articles selected for your language analysis, the tone of a writer/commentator may change during the course of her/his development of a polemic. You should identify this change in your essay discussion.

IDENTIFYING TONE (For Language Analysis)

POSITIVE	NEGATIVE	NEUTRAL
Admiring	Accusing	Academic
Agreeable	Admonishing	Ambivalent
Amiable	Aggravated	Authoritative
Approving	Aggressive	Balanced
Amused	Alarmed	Calm
Casual	Blunt	Candid/frank
Cheerful	Belligerent	Contemplative
Concerned	Condemnatory	Controlled
Consoling	Condescending	Conversational
Conversational	Contemptuous	Equable
Curious	Critical	Factual
Delighted	Despairing	Formal
Empathic	Disingenuous	Impartial
Encouraging	Disturbed	Informal
Enthusiastic	Disgusted	Learned
Excited	Doubtful	Lyrical
Friendly	Foreboding	Nostalgic
Humorous	Frustrated	Objective
Inspiring	Furious	Personal
Jovial	Gloomy	Pragmatic
Optimistic	Insulting	Questioning
Passionate	Judgmental	Reflective
Patriotic	Melancholic	Relaxed
Playful	Mortified	Resigned
Polite	Outraged	Serene
Respectful	Pessimistic	Serious
Reverent	Provocative	Scholarly
Relieved	Quarrelsome	Sober
Soothing	Remorseful	Solemn
Supportive	Sarcastic/Sardonic	Thoughtful
Surprised	Shocked	Uncritical
Sympathetic	Suspicious	Undecided

TOOL 11

BRAINSTORMING ISSUE-BASED ESSAYS CHECKLIST FOR SECONDARY STUDENTS

Essay title:

Essay type: **Argumentative or Persuasive**

Essay's aim/s:		
PERSPECTIVES	MICRO VIEW (Impact on Individuals	MACRO VIEW (Impact on Society)
1. POLITICAL		
2. ECONOMIC		
3. PSYCHOLOGICAL		
4. SOCIAL		
5. MORAL		
6. ENVIRONMENTAL		
7. OTHER		

TOOL 12

TEXT ANALYSIS CHECKLIST

MOTIVATOR	PAGE: QUOTES/ PASSAGES	IMPACT	AUTHOR'S INTENTION
1. Love: passionate			
2. Love: companionate			
3. Hate			
4. Conformity			
5. Rebellion			
6. Greed			
7. Selfishness			
8. Envy			
9. Power			
10. Courage			
11. Fear			
12. Loyalty			
13. Betrayal			
14. Loss			
15. Jealousy			
BELIEF SYSTEM	PGE: QUOTES /PASSAGES	IMPACT	AUTHOR'S INTENTION
16. Fatalist			
17. Non-fatalist			

TOOL 13

12-POINT PLANNING CHECKLIST

Point	Planning Phase 1: COMMENCEMENT—I have:	☑
1.	Read the essay question thoroughly several times and understand its requirements. (See pages 57-8 and 108-9.)	
2.	Identified essay type and style: eg **'argumentative' type, 'creative' type, analytical style,** etc. (See pages 108-9.)	
	Planning Phase 2: BRAINSTORMING—I have:	
3.	Reviewed 'brainstorming' guidelines (page 159); also ensured that, where appropriate, the following have been completed: **Issue-based essays:** brainstormed the perspectives, for example: Political, Environmental, Social, etc, to be addressed; also Micro and Macro Views. (See pages 83-93 and 159-60.) **Creative type essays:** brainstormed action/direct speech/ thoughts and plotted story line. (See pages 111-114.)	
	Planning Phase 3: RESEARCH—I have:	
4.	**Where appropriate:** if essay is assignment-based, not an exam, researched data from a broad cross-section of resources (page 166). **Text analysis essays:** having thoroughly read the text (novel or play, etc), identified and highlighted the human Motivators and Belief Systems in text. (See pages 139-44 and 168-71.)	
	Planning Phase 4: MAKING MY PLAN—I have:	
5.	From my notes (see 'note-taking' chapters, pages 54-65), or otherwise: **made a G-Plan, A-Plan, T-Plan** or **L-Plan** according to suggestions, pages 175-182, 'essay planning' chapter.	
6.	**In the 'first draft' chapter (see page 193):** reviewed the relevant section of the essay type I am planning, to confirm that my Plan has followed its guidelines. **For all essays, I have thought: 'press buttons'.** Continued.	

12-POINT PLANNING CHECKLIST (Continued)

Point	Planning Phase 4: MAKING MY PLAN—I have:	☑
7.	Ensured that the Plan consists of key words or phrases, *not* lengthy sentences. (See note-taking examples, Page 60.)	
8.	**Where Main Ideas feature:** ensured they **can be linked to the essay topic.**	
9.	**Where Main Ideas feature:** clearly noted Main Idea for each paragraph. Ensured Main Ideas have Supporting Details. **For issue-based and text analysis essays:** ensured any points to be used to elaborate Main Ideas can be supported/ substantiated with precise, relevant details. **Paragraph by paragraph:** planned that each Main Idea will build upon the previous Main Idea to give my essay sequential flow (page 191). Considered **conscious** and **subconscious** writing levels (page 192).	
10.	**For creative type essays:** planned to bring the threads of the story together to a *button-pressing* finish (page 105), ensuring resolution of any plot or sub-plots (if used). (See pages 111-112.)	
11.	**For any essays where Main Ideas feature:** planned that the conclusion (one or two paragraphs) will have a summary, with the key Main Ideas *clearly restated.* (Check chapter that deals with relevant essay and 'Skill 8, First draft', page 193.) **For issue-based and text analysis:** planned that the summary will support and strengthen my/the main contention (see relevant essay chapter and also the 'first draft' chapter, page 196). **For language analysis:** planned summary of the issue's current situation (see Emily's 'climate change' essay, page 148). (Also see next point, below.)	
12.	**For issue-based essays:** planned conclusion offering possible future directions or alternative solutions to issue (see page 195). **For language analysis essays:** compared strategies used in articles and how audience type influenced their selection (see 'first draft' chapter, page 198, also L-Plan guidelines, pages 180/182, and Emily's essay, page 148). ⌘	

TOOL 14

Grammar and Punctuation Exercises

▸ Discussed in Chapter 36, page 187:

The main points:

1. Read each passage through, aloud, before commencing.
2. Make sure you *re-write* the following exercises to gain an appreciation of the meaning and flow. Don't simply insert the corrections here.
3. Where appropriate, use correct spelling, grammar and punctuation (see our 'Grammar and Punctuation Tips', page 238, to assist).
4. If necessary, correct the tenses for verbs. Also, fill in the gaps using the correct, *definite* and *indefinite articles.*
5. Two exercises contain dialogue. Don't forget quotation marks and use of indented paragraphs *each time* a different person speaks. If unsure, check a novel for the layout.
6. On completion, be sure to read the passages aloud! Check your answers on pages 258-9.

Exercise 1:
'Energy was required to maintain all ___ processes of life—not only walking blinking breathing speaking thinking and swallowing—but all ___ bodys cells require ___ continuous input of energy for *every* single reaction if one were able to view cell under a microscope it would be seen as being in ___ constant state of movement glucose was ___ major contributor of energy which allow these movements tiny chemical reactions vital to life to occur'

Exercise 2:
'it is ___ moment of truth when we reflect upon ___ dazzling accomplishments of science and technology in modern times to realise they have occurred at great cost to support ___ exploding world population and in its quest for higher crop yields and profits globally we have squander precious groundwater stores depleted soil destroyed forest and pillage our mineral resources the industrial and commercial process associated with burgeoning urban living are constantly exerting untold pressures on natures powers of perpetuity every day chemicals and noxious fumes from cars factories and homes spew into our once clean air creating smog across ___ cities of ___ world from los angeles to london and tokyo and from melbourne to rome'

Exercise 3:

'when they straightened from laughing Megs eyes were shining they returned to their coffee sipping in silence renée thoughts went back to ___ past ___ good times and the tears they had shared in boston and london. a grapefruit . . . and-a-pizza-and-two-mugs-of-hot-chocolate renées mind snapped back to ___ present sorry? a grapefruit ___ pizza and *three* mugs of hot chocolate as Im confessing you may as well know it all meg stared at renée steadily over the rim of her cup For *breakfast* I had ___ grapefruit ___ pizza and three mugs of hot chocolate—with cream she added almost defiantly renée paused then looked at her reprovingly how big was it. what? the grapefruit. Meg snorted into her cup and sent ___ spray of foam across ___ café table they collapsed again quivering with suppressed laughter and grinning ridiculously at each other through watery eyes'

Exercise 4:

'by 4000 bc egyptian civilisation is leading ___ world in cultural and social development it is harnessed ___ waters of the nile and begun to develop the fertile nile valley as a result a egyptian landlords kitchen of ___ period would had displayed ___ cornucopia of foods and wines lamb goose duck eggs legumes root vegetables figs dates walnuts olives grapes and grains such as barley millet and wheat'

Exercise 5:

'in ___ intricate infinitesimal chemical reactions of life oxygen commands ___ primary role this is greatly facilitated by ___ chemical structure that gives it ___ natural affinity to bond with other elements in fact two very important life processes a storage of chemical energy in ___ plants we use as food and its subsequent release in our bodies cells for growth movement and so on is largely due to oxygens reactivity that is it's ready ability to combine with other substances however ___ alliance with oxygen isnt all roses when you look more close and also consider ___ thorn'

Exercise 6:

'unchecked the potential for damage is high in ___ fever of chemical firework shower upon shower of more free radicals and allied reactive oxygen species can be produce emanating bursts of light as they collide with and wreak their havoc upon unsuspecting healthy cells in ___ good deal less time than ___ blink of a eye—___ nanosecond, *or billionth of a second* to be precise—the structure of millions ___ molecules can be permanently altered causing distortions and damage to DNA to protein molecules to enzymes and to cells in fact such is ___ damage that can been caused scientists report that under ___ electron microscope besiege cells can look shrivelled and charred'

Exercise 7:

'the miraculous phenomenon of oxygen producing photosynthesis is ___ process upon which all living things depend humankind animals and plants alike the reason for our dependence is that *unlike* plant life none of our cells possess chlorophyll to trap light nor do they have ___ relevant enzymes to assist carbon dioxide during photosynthesis therefore like all animals we are unable to produce our own glucose yet *glucose is fundamental to the biological machinery of all living organisms* how easy it is for us to lose sight of this simple fact as we immerse ourselves in ___ hurly burly frenetic thrust and pull of our everyday lives that without ___ ingenious biochemical mechanisms of ___ humble green plant there would be none photosynthesis no carbohydrates no fats no proteins no oxygen no forest animals and creatures of ___ field indeed dare it been said no . . . us'

Exercise 8:

'I knew Id made ___ right decision I grinned at Samantha drinking in our surroundings its exquisite Sam samantha smiled back at me her long fingers poised tentatively on ___ thermostat air conditioning or sea breeze Mmm definitely sea breeze samantha glided open ___ balcony door and stepped outside just ___ moment i'll turn on ___ plants watering system to cool ___ air she leaned across ___ mass of green ferns found ___ tap and turned it on ___ fine mist of water suddenly began to spray luxuriantly throughout ___ leaf covered patio and ___ brackish caribbean breeze was immediately transformed into ___ delicious mix of salt and moist fresh air In the distance the sea glittered like sequins I took ___ long deep breath and turned this is truly sublime how will you ever leave the island' ⌘

COMPLETED TEXTS

Completed short essay for upper primary students: 'What concerns me most about growing old.'

▸ From Chapter 21, pages 73-5:

The **Main Ideas** in each paragraph are **bolded.** For clarity, the sentences or clauses that offer linking ideas between paragraphs are underlined. Check out the Main Ideas (bolded), first. Then look at the text again for the linking ideas (underlined), separately. Some words contain both criteria. The four paragraphs are separated for added clarity.

Short essay

Essay topic: 'What concerns me most about growing old'
Essay type: Personal

Until about a century ago, many people didn't live very long. Diseases and deaths in childbirth were largely to blame for this. In those times good hygiene was almost unknown and living conditions were very poor. Today, some people live to be a hundred. Many are in their seventies or eighties. This is largely due to advances in medicine and greatly improved standards of living. But what does growing old really mean? **I wouldn't want to be 90 if I were bedridden or very ill. It would concern me if I couldn't be with friends or do everyday things like playing music or even taking the dog to the park for a game of catch.**

Friends are an important part of growing old. I would hate to be without them. My grandmother, who is 72, is always doing things with her friends like playing Scrabble and going to golf. My grandfather (Papou) really loves his friends. He can often be seen with one or two of his cronies chatting in Greek over coffee in High Street. Sadly, some of his friends have died which means there are fewer people whose company he can enjoy. That's the part I would hate about growing old. Papou always says he never wants to be a burden to his family, but what happens when all your friends have gone? Loneliness can be a terrible thing. It becomes a big issue as you get older. That's really when you need your friends the most.

Another issue I know is that every day things become more difficult as you get older. You slow down a lot. Your bones become more brittle and fragile. If you get arthritis it means you can't do the things you once took for granted. If I lived to be 90, could I still play my Spanish guitar? If my fingers had arthritis, it would be very painful. Growing old wouldn't be much fun for me without my guitar. But worst of all, I would miss taking Spot out to the park for his daily run. I often think about that when I see grey-haired people with their walking sticks and motorised wheel chairs—and especially when I see old Mr. McQuitty shuffle slowly past our house with his little white terrier. There can't be much fun in it. He can't even throw a stick, let alone chase his dog around the park.

Of course, getting old isn't all bad news! My grandparents get to sleep-in most days a week; then they usually have breakfast in bed. In the meantime, at our house, we're driving each another crazy rushing around trying to get ready for school. My sister spends ages in the bathroom flossing her teeth and getting her hair just right. All Nana does is brush her teeth, pull on her golf cap, smile at the mirror and say, 'Who cares?' Not only that, just as we all start to shiver at the first signs of winter, what do my grandparents do? They pack their bags. They load up their golf clubs and then they head off with friends to their favourite sunny holiday spot, leaving dad to watch over their house. No wonder they can't stop smiling!

You will note that in each paragraph our writing never strays from the essay topic, 'What concerns me most about growing old'. The issues covered are:

PARAGRAPH 1: Being bedridden or ill; not enjoying friends or everyday things (like music and fun outings with the dog).

PARAGRAPH 2: Hating to be without friends; friends die, causing loneliness.

PARAGRAPH 3: Every day things: slowing down; brittle bones; arthritis; not playing music; not being able to play with the dog in the park.

PARAGRAPH 4: In discussing what concerns the writer most about growing old, we have painted a pretty dismal picture. The very nature of the topic causes us to be negative. In the concluding paragraph, we want to show the bright side of growing old. So we challenge the topic by declaring our Main Idea that, 'of course, it's not all bad news'. Then we fill in the Supporting Details and finish with a triumphant positive thought: *growing old can mean you can pack up and take off to a place in the sun, leaving winter and looking after the house to the younger members of the family.*

I'll be looking forward to that, won't you? ⌘

Completed Texts for Rhythm Exercises (Includes grammar and punctuation)

▸ From Chapter 36, beginning page 190:

Exercise 1:

'Evidence indicates that refined breads of the Roman era also contained small amounts of sugar and salt, as do our modern breads. However, salt in Roman times played a far less humble role outside a nobleman's kitchen. Salt was treated like gold! In fact, as part of their wages, soldiers of the Imperial Roman Army were paid *salt money* for the sole purchase of salt—thus the derivation of the word *salary.* Indeed, as early as 2200 BCE, salt's value was such that a tax was imposed upon it by a Chinese emperor.'

Exercise 2:

'Erase from your mind images of industrial settings: the smoke stacks, the noxious effluent gushing into once pristine waterways, the cacophony of whirring, thumping, metal machinery and the smell of oil on scorching steel. Expunge visions of cogs and wheels and conveyor belts. Instead, consider this for a moment: somewhere in a microcosm which may seem obscure and separate from your own but which nonetheless is inextricably linked, a wondrous biological phenomenon is occurring. Amidst a complex mixture of fragrant earth, nitrogen-fixing microbes and leguminous plants are playing out their symbiotic roles. Each gains mutual benefit from the other: the microbes live in the root nodules, fixing nitrogen for use by the plant which cannot absorb it from the air; in turn, the microbes draw on nourishment from the roots of their host.'

Exercise 3:

'As you wander from stall to stall, relax and enjoy the experience. Visualise a dish you can prepare at home with the wealth of ingredients on offer. Fresh red peppers, garlic, tomatoes and pungent fresh herbs will have you thinking of a thick sauce nestled in spaghetti. A fragrant pineapple and crisp, brightly-coloured vegetables will send you off looking to buy a new wok. Barrels of red apples and perfumed peaches will have you headed to the park for a feast. And don't overlook the fact, as you pause to smell a mango or gently prod an avocado, that these are Nature's perfect foods; a culmination of the vibrant forces of life that emanate from the elements of the earth: the sun, the air, the water and the soil. Make them a part of you. That is Nature's design.' ⌘

Completed Texts: Grammar and Punctuation Exercises

▸ From page 252, this Appendix:

Corrections are **highlighted** for easier recognition.

Exercise 1:
'Energy **is** required to maintain all **the** processes of life—not only walking, blinking, breathing, speaking, thinking and swallowing—but **the** body**'**s cells require **a** continuous input of energy for *every* single reaction**.** **I**f one were able to view cell**s** under a microscope**,** **they** would be seen as being in **a** constant state of movement**.** **G**lucose **is a** major contributor of energy which allows these movements **(**tiny chemical reactions vital to life**)** to occur.'

Exercise 2:
'It is **a** moment of truth, when we reflect upon **the** dazzling accomplishments of science and technology in modern times, to realise they have occurred at great cost. **T**o support **an** exploding world population, and in **its** quest for higher crop yields and profits, globally, we have squander**ed** precious groundwater stores, depleted soil**s**, destroyed forest**s** and pillage**d** our mineral resources.

The industrial and commercial process**es** associated with burgeoning urban living are constantly exerting untold pressures on nature's powers of perpetuity**.** **E**very day, chemicals and noxious fumes from cars, factories and homes spew into our once**-**clean air, creating smog across **the** cities of **the** world from **L**os **A**ngeles to **L**ondon and **T**okyo, and from **M**elbourne to **R**ome.'

Exercise 3:
'**W**hen they straightened from laughing, Meg**'**s eyes were shining. **T**hey returned to their coffee**,** sipping in silence. **R**enée's thoughts went back to **the** past**:** **the** good times and the tears they had shared in **B**oston and **L**ondon.

"A grapefruit . . . and-a-pizza-and-two-mugs-of-hot-chocolate!**"**

Renée**'**s mind snapped back to **the** present. **"S**orry?**"**

"A grapefruit, **a** pizza and *three* mugs of hot chocolate. **A**s **I'**m confessing, you may as well know it all.**"** **M**eg stared at Renée steadily over the rim of her cup. "For *breakfast.* I had **a** grapefruit, **a** pizza and three mugs of hot chocolate—with cream**!"** she added, almost defiantly.

Renée paused, then looked at her reprovingly. **"H**ow big was it**?"**

"What?**"**

"The grapefruit!**"**

Meg snorted into her cup and sent **a** spray of foam across **the** café table. They collapsed again quivering with suppressed laughter and grinning ridiculously at each other through watery eyes.'

Exercise 4:

'By 4000 **BC**, Egyptian civilisation **was** leading **the** world in cultural and social development. **It had** harnessed **the** waters of the Nile and begun to develop the fertile Nile valley. As a result, **an** Egyptian landlord's kitchen of **the** period would **have** displayed **a** cornucopia of foods and wines: lamb, goose, duck eggs, legumes, root vegetables, figs, dates, walnuts, olives, grapes, and grains such as barley, millet and wheat.'

Exercise 5:

'In **the** intricate, infinitesimal chemical reactions of life, oxygen commands **a** primary role. This is greatly facilitated by **a** chemical structure that gives it **a** natural affinity to bond with other elements. In fact, two very important life processes, **the** storage of chemical energy in **the** plants we use as food, and its subsequent release in our bodies' cells for growth, movement and so on, is largely due to oxygen's reactivity: that is, **its** ready ability to combine with other substances. However, **an** alliance with oxygen **isn't** all roses when you look more closely and also consider **the** thorns.'

Exercise 6:

'Unchecked, the potential for damage is high. In **a** fever of chemical fireworks, shower upon shower of more free radicals and allied reactive oxygen species can be produced, emanating bursts of light as they collide with, and wreak their havoc upon, unsuspecting healthy cells. In **a** good deal less time than **the** blink of **an** eye—**a** nanosecond, *or billionth of a second,* to be precise—the structure of millions **of** molecules can be permanently altered, causing distortions and damage to DNA, to protein molecules, to enzymes and to cells. In fact, such is **the** damage that can **be** caused, scientists report that under **the** electron microscope, besieged cells can look shrivelled and charred.'

Exercise 7:

'The miraculous phenomenon of oxygen-producing photosynthesis is **a** process upon which all living things depend: humankind, animals and plants alike. The reason for our dependence is that, *unlike* plant life, none of our cells possesses chlorophyll to trap light; nor do they have **the** relevant enzymes to assist carbon dioxide during photosynthesis. Therefore, like all animals, we are unable to produce our own glucose. Yet—*glucose is fundamental to the biological machinery of all living organisms.*

How easy it is for us to lose sight of this simple fact as we immerse ourselves in **the** hurly burly, frenetic, thrust-and-pull of our everyday lives: **t**hat without **the** ingenious biochemical mechanisms of **the** humble green plant, there would be **no** photosynthesis, no carbohydrates, no fats, no proteins, no oxygen, no forest animals and creatures of **the** field, indeed, dare it **be** said, no . . . us!'

Exercise 8:

' **"**I knew I'd made **the** right decision,**"** I grinned at Samantha, drinking in our surroundings**. "**It's exquisite, Sam.**"**

Samantha smiled back at me, her long fingers poised tentatively on **the** thermostat. **"A**ir-conditioning or sea breeze**?"**

"Mmm. **D**efinitely sea breeze."

Samantha glided open **the** balcony door and stepped outside. **"J**ust **a** moment. **I**'ll turn on **the** plants**'** watering system to cool **the** air.**" S**he leaned across **a** mass of green ferns, found **a** tap and turned it on**. A** fine mist of water suddenly began to spray luxuriantly throughout **the** leaf-covered patio and **the** brackish **C**aribbean breeze was immediately transformed into **a** delicious mix of salt and moist fresh air**.**

In the distance, the sea glittered like sequins.

I took **a** long deep breath and turned**. "**This is truly sublime! **H**ow will you ever leave the island**?"** ' ⌘

References

1. Slade, M. and Trent, F. Are they all the same? A project to examine success among adolescent males in secondary and tertiary education. School of Education, Flinders University, Adelaide. *Presented at the Australian Association for Research in Education Conference, Sydney,* 2000.
2. Slade, Malcolm. Listening to the Boys, *Shannon Press,* 2002. ISBN 0-9580704-0-7
3. Bonnor, Chris. Creating and choosing good schools. *Inside Story: edited at Swinburne University of Technology.* www.inside.org.au/?s=creating+and+choosing+good+schools, July 12, 2012.
4. Dearing, R. The University of Leeds. *The National Committee of Inquiry into Higher Education,* 1997.
5. Ross, T. Pupils 'drilled to pass exams are left without key skills'. *London Evening Standard,* July 21, 2008.
6. Gallagher, I. Generation betrayed by bogus promises: Our failing schools are 'forcing UK firms to choose foreign workers'. *Daily Mail,* November 20, 2011.
7. Stevenson, H.W. and Stigler, J.W. The Learning Gap, *Touchstone (Simon & Schuster),* 1992. ISBN 0-671-70983-6; ISBN 0-671-88076-4 (PBK)
8. Usher, A. AYP Results for 2010-2011. *Center on Education Policy,* December, 2011.
9. Levin, Henry M. and Rouse, Cecilia E. The True cost of High School Dropouts. *The Opinion Pages, The New York Times,* January 25, 2012.
10. Cree, A, Kay, A., Steward, J. Economic and social cost of illiteracy: a snapshot of illiteracy in a global context. *Final report from the World Literacy Foundation,* April, 2012.
11. Balfanz, R., Bridgeland, J. M., Moore, L. A., Hornig Fox, J. Building a Grad Nation: Progress and Challenge in Ending the High School Dropout Epidemic. *Everyone Graduates Center, John Hopkins University,* Nov., 2010.
12. Gow, L. and Kember, D. Does higher education promote independent learning? *Higher Education,* 1990; 19: 307-322.
13. Hare, J. Policy forces unis to aim low. *The Australian,* July 31, 2012.
14. Sharma, Y. Global: The world's talent pool is changing – OECD. *University World News,* September 18, 2011; issue 189.
15. Paton, Graeme. University drop-out rates soar by 13pc in a year. (Quoting the Higher Education Statistics Agency.) *The Telegraph,* March 29, 2012.
16. Cariozo, L. Why college students stop short of a degree. (Quoting Harvard Graduate School of Education, 'Pathways to Prosperity' study), *Reuters,* March 27, 2012.
17. Fox, D. Personal theories of teaching. *Studies in Higher Education,* 1983; 8 (2): 151-163.
18. Dart, B. and Boulton-Lewis, G. Teaching and Learning in Higher Education. *Acer Press,* 1998; p. 23.
19. Bruce, R. Thinkers have the edge, *The Age,* August 11, 2003.
20. Stigler, J.W., Hiebert, J. The Teaching Gap. *The Free Press (Simon & Schuster),* 1999. ISBN 0-684-85274-8
21. Stevenson, H.W. and Stigler, J.W. The Learning Gap, op. cit.
22. Bruner, J. The Culture of Education. *Harvard University Press,* 1996. ISBN 0-674-17953-6
23. Seaton, A. New wine demands new bottles. *EQ Australia* (magazine of the Curriculum Corporation) Spring, September, 2001; Issue 3.
24. Maruta, T., Colligan, R.C., Malinchoc, M., Offord, K.P. Optimists vs pessimists: survival rate among medical patients over a 30-year period. *Mayo Clin Proc,* Feb 2000; 75(2): 133-4, 140-3.

My warmest thanks to my editor and partner, Prue Sobers, whose ideas, energy and attention to detail so often breathed life and personality into an otherwise dry passage, and who contributed greatly to the shaping of this book.

Greg Nicholson

About the author

Psychologist, educator and author, Greg Nicholson, was born in Melbourne, Australia. During his early career, he held a broad range of teaching posts, including school principal with the Department of Education, graduating as a psychologist in 1990.

Greg has played key roles in a number of academic and youth welfare programs including the Ardoch Youth Foundation and The Sir Edward Dunlop Program, a creative educational program for secondary students of which he was Chairman.

Greg founded Edworks® in 1990. As company director, he is an active participant, innovator and policy maker.

Visit Edworks Tutoring at www.edworksglobal.com.

INDEX OF SKILLS for WORKING SMART

For easy reference, the specific study skills discussed in this book are listed according to the chapters and pages on which they appear:

Index

The gull sees farthest who flies highest.

Jonathan Livingston Seagull RICHARD BACH

Made in the USA
Columbia, SC
08 December 2020

26006770R00174